Realtime, Conflict-Free
Machine Shorthand for Expanding Careers

REALTIME DICTIONARY OF BRIEFS & PHRASES

FOR REPORTING, CAPTIONING & OTHER IT PROFESSIONS

StenEd® Theory is approved
by the NCRA Theory Task Force

Beverly Loeblein Ritter   Patricia Pooser Rhyne

© Copyright, 1989, 1992, 1997, 1998, 2004
Stenotype Educational Products, Inc.

Revised Edition

1st Printing 2004
2nd Printing 2005

*This book, or any parts thereof,
may not be reproduced in any form
without permission of the publisher.*

Stenotype Educational Products, Inc.
P.O. Box 959, Melrose, Florida 32666
Phone: 1-888-StenEd1 or 1-352-475-3332
Fax: 1-352-475-2152

www.stened.com

ISBN #0-938643-74-6
StenEd #553

PREFACE

This text was originally compiled at the request of many students, teachers, and reporters who wanted a concise, easy-to-reference list of short forms (also called "briefs" or "arbitraries") that would be conflict free based on the entire StenEd theory.

The Dictionary of Briefs & Phrases has been greatly enlarged because of the increased importance of realtime writing and the NCRA requirement to teach/learn a conflict-free theory. All outlines in this text have been tested against the main and medical StenEd translating dictionaries to insure that all published StenEd outlines are free of conflicts.

This updated text contains over 12,000 entries. Most of these briefs are optional. The few that are required (e.g., the high-frequency word "be" is always written B-) are so indicated in StenEd's Realtime Theory text. All others are to be used only if they are easy and natural for you to stroke and remember and thus cause no hesitation in your writing.

Keep in mind that heavy use of briefs and phrases is not necessary for high-speed writing. Many of the fastest and most accurate writers—some of the most successful captioners and realtime reporters whose reputation is built on getting a clean translation as they write—are very selective in their use of short forms. But if a short form is easy for you to remember and to stroke, feel free to use it.

ACKNOWLEDGMENT

Thanks to all of you who submitted briefs and phrases for StenEd review and testing. A special thanks goes to Sharon Diaz, theory teacher extraordinaire, of Denver Academy of Court Reporting in Colorado. We're sure StenEd students everywhere will thank you, Sharon, for your time and expertise in developing many of these short forms.

INTRODUCTION

This text contains a "short and sweet" listing of StenEd briefs and phrases. All of these short forms (also called "arbitraries") are also included in StenEd's Realtime Professional Dictionary. The outlines in this text are represented in raw steno (e.g., save = SA*EUF, not SAIV) so there is no confusion as to which keys are to be stroked.

Warning: Do not incorporate too many briefs until you have completed the StenEd Realtime Theory and understand StenEd writing principles and the importance of remaining conflict free.

This text is not a summary of StenEd writing principles. It is simply a listing of StenEd-allowed briefs and phrases. When a word or phrase has multiple briefs, often only the most efficient ones are listed in this text. See the Professional Dictionary for a complete listing of all StenEd outlines and theory principles.

We have been very careful to insure that StenEd is 100 percent free of conflicts. If you want to incorporate an outline not contained in a StenEd text, be sure to check it against the Reverse Dictionary and/or the StenEd CAT translating dictionary to make absolutely sure it does not conflict with anything else in StenEd.

We have generally not included words that may look like briefs but, because they follow basic StenEd principles, are actually the written-out form—even though many of these forms are only one stroke.

Following is a very abbreviated listing of "some" of the stroke-saving principles presented in the StenEd theory. (Some options are included that some StenEd writers may not use.) The StenEd Realtime Theory lesson number in which the principle is introduced is also listed. Remember, most of the words in the following categories are not contained in this dictionary because they follow StenEd theory principles and, thus, are not "arbitrary" briefs or phrases.

Some Stroke-Saving StenEd® Principles

Following are the types of outlines that follow the StenEd theory principles—particularly Lessons 19-40 in the theory text. Many of the words following these principles are not included in this book of short forms since they are theory principles, not briefs. Remember, the following is only a **partial list** of StenEd principles. For a complete theory summary, refer to *StenEd's Realtime Theory* text and/or the *StenEd's Realtime Professional Dictionary*.

Unaccented syllables

abdomen	ABD/PHEPB	immigrant	EUPL/TKPWRAPBT
alteration	ALT/RAEUGS	incident	EUPBS/TKEPBT
artificial	ART/TPEURBL	Korea	KRAOE/KWRA
barricade	PWAEUR/KAEUD	recreation	REBG/RAEUGS
charisma	KREUZ/PHA	monolith	PHOPB/HR*EUT

Lesson 19: -ver & -fer, -ven & -vern

braver	PWRA*EUFR	driven	TKR*EUFPB
briefer	PWRAOEFR	govern	TKPWO*FRPB

Lesson 20: negative contractions

doesn't	TKUPBT	hasn't	HAPBT
didn't	TK-PBT	haven't	SR-PBT

Lesson 21: ex- before vowels, h, or sibilant c

exact	KPABGT	exempt	KPEPLT
exaggerate	KPAPBLG/RAEUT	exist	KP*EUS
excerpt	KPERPT	exuberant	KPAOUB/RAPBT

Lesson 22: shun sounds

attention	AEU/TEPBGS	penetration	PEPB/TRAEUGS
deduction	TKE/TK*UBGS	permission	PER/PHEUGS
digestion	TKEU/SKWR*EGS	promotion	PRO/PHOEGS

Lesson 23: coll-, comm-, corr-

collateral	KHRAT/RAL	commotion	KPHOEGS
collect	KHREBGT	correct	KREBGT
commander	KPHAPBD/ER	corroboration	KROB/RAEUGS

Lesson 24: -st, -xt, -th

existed	KP*EUS/-D	next	TPH*EBGS	earth	*ERT
satirist	SAT/R*EUS	text	T*EBGS	path	PA*T

Lesson 26: shal & shus sounds

social	SOERBL	ambitious	APL/PWEURBS
judicial	SKWRAOU/TKEURBL	nauseous	TPHAURBS
specialist	SPERBL/*EUS	fractious	TPRABG/-RBS

Lesson 27: int- & ent-, inter- & enter-

entire	SPWAOEUR	intern	SPWERPB
intestinal	SPW*ES/TPHAL	entertain	SPWER/TAEUPB
intend	SPWEPBD	intermission	SPWER/PHEUGS

Lesson 28: -ent, -ant, -ance

current	KURPBT	truant	TRAOUPBT
different	TKEUFRPBT	defiant	TKE/TPAOEUPBT
patient	PAEURBT	defiance	TKE/TPAOEUPBS
deficient	TKE/TPEURBT	reliance	RE/HRAOEUPBS

Lesson 29: -fl(e), bl(e), -el, -al, -il

baffle	PWAFL	denial	TKE/TPHAOEUL
rifle	RAOEUFL	electoral	E/HREBG/TORL
scuffle	SKUFL	final	TPAOEUPBL
able	AEUBL	oral	ORL
curable	KAOURBL	penal	PAOEPBL
favorable	TPA*EUFRBL	journal	SKWRURPBL
gavel	TKPWA*FL	civil	S*EUFL
quarrel	KWARL	evil	AO*EFL
tunnel	TUPBL	sterile	STERL

Lesson 30: -ism, -mp, -rve, -nch, -rch

terrorism	TER/REUFPL	camp	KAFRP
plagiarism	PHRAEUPBLG/REUFPL	slump	SHRUFRP
vandalism	SRAPBD/HREUFPL	emphasis	EFRP/SEUS

(The following are optional StenEd techniques)

carve	KAFRB	bench	PWEFRPBLG	march	PHA*RPBLG
nerve	TPHEFRB	lunch	HRUFRPBLG	porch	PO*RPBLG
observe	OB/SEFRB	ranch	RAFRPBLG	search	S*ERPBLG

Lesson 31: -bility, -ology, -ary, -ory, -ically, -edly, -ingly, -fully, -ously, -ography

ability	ABLT	advisedly	AD/SRAOEUZ/TKHREU
liability	HRAOEUBLT	heatedly	HAOET/TKHREU
ecology	E/KOLG	grudgingly	TKPWRUPBLG/TKPWHREU
technology	TEBG/TPHOLG	knowingly	TPHOE/TKPWHREU
budgetary	PWUPBLG/TAEUR	lawfully	HRAU/TPHREU
customary	K*US/PHAEUR	playfully	PHRAEU/TPHREU
category	KAT/TKPWOEUR	famously	TPAEUPL/SHREU
mandatory	PHAPBD/TOEUR	nervously	TPHEFRB/SHREU
politically	PHREUT/KHREU	stenography	STEPB/OG/TPEU
typically	TEUP/KHREU	xerography	SAO*ER/OG/TPEU

Lesson 32: under-

	underage	UPBDZ/AEUPBLG
	underline	UPBDZ/HRAOEUPB
	underrate	UPBDZ/RAEUT

© 2004 *StenEd*® Realtime Briefs & Phrases

Lesson 33: unaccented medial -yu-, -rial, -rian

circular	SEURBG/HRAR	editorial	ED/TOEURL
fabulous	TPAB/HROUS	historian	HEUS/TOEURPB
stipulate	STEUP/HRAEUT	librarian	HRAOEU/PWRAEURPB

Lesson 37: -ful, -ment, -ishment, -fulness, -ishness, -iveness, -some, -ographer, -ologist, -itis

lawful	HRAUFL	abusiveness	AEU/PWAOUS/*EUFPBS
playful	PHRAEUFL	forgiveness	TPOR/TKPW*EUFPBS
moment	PHOEPLT	tiresome	TAOEUR/SPH-
payment	PAEUPLT	wholesomeness	WHOEL/SPH*PBS
garnishment	TKPWARPB/SH-PLT	lexicographer	HREBGS/KOG/FER
nourishment	TPHUR/SH-PLT	typographer	TAOEUP/OG/FER
cheerfulness	KHAOER/TPHR*PBS	criminologist	KREUPL/TPHO*LGS
truthfulness	TRAO*UT/TPHR*PBS	ecologist	E/KO*LGS
foolishness	TPAOL/SH*PBS	dermatitis	TKERPL/TAOEUTS
selfishness	SEFL/SH*PBS	tonsillitis	TOPBS/HRAOEUTS

Lesson 38: miscellaneous prefixes (prefix is underlined)

aftermath	AFR/PHA*T	megaphone	PHEG/TPOEPB
antedate	AEPBT/TKAEUT	monotone	PHOPB/TOEPB
antisocial	A*EPBT/SOERBL	multivitamin	PHULT/SRAOEUT/PHEUPB
automatic	AUT/PHAT/EUBG	photocopier	TPOET/KOP/KWRER
countersign	KO*UPBT/SAOEUPB	prototype	PROET/TAOEUP
electronic	HREBG/TROPB/EUBG	pseudoscience	SAOUD/SAOEUPBS
hypertension	HAO*EUP/TEPBGS	psychopath	SAOEUBG/PA*T
hypodermic	HO*EUP/TKERPL/EUBG	self-serving	SEFL/SEFRB/-G
intrastate	SPWRA/STAEUT	semicircle	SEPL/SEURBG/-L
introduce	SPWRO/TKAOUS	superman	SAO*UP/PHAPB

Lesson 39: -self

herself	H*ERS	myself	PHAO*EUS
himself	H*EUPLS	yourself	KWRO*URS

As always, if an **optional** brief or phrase is hard to remember or stroke, you don't have to use it. It fact, it would be counterproductive to force yourself to use a short form that is not natural for you. As an example, *EUFPBS can be written for "iveness," but many writers find it too difficult to stroke. Therefore, one could write "effectiveness" as EFBGT/*EUF/-PBS rather than EFBGT/*EUFPBS. That extra stroke can actually save time and frustration (and a possible shadowed -R).

Remember, principles taught (or presented as an option) in StenEd theory are not generally included in this *Dictionary of Conflict-Free Briefs & Phrases*.

Phrases are listed after their initial word. A sample entry follows.

at *(as wd)*	AT
at all times	TAULTS

a (as wd)	A
A. (answer bank)	-FRPBLGTS
A. No.	TPH-FRPBLGTS
A. No, ma'am.	TPHAFRPBLGTS
A. No, sir.	TPHEUFRPBLGTS
A. Oh	OEFRPBLGTS
A. Oh,	O*EFRPBLGTS
A. So	SOFRPBLGTS
A. So,	SO*FRPBLGTS
A. Yes.	KWR-FRPBLGTS
A. Yes, ma'am.	KWRAFRPBLGTS
A. Yes, sir.	KWREUFRPBLGTS
A&E (Arts & Entertainment)	ARBGS/SKP*E
A&E	ARBGS/TPH*E
AARP (American Association of Retired Persons)	AEU/ARP
AARP	ARBGS/A*RP
ABA (American Bar Association)	ARBGS/PWA*
abandon	PWAUPB
abandonee	PWAUPB/TPHAOE
abandonment	PWAUPLT
abbreviate	PWRAO*EFT
abbreviation	PWRAO*EFGS
abc	A*/PW*BG
ABC	ARBGS/PW*BG
abc's	A*/PW*BG/AOES
ABC's	ARBGS/PW*BG/AOES
abdomen	ABD
abdominal	ABD/TPHAL
abdominally	ABD/HREU
abdominally	ABD/TPHAL/HREU
ABM (antiballistic missile)	ARBGS/PW*PL
abort	PWORT
abortion	PWORGS
abortionist	PWORGS/*EUS
abortive	PWORT/*EUF
about (as wd)	ABT
about how large	PWHOURPBLG
about how long	PWHOUPBG
about how many	PWHOUPL
about how much	PWHOUFP
about how often	PWHOUFPB
above (as wd)	PWO*F
above and beyond	SROPBD
aboveground	PWO*F/TKPWROUPBD
Abraham	AEUB/HAPL
absolve	AB/SO*F
accelerate	SHRERT
acceleration	SHRERGS
accelerator	SHRERT/TOR
accept	SEP
acceptability	SEPBLT
acceptability	SEP/-BLT
acceptable	SEPBL
acceptable	SEP/-BL
acceptably	SEP/PWHREU
acceptance	SEP/TAPBS
accidence	STKEPBS
accident (as wd)	STKEPBT
accident happen	STKAP
accident happened	STKAPD
accident in question	STKEUBG
accident occur	STKUR
accident occurred	STKURD
accident occurring	STKURG
accident occurs	STKURS
accident report	STKORT
accident scene	STKAEPB
accident took place	STKAOPLS
accidental	STKEPB/TAL
accidental	STKEPBL
accidentally	STKEPB/TAL/HREU
accidentally	STKEPBL/HREU
accidentally	STKEPBT/HREU
accidents	STKEPBTS, STKEPBT/-S
accompaniment	AEU/KPAEPB/-PLT
accompany	AEU/KPAEPB
accomplish	PHREURB
accomplishment(s)	PHREURB/-PLT(S)
according (as wd)	KORG
according to	KORGT
accordingly	KORG/HREU
account(s)	K-T(S)
accountability	K-T/-BLT
accountable	K-T/-BL
accountably	K-T/PWHREU
accountancy	K-T/APB/SEU
accountancy	K-T/TAPB/SEU
accountant	K-T/TAPBT
accounted	K-TD
accounting	K-T/-G
accredit	AEU/KRET
accreditation	AEU/KRET/TAEUGS
accuracy	ABG/SEU
accurate	ABG/RAT
accurately	ABG/RAT/HREU
Ace bandage	AEUS/PW-PBLG
achiness	AEU/K*EUPBS
achiness	AEUBG/K*EUPBS
acknowledge	ABG/TPHOPBLG
acknowledgment(s)	ABG/TPHOPBLG/-PLT(S)
ACLU (American Civil Liberties Union)	ARBGS/KHR*U
ACLU	ARBGS/KR*RBGS/HR*U
acquittal	AEU/KWEULT
acrimonious	ABG/PHOEPB/KWROUS
acrimony	ABG/PHO/TPH*EU
acrimony	ABG/PHOE/TPH*EU
acrobat	ABG/PWAT
acrobatic(s)	ABG/PWAT/EUBG(S)
acronym	ABG/TPHEUPL
across (as wd)	AEU/KROSZ
across the street	KROTS
activity	ABG/T*EUFT
activity	ABGT/*EUFT
actual	TWAUL
actuality	TWAUL/TEU
actuality	TWAULT

© 2004 *StenEd®* Briefs & Phrases (Excerpted from StenEd's Realtime Professional Dictionary)

actualize	TWAUL/AOEUZ	adulterous	TKULT/ROUS
actualize	TWAULZ	adultery	TKULT/REU
actually	TWAEUL	adulthood	TKULTD
actually	TWAUL/HREU	adulthood	TKULT/HAOD
ad interim	A*D/SPWERPL	advance	SRAPBS
ad referendum	A*D/REFRPBD/UPL	advancement(s)	SRAPBS/-PLT(S)
ad referendum	AD/REFRPB/TKUPL	advantage	SRAPBG
ad respondendum	A*D/SPOPB/TKEPBD/UPL	advantageous	SRAPBG/OUS
ad respondendum	A*D/SPOPBD/EPBD/UPL	advantageously	SRAPBG/OUS/HREU
ad respondendum	AD/SPOPB/TKEPB/TKUPL	advantageously	SRAPBG/SHREU
ad respondendum	AD/SPOPBD/EPB/TKUPL	adventure(s)	SR*EFP(-/S)
ad testificandum	A*D/TEF/KAPBD/UPL	adventurer(s)	SR*EFP/ER(S)
ad testificandum	AD/TEF/KAPB/TKUPL	adventurous	SR*EFP/OUS
ad valorem	A*D/TPHROERPL	advertise	TEUZ
ad valorem	AD/TPHROERPL	advertisement(s)	TEUZ/-PLT(S)
ADA *(Americans with Disabilities Act, American*		advertiser(s)	TEUZ/ER(S)
Dental Association)	ARBGS/TKA*	AFB *(air force base)*	ARBGS/TP*B
ADD *(attention deficit disorder)*		AFDC *(Aid to Families with Dependent Children)*	
	ARBGS/TK*D		ARBGS/TP*RBGS/TK*BG
adjudgment	AEU/SKWRUPLT	affability	AFBLT
admeasure	AD/PH-RB	affable	AFBL
admeasurement	AD/PH-RB/-PLT	affect	AFBGT
administer(s)	AD/PH*R(S)	affectation	AFBG/TAEUGS
administer(s)	PH*R(S)	affectation	AFBGT/TAEUGS
administered	AD/PH*RD	affection	A*FBGS
administered	PH*RD	affectionate	A*FBGS/TPHAT
administering	AD/PH*RG	affective	AFBG/T*EUF
administering	PH*RG	affective	AFBGT/*EUF
administrate	AD/PH*RT	affidavit(s)	AFD(Z)
administrate	PH*RT	affirmative *(as wd)*	AEU/TPEURPL/T*EUF
administration	AD/PH*RGS	affirmative action	A*FRBGS
administration	PH*RGS	afford(s)	AFRD(Z)
Administration	A*D/PH*RGS	affordability	AFRD/-BLT
administrative	AD/PH*RT/*EUF	affordable	AFRD/-BL
administrative	PH*RT/*EUF	AFL *(American Football League)*	
administratively	AD/PH*RT/*EUF/HREU		ARBGS/TP*L
administratively	PH*RT/*EUF/HREU	AFL-CIO *(American Federation of Labor & Congress*	
administrator	AD/PH*RT/TOR	*of Industrial Organizations)* AFL/KRO*EU	
administrator	PH*RT/TOR	aforedescribed	AEU/TPOER/TKRAOEUB/-D
administratrices	AD/PH*RT/SAOEZ	aforedescribed	AEU/TPOER/TKRAOEUBD
administratrices	PH*RT/SAOEZ	aforethought	AEU/TPOER/THAUT
administratrix	AD/PH*RT/REUBGS	Aframerican	AF/RA/PHERPB
administratrix	PH*RT/REUBGS	Aframerican	AF/TPRA/PHERPB
admissibility	PHEUBLT	Africa	AFR/KA
admissible	PHEUBL	African	AFR/KAPB
admit(ted) *(as wd)*	AD/PHEUT(/-D)	African-American	TPREUPL
admitted in evidence	TKPH*EFD, TKPHEFD	Afro-American	TPROEPL
admitted into evidence	TKPHO*EFD, TKPHOEFD	after *(as wd)*	AF
adopt	TKOPT	after that accident	AFRBGS
adoptable	TKOPT/-BL	after the accident	AEFRBGS
adoptee	TKOP/TAOE	after this accident	AEUFRBGS
adoptee	TKOPT/TAOE	afternoon	AFRPB
adoption	TKOPGS	afterthought	AFR/THAUT
adoptive	TKOPT/*EUF	again	TKPWEPB
ADP *(automatic data processing)*		against	TKPW*EPBS
	ARBGS/TK*P	agency	AGT/SEU
adult	TKULT	agent	AGT
adulter	TKULT/ER	Agent Orange	AGT/ORPBG
adulterant	TKULT/ERPBT	aggravate(d) *(as wd)*	AG/SRAEUT(/-D)
adulterant	TKULT/RAPBT	aggravated assault	TKPWRAULT
adulterate	TKULT/RAEUT	aggravated assault	
adulteration	TKULT/RAEUGS	and battery	TKPWRAUBLT
adulterer	TKULT/RER	aggravation	AG/SRAEUGS

ago	AG	am I right?	PHEURGT
agreed	AEU/TKPWRAOED	a.m.	A*PL
agreeing	AEU/TKPWRAOEG	AMA *(American Medical Association)*	
agrees	AEU/TKPWRAOES		ARBGS/PHA*
agricultural	AG/KHURL	ambience	APL/PWAOEPBS
agriculture	AG/KHUR	ambient	APL/PWAOEPBT
AIDS *(Acquired Immune Deficiency Syndrome)*		ambiguity	TKPWAOUT
	A*EUDZ	ambiguous	TKPWAOUS
AIDS-related complex	A*EUDZ/RELT/-D/	ambiguously	TKPWAOUS/HREU
	KPHREBGS	ambulance	PWHRAPBS
air *(as wd)*	AEUR	ambulance	APL/PWHRAPBS
air-condition	AEUR/K-PB	ambulant	APL/PWHRAPBT
air conditioner(s)	AEUR/K-PB/ER(S)	ambulate	APL/PWHRAEUT
air-conditioning	AEUR/K-PBG	ambulation	APL/PWHRAEUGS
aircraft	AEURBGT	AMC *(American Movie Classics)*	
air force	AEUFRS		ARBGS/PH*BG
Air Force	A*EUFRS	amend(s)	APLD(Z)
air force base	AEUFRBS	amendable	APLD/-BL
Air Force Base	A*EUFRBS	amendment(s)	AEPLT(S)
airplane	AEURP	amendment(s)	APLD/-PLT(S)
air pollution	AEURPLGS	America	PHERBG
airport	AEURPT	American Express	PHERPB/EBGS/PRESZ
airworthiness	AEUR/WOR/TH*EUPBS	American Samoa	PHERPB/SPHOE/WA
aka *(also known as)*	A*/KA*	American	PHERPB
a.k.a.	A*PD/KA*	Americana	PHERPB/TPHA
a.k.a.	AEUBG/KWRAEU	Americanism	PHERPB/EUFPL
a.k.a.	A*PD/KA*	Americanize	PHERPB/AOEUZ
AKA	ARBGS/KA*	among	PHOPBG
Alabama	A*L/A*L	amongst	PHO*PBGS
Alaska	A*BG/A*BG	amount	APLT
albeit	AL/PWAOET	amphitheater	AFRP/THAOET/ER
Albuquerque	KWERBG	ample	AFRPL
alcohol *(as wd)*	KHOL	ampler	AFRPL/ER
alcohol and drugs	KHRAPBDZ	amplest	AFRPL/*ES
alcohol or drugs	KHRORDZ	amplification	AFRP/TPEU/KAEUGS
alcoholic(s)	KHROEUBG(/-S)	amplifier(s)	AFRP/TPEU/ER(S)
alcoholic(s)	KHOL/EUBG(S)	amplify	AFRP/TPEU
alcoholic beverage	KHROEUPBLG	amplitude	AFRP/TAOUD
alcoholism	KHROEUFPL	AMT *(alternative minimum tax)*	
alcoholism	KHOL/EUFPL		ARBGS/PH*T
ALI *(American Law Institute)*	ARBGS/HR*EU	an ex- *(pre)*	TPHEBGS/H-F
all *(as wd)*	AUL	an ex *(space follows)*	TPHEBGS
all right	HR-RT	ANA *(American Nurses Association)*	
all right, sir	HR-RTS		ARBGS/TPHA*
all the	AULT	analogize	APBL/SKWRAOEUZ
all-American	AUL/H-F/PHERPB	analogous	APBL/TKPWOUS
almightily	AL/PHAOEUT/HREU	analogy	AEU/TPHALG
almighty	AL/PHAOEU/TEU	analogy	APBL/SKWREU
almighty	AL/PHAOEUT/TEU	analyses	APBL/SAOEZ
Almighty	A*L/PHAOEU/TEU	analysis	APBL/SEUS
Almighty	A*L/PHAOEUT/TEU	and *(as wd)*	APBD, SKP-
almost	HR-PL	-and- *(suf/pre)*	/SKPH-F
alms	AUPLS	and a	SKPA
alongside	AEU/HROPBGDZ	and a half	TPHAF
already	HR-R	-and-a-half *(suf)*	TPHA*F
also *(as wd)*	ALS	and all	SKPAUL
also known as	AEUBG/TPHAEU	and all the	SKPAULT
altogether	AL/TOGT	and also	SKPALS
always	AULS, AULZ	and are	SKP-R
am *(as wd)*	APL	and be	SKP-B
am I correct	PHEUBGT	and can	SKP-BG
am I correct?	PHEURBGT	and could	SKP-BGD
am I right	PHEURT	and feel	SKP-FL

and felt	SKP-FLT	and I	SKPEU
and find	SKP-FPBD	and I'd	SKP*EUD
and had	SKP-D	and I'll	SKP*EUL
and have	SKP-F	and I'm	SKP*EUPL
and have been	SKP-FB	and I've	SKP*EUF
and have the	SKP-FT	and I am	SKPEUPL
and he	SKPE	and I am the	SKPEUPLT
and he'd	SKP*ED	and I believe	SKPEUBL
and he'll	SKP*EL	and I believe the	SKPEUBLT
and he's	SKP*ES	and I believed	SKPEUBLD
and he believed	SKPEBLD	and I can	SKPEUBG
and he believes	SKPEBLS	and I cannot	SKPEUBG/TPHOT
and he can	SKPEBG	and I can't	SKPEUBG/-PBT, SKPEU/K-PBT
and he cannot	SKPEBG/TPHOT		
and he can't	SKPEBG/-PBT, SKPE/K-PBT	and I could	SKPEUBGD
		and I could not	SKPEUBGD/TPHOT
and he could	SKPEBGD	and I couldn't	SKPEUBGD/-PBT
and he could not	SKPEBGD/TPHOT	and I feel	SKPEUFL
and he couldn't	SKPEBGD/-PBT	and I felt	SKPEUFLT
and he feels	SKPEFLS	and I find	SKPEUFPBD
and he felt	SKPEFLT	and I go	SKPEUG
and he had	SKPED	and I had	SKPEUD
and he had not	SKPED/TPHOT	and I had not	SKPEUD/TPHOT
and he hadn't	SKPED/-PBT, SKPE/H-PBT	and I hadn't	SKPEUD/-PBT, SKPEU/H-PBT
and he happened	SKPEPD	and I happen	SKPEUP
and he happens	SKPEPS	and I happened	SKPEUPD
and he has	SKPEZ	and I have	SKPEUF
and he has not	SKPEZ/TPHOT	and I have been	SKPEUFB
and he hasn't	SKPEZ/-PBT, SKPE/HAPBT	and I have been the	SKPEUFBT
		and I have believed	SKPEUFBLD
and he is	SKPES	and I have gone	SKPEUFG
and he is not	SKPES/TPHOT	and I have had	SKPEUFD
and he isn't	SKPES/-PBT, SKPE/S-PBT	and I have the	SKPEUFT
		and I haven't	SKPEUFPBT
and he recalled	SKPERLD	and I haven't	SKPEUF/-PBT, SKP-/EUFPBT
and he recalls	SKPERLS		
and he recollected	SKPERBGD	and I recall	SKPEURL
and he recollects	SKPERBGS	and I recall the	SKPEURLT
and he remembered	SKPERPLD	and I recalled	SKPEURLD
and he remembers	SKPERPLS	and I recollect	SKPEURBG
and he said	SKPEBS	and I recollect the	SKPEURBGT
and he say	SKPEBZ	and I recollected	SKPEURBGD
and he says	SKPEBSZ	and I remember	SKPEURPL
and he shall	SKPERB	and I remember the	SKPEURPLT
and he should	SKPERBD	and I remembered	SKPEURPLD
and he should not	SKPERBD/TPHOT	and I said	SKPEUBS
and he shouldn't	SKPERBD/-PBT	and I say	SKPEUBZ
and he thinks	SKPEPBGS	and I says	SKPEUBSZ
and he understands	SKPEPBDZ/-S	and I shall	SKPEURB
and he understood	SKP*EPBDZ	and I should	SKPEURBD
and he understood	SKPE/UPBD	and I should not	SKPEURBD/TPHOT
and he wanted	SKPEPTD	and I shouldn't	SKPEURBD/-PBT
and he wants	SKPEPTS	and I think	SKPEUPBG
and he was	SKPEFS	and I think the	SKPEUPBGT
and he was not	SKPEFS/TPHOT	and I understand	SKPEUPBDZ
and he wasn't	SKPEFS/-PBT, SKPE/WUPBT	and I understood	SKP*EUPBDZ
		and I want	SKPEUPT
and he will	SKPEL	and I wanted	SKPEUPTD
and he will go	SKPELG	and I was	SKPEUFS
and he would	SKPELD	and I was not	SKPEUFS/TPHOT
and he would not	SKPELD/TPHOT	and I wasn't	SKPEUFS/-PBT, SKPEU/WUPBT
and he wouldn't	SKPELD/-PBT		

and I will	SKPEUL	and she say	SKPHEBZ
and I will go	SKPEULG	and she says	SKPHEBSZ
and I would	SKPEULD	and she shall	SKPHERB
and I would not	SKPEULD/TPHOT	and she should	SKPHERBD
and I wouldn't	SKPEULD/-PBT	and she should not	SKPHERBD/TPHOT
and is	SKPEUS	and she shouldn't	SKPHERBD/-PBT
and isn't	SKPEUS/-PBT	and she thinks	SKPHEPBGS
and it	SKPEUT	and she understands	SKPHEPBDZ/-S
and it'll	SKP*EULT	and she understood	SKPH*EPBDZ
and it will	SKPEULT	and she understood	SKPHE/UPBD
and its	SKPEUTS	and she wanted	SKPHEPTD
and it's	SKP*TS	and she wants	SKPHEPTS
and it is	SKP-TS	and she was	SKPHEFS
and now	SKPOU	and she was not	SKPHEFS/TPHOT
and of course	SKPOFBG	and she wasn't	SKPHEFS/-PBT,
and off	SKPAUF		SKPHE/WUPBT
and on	SKPOPB	and she will	SKPHEL
and/or	SKPOR	and she will go	SKPHELG
and over	SKPOFR	and she would	SKPHELD
and over	SKPOEFR	and she would not	SKPHELD/TPHOT
and recall	SKP-RL	and she wouldn't	SKPHELD/-PBT
and recalled	SKP-RLD	and should	SKP-RBD
and recollect	SKP-RBG	and the	SKP-T
and recollected	SKP-RBGD	and was	SKP-FS
and remember	SKP-RPL	and we	SKPWE
and remembered	SKP-RPLD	and we'd	SKPW*ED
and shall	SKP-RB	and we'll	SKPW*EL
and she	SKPHE	and we're	SKPW*ER
and she'd	SKPH*ED	and we've	SKPW*EF
and she'll	SKPH*EL	and we had	SKPWED
and she's	SKPH*ES	and we will	SKPWEL
and she believed	SKPHEBLD	and we are	SKPWER
and she believes	SKPHEBLS	and we have	SKPWEF
and she can	SKPHEBG	and were	SKP-RP
and she can't	SKPHEBG/-PBT,	and what happened	SKPWHAPD
	SKPHE/K-PBT	and what happens	SKPWHAPS
and she cannot	SKPHEBG/TPHOT	and what has	SKPWHAZ
and she could	SKPHEBGD	and what have	SKPWHAF
and she could not	SKPHEBGD/TPHOT	and what, if anything,	SKPWHAFPBG
and she couldn't	SKPHEBGD/-PBT	and what is	SKPWHAS
and she feels	SKPHEFLS	and what was	SKPWHAFS
and she felt	SKPHEFLT	and what will	SKPWHAL
and she had	SKPHED	and will	SKP-L
and she had not	SKPHED/TPHOT	and would	SKP-LD
and she hadn't	SKPHED/-PBT,	and you	SKPU
	SKPHE/H-PBT	and you'd	SKP*UD
and she happened	SKPHEPD	and you'll	SKP*UL
and she happens	SKPHEPS	and you're	SKP*UR
and she has	SKPHEZ	and you've	SKP*UF
and she has not	SKPHEZ/TPHOT	and you are	SKPUR
and she hasn't	SKPHEZ/-PBT,	and you are not	SKPUR/TPHOT
	SKPHE/HAPBT	and you are the	SKPURT
and she is	SKPHES	and you aren't	SKPUR/-PBT,
and she is not	SKPHES/TPHOT		SKPU/R-PBT
and she isn't	SKPHES/-PBT,	and you believe	SKPUBL
	SKPHE/S-PBT	and you believe the	SKPUBLT
and she recalled	SKPHERLD	and you believed	SKPUBLD
and she recalls	SKPHERLS	and you can	SKPUBG
and she recollected	SKPHERBGD	and you cannot	SKPUBG/TPHOT
and she recollects	SKPHERBGS	and you can't	SKPUBG/-PBT,
and she remembered	SKPHERPLD		SKPU/K-PBT
and she remembers	SKPHERPLS	and you could	SKPUBGD
and she said	SKPHEBS	and you could not	SKPUBGD/TPHOT

and you couldn't	SKPUBGD/-PBT	anonymously	TPHOPLS/HREU
and you feel	SKPUFL	another	AOT
and you felt	SKPUFLT	answer(s) *(as wd)*	APBS(/-S)
and you find	SKPUFPBD	answer read	STPHAED
and you go	SKPUG	(Answer read.)	STPHA*ED
and you had	SKPUD	answer to interrogatory	STROG
and you had not	SKPUD/TPHOT	answerable	APBS/-BL
and you hadn't	SKPUD/-PBT, SKPU/H-PBT	answers to interrogatories	STROGS
and you happen	SKPUP	antiabortion	A*EPBT/PWORGS
and you happened	SKPUPD	antiaircraft	A*EPBT/AEURBGT
and you have	SKPUF	anti-American	A*EPBT/PHERPB
and you have been	SKPUFB	antibiotic(s)	AEBT(S), AEBT(/-S)
and you have been the	SKPUFBT	antibiotic(s)	A*EPBT/PWOT/EUBG(S)
and you have believed	SKPUFBLD	anticompetitive	A*EPBT/KPET/T*EUF
and you have gone	SKPUFG	antidepressant	AEPT(S), AEPT(/-S)
and you have had	SKPUFD	antidepressant	A*EPBT/TKPRES/SAPBT
and you have not	SKPUF/TPHOT	anti-intellectual	A*EPBT/SPWHREBG/KHUL
and you have the	SKPUFT	antiserum	A*EPBT/SAOERPL
and you haven't	SKPUFPBT	anxious	APBGS
and you haven't	SKPUF/-PBT, SKPU/SR-PBT	anxiously	APBGS/HREU
		any *(as wd)*	TPHEU
and you recall	SKPURL	any and all	TPHEUPBL
and you recall the	SKPURLT	anybody	TPHEUB
and you recalled	SKPURLD	anybody else	TPHEUBLS
and you recollect	SKPURBG	anybody else	TPHEUB/ELS
and you recollect the	SKPURBGT	any fact	TPHEUFT
and you recollected	SKPURBGD	any further	TPHEUFR
and you remember	SKPURPL	any further questions	TPHEUFRGS
and you remember the	SKPURPLT	anyhow	TPHEU/HOU
and you remembered	SKPURPLD	anyhow	TPHEU/HO*U
and you said	SKPUBS	any knowledge	TPHEUPBLG
and you say	SKPUBZ	any knowledge	TPHEU/TPHOPBLG
and you says	SKPUBSZ	anymore	TPHEUPL
and you shall	SKPURB	any more	TPHEU/PH-R
and you should	SKPURBD	any more questions	TPHEURGS
and you should not	SKPURBD/TPHOT	any objection	TPH*EUBGS
and you shouldn't	SKPURBD/-PBT	anyone	TPHEUPB
and you think	SKPUPBG	any one	TPHEU/WUPB
and you think the	SKPUPBGT	anyone else	TPHEUPBLS
and you understand	SKPUPBDZ	anyone else	TPHEUPB/ELS
and you understood	SKP*UPBDZ	any particular time	TPHEUPT
and you want	SKPUPT	anyplace	TPHEUPLS
and you wanted	SKPUPTD	any place	TPHEU/PHRAEUS
and you were	SKPURP	anything	TPHEUG
and you were not	SKPURP/TPHOT	any thing	TPHEU/THEUPBG
and you were the	SKPURPT	anything further	TPHEUFRG
and you weren't	SKPURP/-PBT, SKPU/W-RPBT	anytime	TPHAOEUPL
		any time	TPHEU/TAOEUPL
and you will	SKPUL	anyway	TPHA*E
and you will go	SKPULG	anyway	TPHEU/WA*EU
and you would	SKPULD	any way	TPHAE
and you would not	SKPULD/TPHOT	any way	TPHEU/WAEU
and you wouldn't	SKPULD/-PBT	anywhere	TPHEUR
ands	APBDZ, SKP-S	any where	TPHEU/WR-
an ex *(space follows)*	TPHEBGS	anywhere else	TPHEURLS
Anglo-American	APBG/HRO/PHERPB	anywhere else	TPHEUR/ELS
angriness	APBG/R*EUPBS	AOL *(America Online)*	AO*L
Ankara	APBG/RA	AOL	ARBGS/O*L
ankle(s)	A*PBG/-L(S)	APA *(American Psychiatric/Psychological Association)*	ARBGS/PA*
anklet	A*PBG/HRET	apartment(s)	PARPLT(S), PARPLT(/-S)
annals	APBLS		
anonymous	TPHOPLS	APB *(all points bulletin)*	ARBGS/P*B

APL *(A Programming Language)*		Army *(as wd)*	A*ERPL
	ARBGS/P*L	army base	AERPBLS
apnea	AP/TPHA	Army Base	A*ERPBLS
APO *(Army [Air Force] Post Office)*		Arnold	ARPBLD
	ARBGS/PO*	around *(as wd)*	ARPBD
appellant	PAEPBT	arraign	AEURPBG
appellant	AEU/PHRAPBT	arraignment(s)	AEURPBG/-PLT(S)
appellate *(as wd)*	PAELT	arrange	ARPBG
appellate *(as wd)*	AEU/PHRAT	arrangement(s)	ARPBG/-PLT(S)
appellate court	PHROURT	arranger(s)	ARPBG/ER(S)
Appellate Court	PHRO*URT	arrearage	AEU/RAOERPBLG
appellation	AEU/PHRAEUGS	arrears	AEU/RAOERS
appellee	AEU/PHRAOE	arrest	A*EURS
appellor	AEU/PHROR	arterial	AR/TAOERL
(Applause.)	PHRA*UZ	arthritic	THREUBG
(Applause and laughter.)	PHRA*UFRZ	arthritis	THRAOEUTS
applicability	PHREUBLT	article	ARL
applicable	PHREUBL	as *(as wd)*	AZ
applicant	PHREUBGT	as a matter of	SPHAF
application	PHR*EUBGS	as a matter of fact	SPHAFT
appointment(s)	POEUPLT(S),	as a matter of law	SPHAFL
	POEUPLT(/-S)	as a matter of record	SPHAFRD
apposition	AEU/POGS	as a principle of law	SPROFL
apposition	AP/POGS	as a result	SRULT
appreciable	PRAOERBL	as a rule	SRUL
appreciably	PRAOERB/PWHREU	as bad as	SPWADZ
appreciate	PRAOERBT	as big as	SPWEUGS
appreciation	PRAOERBGS	as dead as	STKEDZ
appreciative	PRAOERB/T*EUF	as far as	STPARS
appropriate	PROEPT	as follows	STPOLS
appropriately	PROEPT/HREU	as good as	STKPWAODZ
appropriation	PROEPGS	as I sit here today	S*EU/SH*TD
approval	AEU/PRO*FL	as I understand	SEUPBDZ
approve	AEU/PRO*F	as I understood	S*EUPBDZ
approvingly	AEU/PRO*F/TKPWHREU	as long as	SHROPBGS
approximate	PR*BGS	as much	S-FP
approximately	PR*BGS/HREU	as much as	S-FPS
approximation	PR*BGS/PHAEUGS	as near as	STPHAOERS
APR *(annual percentage rate)*		as opposed to	SOPT
	ARBGS/P*R	as quick as	SKWEUBGS
April	PREUL	as soon as	SAOPBS
aquarium	AEU/KWAEURPL	as the result	STRULT
arbitrament	ARB/TRAPLT	as we sit here today	SWE/SH*TD
archaic	AR/KAEUBG	as we understand	SWEPBDZ
are *(as wd)*	R-	as we understood	SW*EPBDZ
are also	R-LS	as well	SW*EL
are not	R-/TPHOT	as well as	SWELS
are the	R-T	as well as	SW*ELS
aren't	R-PBT	as you sit here today	S*U/SH*TD
arguable	ARG/-BL	as you were	SURP
arguably	ARG/PWHREU	ASAP *(as soon as possible)*	AEU/SAP
argue	ARG	ASCII *(American Standard Code for Information*	
argument(s)	ARGT(S), ARGT(/-S)	*Interchange)*	AS/KAOE
argument(s)	ARG/-PLT(S)	asexual	AEU/SWAUL
argumentative	ARGT/*EUF	ashamed	AEU/SHAEUPLD
argumentative	ARG/-PLT/*EUF	ask(s)	SK-S
Arizona	A*Z/A*Z	asked	SK-D
Arkansas	A*R/A*R	asked and answered	SK-PBD
Arkansas	ARBG/SAU	asker(s)	SK-R(S)
Arlington	ARLG/TOPB	asker(s)	SK-/ER(S)
ARM *(adjustable rate mortgage)*		asking	SK-G
	ARBGS/R*PL	ASL *(American Sign Language)*	
army *(as wd)*	AERPL		ARBGS/S*L

ASPCA *(American Society for the Prevention of Cruelty to Animals)*	ARBGS/S*P/KRA*	auditorium	AUD/TOEURPL
assault *(as wd)*	AEU/SAULT	aught	A*UT
assault and battery	SAUB	August	AUG
assistance	STA*PBS	authoritarian	THOR/TAEURPB
assistant *(as wd)*	STA*PBT	authoritarianism	THOR/TAEURPB/EUFPL
assistant district attorney	STKROERPB	authoritative	THOR/TAEUT/*EUF
		authority	THORT
Assistant District Attorney	STKRO*ERPB	authority	THOR/TEU
		authorization	THORGS
assistant district attorney general	STKROERPBG	authorize	THORZ
		autobiographic	AUT/PWAO*EU/TKPWRAFBG
Assistant District Attorney General	STKRO*ERPBG	automobile *(as wd)*	AUBL
		automobile accident	AUBGS
associate	SOERBT	autopsy	AUPS
association	SOERBGS	availability	SRAEUBLT
Association	SO*ERBGS	available	SRAEUBL
associative	SOERB/T*EUF	avenge	AEU/SREPBG
at *(as wd)*	AT	avenger(s)	AEU/SREPBG/ER(S)
at a time	TAEUT	avengingly	AEU/SREPBG/TKPWHREU
at all times	TAULTS	avenue	A*F
at any time	T*PBT	Avenue	K-P/A*F
at least	THRA*ES, THRAO*ES	aver	A*FR
at no time	T-PBT	average	A*FRPBLG
at once	TWUPBS	averment	A*FRPLT
at that particular time	TAPT	averment	A*EUFRPLT
at that point	TA*PT	aversion	A*FRGS
at that time	TA*T	avert	A*FRT
at the point	T*EPT	avid	A*FD
at the present time	TEPT	awareness	AEU/WA*EURPBS
at the same time	TAEUPLT	awning	AUPBG
at the scene	TEZ	AWOL *(absent without leave)*	AEU/WOL
at the time	T*ET	AWOL	ARBGS/WO*L
at this particular time	TEUPT		
at this point	T*EUPT		
at this time	T*EUT		
at what point	TWHA*PT		
at what time	TWHAT		
at which time	TKH-T		
AT&T *(American Telephone & Telegraph)*	A-RBGS/T*RBGS/SKP*T, A-RBGS/T*RBGS/TPH*T		
ATLA *(American Trial Lawyers Association)*	ARBGS/THRA*		
ATM *(automated/automatic teller machine)*	ARBGS/T*PL		
atrium	AEU/TRAOEPL		
attorney *(as wd)*	TOERPB		
Attorney *(as wd)*	TO*ERPB		
attorney-at-law	TOERPB/AT/HRAU		
attorney-client	TOERBGT		
attorney-client privilege	TOERPBLGT		
attorney general	TOERPBG		
attorney general	TOERPB/SKWREPB		
Attorney General	TO*ERPBG		
Attorney General	TO*ERPB/SKWR*EPB		
attorneys general	TOERPBGS		
attorneys general	TOERPBS/SKWREPB		
attributable	AEU/TREUBT/-BL		
attribute	AEU/TREUBT		
ATV *(all-terrain vehicle)*	ARBGS/T*F		
audiocassette	AUBG		
audiotape	AUP		

babysat	PWAEUB/SAT
baby-sat	PWAEUB/H-F/SAT
babysit	PWAEUB/SEUT
baby-sit	PWAEUB/H-F/SEUT
babysitter(s)	PWAEUB/SEUT/ER(S)
baby-sitter(s)	PWAEUB/H-F/SEUT/ER(S)
baccalaureate	PWABG/HRAURT
bachelor('s) *(as wd)*	PWAFP/HROR(/AOES)
Bachelor's degree	PWHR-D
back *(as wd)*	PWABG
back and forth	PWA*FRT
background(s)	PW-GD(Z)
back on the record	PWOERBGD
backseat	PWABGS
backside	PWABGDZ
backup	PWA*UP
back up	PWAUP
bacterium	PWABG/TAOERPL
bagginess	PWAG/TKPW*EUPBS
bailiff(s)	PWHR-F(S)
Bailiff(s)	PWHR*F(S)
THE BAILIFF: *(colloquy)*	PWHR-F/PWHR-F, PWAEUL/PWAEUL
balance	PWHRA*PBS
ballistic(s)	PWHR*EUS/EUBG(S)
balloon	PWHRAOPB
balminess	PWAU/PH*EUPBS
balminess	PWAUPL/PH*EUPBS
bandage(s)	PW-PBLG(S)
bandaged	PW-PBLGD
band-aid(s)	PW-PBD(Z)
Band-Aid(s)	PW*PBD(Z)
B&E *(breaking and entering)*	PW-RBGS/SKP*E
B&E	PW-RBGS/TPH*E
bank *(as wd)*	PWA*PBG
bank *(as wd)*	PWAPB/-BG
bank account(s)	PW-BGT(S)
bank robber	PWRORB
bank robbery	PWROERB
bankable	PWA*PBG/-BL
bankbook	PWA*PBG/PWAOBG
banker(s)	PWA*PBG/ER(S)
bankroll	PWROL
bankrupt	PWRUPT
bankruptcy	PWRUPS
bankruptcy	PWRUPT/SEU
barbaric	PWAR/PWAEURBG
bargainee	PWARG/TPHAOE
bargainer	PWARG/TPHER
barium	PWAEURPL
barometer	PWROPL/TER
barometer(s)	PWROPLT/ER(S)
barracks	PWAR/ABGS
barrage	PWRAPBLG
barren	PWAEURPB
barrister(s)	PWA*EURS/ER(S)
barrister(s)	PWA*RS/ER(S)
baseball	PWAEUBL
BASIC	PWA*EUS/EUBG
basketball	PWABGT/PWAL
bathroom	PWA*RPL
bawdiness	PWAU/TK*EUPBS
bawdiness	PWAUD/TK*EUPBS
Bayer	PWA*EUR
bazillion	PWA/S*L
BBA *(Bachelor of Business Administration)*	PW-RBGS/PWA*
BBC *(British Broadcasting Corporation)*	PW-RBGS/PW*BG
BBS *(bulletin board system)*	PW-RBGS/PW*S
BCE *(before Christian/common era, B.C.)*	PW-RBGS/KR*E
be	PW-
be the	PW-T
beadiness	PWAOE/TK*EUPBS
beadiness	PWAOED/TK*EUPBS
bear *(as wd)*	PWAER
bear in mind	PWAERPLD
beatific	PWAOE/TEUFBG
beautiful	PWAOUFL
beautifully	PWAOUFL/HREU
became	PWAEUPL
because *(as wd)*	PWAUZ
because of	PWAUF
because of the	PWAUFT
become(s)	PW-BG(S)
B complex	PW-RBGS/KPHREBGS
bedroom	PW*ERPL
beefiness	PWAOE/TP*EUPBS
beefiness	PWAOEF/TP*EUPBS
been	PW-PB
before *(as wd)*	PW-FR
before and after	PWRAFR
before or after	PWROFR
before that accident	PWAFRBGS
before the accident	PWEFRBGS
before the	PW-FRT
before this accident	PWEUFRBGS
beforehand	PW-FRPBD
beforehand	PW-FR/HAPBD
beg *(as wd)*	PWEG
beg your pardon	PWURPD
began	TKPWAPB
begin	TKPWEUPB
beginner(s)	TKPWEUPB/ER(S)
beginning(s)	TKPWEUPBG(S), TKPWEUPBG(/-S)
beginning(s)	TKPWEUPB/-G(S)
begun	TKPW-PB
behalf	PWHAF
behave	PWHA*EUF
behavior	PWHA*EUF/KWROR
behavioral	PWHA*EUF/KWRORL
behind	PWHAOEUPBD
being *(as wd)*	PW-G
being duly impaneled and sworn	PWUPLS
being duly sworn and impaneled	PWURPBLD

beings	PW-GS	bill of indictment	PWOFPLT
belated	PWE/HRAEUTD	bill of lading	PWOFLG
belief	PWHRAOEF	bill of particulars	PWOFPS
believability	PWHRAO*EFBLT	Bill of Rights	PWOFRTS
believable evidence	PWHR*EFD, PWHREFD	bill of sale	PWOFS
		billion(s) *(as wd)*	PW-L(S)
believable	PWHRAO*EFBL	billion dollar(s)	PW-LD(Z)
believably	PWHRAO*EF/PWHREU	billionaire	PW-L/TPHAEUR
believe *(as wd)*	PWHRAO*EF	billionth	PW*LT
believe it or not	PWHRORPBT	biofeedback	PWAOEUFB
believer(s)	PWHRAO*EFR(/-S)	biographic	PWAO*EU/TKPWRAFBG
believer(s)	PWHRAO*EF/ER(S)	biological warfare	PWAFR
believingly	PWHRAO*EF/TKPWHREU	biological weapon(s)	PWEP(S)
belligerence	PWHREUPBLG/ERPBS	biophysical	PWAO*EU/TP-L
belligerence	PWHREUPBLG/REPBS	biophysical	PWAOEU/KWRO/TP-L
belligerency	PWHREUPBLG/ERPB/SEU	biopsy	PWAOEUPS
belligerency	PWHREUPBLG/REPB/SEU	birdbrained	PWEURD/PWRAEUPBD
belligerent	PWHREUPBLG/ERPBT	Birmingham	PWEURPLG/HAPL
belligerent	PWHREUPBLG/REPBT	bisexual	PW*EU/SWAUL
belong	PWHROPBG	black *(as wd)*	PWHRABG
belonging(s)	PWHROPBG/-G(S)	black market *(n)*	PWHRARBGT
beloved	PWE/HR*UFD	black marketeer *(n)*	PWHRARBGT/TAOER
beloved	PWE/HRO*FD	black marketer(s) *(n)*	PWHRARBGT/ER(S)
below	PWHRO*E	blackball	PWHRABL
beltway	PWAE	blameworthiness	PWHRAEUPL/WOR/TH*EUPBS
Beltway	PWA*E		
beneath	TPHAO*ET	blank	PWHRA*PBG
Bernard	PWERPBD	blanker	PWHRA*PBG/ER
beside(s)	PW-DZ(/-S)	blankest	PWHRA*PBG/*ES
best *(as wd)*	PW*ES	blanket	PWHRA*PBGT
best of my ability	PWEUBLT	blanket	PWHRA*PBG/ET
best of my knowledge	PWEUPBLG	blankly	PWHRA*PBG/HREU
best of my recollection	PWEURBG	bleariness	PWHRAOE/R*EUPBS
best of your ability	PWURBLT	bleariness	PWHRAOER/R*EUPBS
best of your knowledge	PWURPBLG	blink	PWHR*EUPBG
best of your recollection	PWURBG	blinker(s)	PWHR*EUPBG/ER(S)
bestowal	PWE/STOEL	blood *(as wd)*	PWHRAOD
betrayal	PWE/TRAEUL	blood alcohol	PWHROL
between *(as wd)*	TWAOEPB	blood alcohol level	PWHRO*FL, PWHROFL
between the	TWAOEPBT	blood clot	PWHR-LT
beverage	PW*EFRPBLG	blood count	PWHR-BGT
beyond *(as wd)*	KWROPBD	blood pressure	PWHR-P
beyond a reasonable doubt	KWR-RD	blood sugar	PWHRAOUG
		blood test	PWHR*ES
beyond all doubt	KWR-LD	blood type	PWHRAOEUP
beyond all reasonable doubt	KWR-RLD	blood vessel	PWHR*FL
		bloodiness	PWHRAOD/TK*EUPBS
beyond any reasonable doubt	KWR-RPBD	bloodstream	PWHRAOEPL
		BLT *(bacon, lettuce, and tomato)*	PW-RBGS/HR*T
beyond every reasonable doubt	KWR-FRD		
		blue *(as wd)*	PWHRU, PWHRAO*U
beyond reasonable doubt	KWR*RD	blueberry	PWHRU/PWER/REU
bias	PWAOEUS	bluebird(s)	PWHRU/PWEURD(Z)
biblical	PWEUBL/KAL	blue-collar *(j)*	PWHRUBG
biceps	PW*EU/SEPS	blue collar *(n)*	PWHRU/KHRAR
bicycle	PWOEUBG	Blue Cross	PWHRUBGS
bicyclist	PWOEUBG/*EUS	Blue Cross/Blue Shield	PWHRUBGS/PWHRULD
b.i.d. *(med [twice a day])*	PW*EUD	blue-eyed *(j)*	PWHRU/KWRAOEUD
bidirectional	PW*EU/TKR*EBGS/TPHAL	bluegrass	PWHRU/TKPWRASZ
bilge	PWEULG	blue-green	PWHRU/(H-F/)TKPWRAOEPB
bill *(as wd)*	PWEUL		
Bill *(as wd)*	PW*EUL	blue laws	PWHRU/HRAU/-S
Bill Clinton	PWHR*EUBG	blueprint	PWHRUPT

blueprint	PWHRU/PREUPBT	breathiness	PWR*ET/TH*EUPBS
bluer	PWHRU/ER	breeziness	PWRAOE/S*EUPBS
Blue Shield	PWHRULD	breeziness	PWRAOEZ/S*EUPBS
bluest	PWHRU/*ES	breeziness	PWRAOEZ/*PBS
bluish	PWHRU/EURB	bric-a-brac	PWREUBG/PWRABG
bluishness	PWHRU/SH*PBS	bright *(as wd)*	PWRAOEUGT
blurriness	PWHRUR/R*EUPBS	bright light(s)	PWR-LT(S)
BMOC *(big man on campus)*	PW-RBGS/PH*RBGS/O*BG	bring	PWREU
BMOC	PW-RBGS/PHO*BG	brink	PWR*EUPBG
board *(as wd)*	PWAORD	British	PWREURB
board of arbitration	PWR-RBGS	British Isles	PWREURB/AOEULS
Board of Arbitration	PWR*RBGS	broken	PWROEPB
board of commissioners	PWR-RPLGS	brokenhearted	PWROEPB/HARTD
Board of Commissioners	PWR*RPLGS	brother(s) *(as wd)*	PWROER(/-S)
board of directors	PWR-DZ	brother and sister	PWRA*S
Board of Directors	PWR*DZ	brothers and sisters	PWRA*SZ, PWRA*S/-S
board of education	PWR-PBLGS	brother or sister	PWRO*S
Board of Education	PWR*PBLGS	brothers or sisters	PWRO*SZ, PWRO*S/-S
board of trustees	PWR-TS	brotherhood	PWROER/HAOD
Board of Trustees	PWR*TS	brother-in-law	PWROERPBL
boardroom	PWAO*RPL	brothers-in-law	PWROERPBLS
bodily *(as wd)*	PWOD/HREU	brother-in-laws	PWROERPBL/-S
bodily harm	PWORPL	brotherly	PWROER/HREU
bodily injury	PWOPBLG	brought	PWRAUT
Boeing	PWOEPBG	brown-eyed *(j)*	PWROUPB/KWRAOEUD
bogginess	PWOG/TKPW*EUPBS	Btu *(British thermal unit)*	PW-RBGS/T*U
Bolivia	PWHR*EUF/KWRA	B.t.u. *(British thermal unit)*	PW-FPLT/T*U
bon voyage	PWOPB/SROEUPBLG	bubbliness	PWUB/HR*EUPBS
bona fide	PWOEPB/TPAOEUD	bucket	PWUBGT
boogie-woogie	PWAOG/WAOG/TKPWAOE	budget	PWUPBLGT
(Booing.)	PWAO*G	buenas noches	PWAEUPBS/TPHOEFPS
boondocks	PWAOPB/TKOBGS	Buenos Aires	PWAEUPBS/AEURZ
booziness	PWAO/S*EUPBS	buenos dias	PWAEUPBS/TKAOES
booziness	PWAOZ/*PBS	Bufferin	PWUFRPB
booziness	PWAOZ/S*EUPBS	bugginess	PWUG/TKPW*EUPBS
boric	PWOERBG, PWORBG	bulge	PWULG
Bosnia-Herzegovina	PWOZ/HERZ	bulimia	PWHRAOEPL/KWRA
bought	PWAUT	bulkiness	PWUL/K*EUPBS
boulevard(s)	PWHR-FD(Z), PWHR*FD(Z)	bullet	PWULT
bowel	PWO*UL	bulletproof	PWHRAOF
bower	PWO*UR	bum-bailiff	PWUPL/PWHR-F
boxiness	PWOBG/S*EUPBS	bumpiness	PWUFRP/P*EUPBS
boxiness	PWOBGS/S*EUPBS	bumpiness	PWUPL/P*EUPBS
boyfriend	PWOEUF	bunk	PW*UPBG
bpd *(barrels per day)*	PW*/P*D	bunker(s)	PW*UPBG/ER(S)
bpi *(bits/bytes per inch)*	PW*/P*EU	buoyancy	PWOEUPB/SEU
BPOE *(Benevolent and Protective Order of Elks)*		buoyant	PWOEUPBT
	PW-RBGS/PO*E	burden(s) *(as wd)*	PWURD(Z)
BPOE	PW-RBGS/P*RBGS/O*E	burden of proof	PWR-P
bps *(bits per second)*	PW*PS	burden of proving	PWR-PG
bps	PW*/P*S	burdensome	PWURD/SPH-
braininess	PWRAEU/TPH*EUPBS	burglar	PWHRAR
braininess	PWRAEUPB/TPH*EUPBS	burglarize	PWHRAR/AOEUZ
brake *(as wd)*	PWRAEUBG	burglary	PWHRAR/REU
brake light(s)	PW-LT(S)	burliness	PWUR/HR*EUPBS
brassiness	PWRAS/S*EUPBS	Bush	PW*URB
brawniness	PWRAU/TPH*EUPBS	Bush Administration	PW*URGS
brawniness	PWRAUPB/TPH*EUPBS	business	PWEUZ
breast *(as wd)*	PWR*ES	businesslike	PWEUZ/HRAO*EUBG
breast implant	PWHRAPBT	businessman	PWEUZ/PHAPB
Breathalyzer	PWHRAOEURZ	businessmen	PWEUZ/PHEPB
Breathalyzer	PWRAOEUZ/ER	businesswise	PWEUZ/WAO*EUZ
		businesswoman	PWEUZ/WOPL

businesswomen	PWEUZ/WEUPL
but	PWU
BVD *(underwear)*	PW-RBGS/SR*D
BVD's	PW-RBGS/SR*D/AOES
BVDs	PW-RBGS/SR*D/-S
BWI *(British West Indies)*	PW-RBGS/W*EU
by *(as wd)*	PWEU
by and large	PWHRARPBLG
bylaw	PWHRAU
byline	PWHRAOEUPB
BYO *(bring your own)*	PW-RBGS/KWRO*
BYOB *(bring your own bottle)*	PW-RBGS/KWR*RBGS/O*B
BYOB	PW-RBGS/KWRO*B
by-product	PW*EU/PRUBGT
by-product	PWEU/H-F/PRUBGT

CAB *(Civil Aeronautics Board)*	KR-RBGS/A*B
CAD *(computer-aided design)*	KR-RBGS/A*D
calamitous	KHRAPL/TOUS
calamity	KHRAPL/TEU
calculate	KAL/KHRAEUT
calculation	KAL/KHRAEUGS
calculator	KAL/KHRAEU/TOR
calendar	KAL/TKAR
California	KRA*/KRA*
California	KRAFPLT
Californian	KRA*/KRA*/KWRAPB
Californian	KRAFPLT/KWRAPB
call *(as wd)*	KAUL
call your attention	KAURGS
calling your attention	KAURPBGS
calls for a conclusion	KA*UGS
calls for a legal conclusion	KA*ULGS
calls for a legal opinion	KA*UPL
calls for speculation	KA*UPS
calligrapher	KHREUG/TPER
calligraphist	KHREUG/TP*EUS
calligraphy	KHREUG/TPEU
caloric	KA/HROERBG
caloric	KA/HRORBG
calypso	KHREUP/SOE
Camaro	KPHAEUR/ROE
Camaro	KPHAR/ROE
camellia	KPHAOEL/KWRA
can *(v)*	K-
can be	K-B
can be the	K-BT
can believe	K-BL
can believe the	K-BLT
can feel	K-FL
can find	K-FPBD
can go	K-G
can have	K-F
can have been	K-FB
can he be	KEB
can he be the	KEBT
can he believe	KEBL
can he believe the	KEBLT
can he feel	KEFL
can he find	KEFPBD
can he have	KEF
can he have the	KEFT
can he recall	KERL
can he recall the	KERLT
can he recollect	KERBG
can he recollect the	KERBGT
can he remember	KERPL
can he remember the	KERPLT
can he think	KEPBG
can he think the	KEPBGT
can he understand	KEPBDZ
can I be	KEUB

can I be the	KEUBT	Canal Zone	KAPBL/SO*EPB
can I believe	KEUBL	Canberra	KAPB/PWRA
can I believe the	KEUBLT	candidacy	KAPBD/SEU
can I feel	KEUFL	candidate	KAPBD/TKAEUT
can I find	KEUFPBD	candidate	KAPBD/TKAT
can I have	KEUF	canker(s)	KA*PBG/ER(S)
can I have the	KEUFT	cankerous	KA*PBG/ROUS
can I recall	KEURL	cannabis	KAPB/PWEUS
can I recall the	KEURLT	cannibal	KAPB/PWAL
can I recollect	KEURBG	cannibalism	KAPB/PWHREUFPL
can I recollect the	KEURBGT	cannot	K-/TPHOT
can I remember	KEURPL	capability	KAEUPBLT
can I remember the	KEURPLT	capable	KAEUPBL
can I think	K-/EUPBG	capacious	KPAEURBS
can I think the	K-/EUPBGT	capaciously	KPAEURBS/HREU
can I understand	K-/EUPBDZ	capaciousness	KPAEURBS/*PBS
can I want	KEUPT	capacitor	KPAS/TOR
can recall	K-RL	capacity	KPAS/TEU
can recall the	K-RLT	capitalization	KAPT/SA*EUGS
can recollect	K-RBG	capitular	KPEUFP/HRAR
can recollect the	K-RBGT	capitulary	KPEUFP/HRAEUR
can remember	K-RPL	capitulate	KPEUFP/HRAEUT
can remember the	K-RPLT	capitulation	KPEUFP/HRAEUGS
can she be	SKEB	capitulator	KPEUFP/HRAEU/TOR
can she be the	SKEBT	capricious	KPRAOERBS
can she believe	SKEBL	capricious	KPREURBS
can she believe the	SKEBLT	capriciously	KPRAOERBS/HREU
can she feel	SKEFL	capriciously	KPREURBS/HREU
can she find	SKEFPBD	capriciousness	KPRAOERBS/*PBS
can she have	SKEF	capriciousness	KPREURBS/*PBS
can she have the	SKEFT	captivity	KAPT/*EUFT
can she recall	SKERL	carbon *(as wd)*	KAR/PWOPB
can she recall the	SKERLT	carbon dioxide	KOEUBGS
can she recollect	SKERBG	carbon monoxide	KPHOEUBGS
can she recollect the	SKERBGT	carbonization	KARB/SA*EUGS
can she remember	SKERPL	cardiogram	KARD/TKPWRAPL
can she remember the	SKERPLT	cardiograph	KARD/TKPWRAF
can she think	SKEPBG	careen	KRAOEPB
can she think the	SKEPBGT	career	KRAOER
can she understand	SKEPBDZ	careless	KAEURLS
can understand	K-PBDZ	carelessly	KAEURLS/HREU
can want	K-PT	carelessness	KAEURLS/*PBS
can you be	K-/KWROU/PW-	Caribbean	KAEUR/PWAOEPB
can you be the	KUBT	Caribbean	KREUB/KWRAPB
can you believe	KUBL	caricature(s)	KARBG/KHUR(S)
can you believe the	KUBLT	carjack	KARPBLG
can you describe	K*UDZ	carjacker(s)	KARPBLG/ER(S)
can you feel	KUFL	carol	KAEURL
can you find	KUFPBD	carotid	KROT/EUD
can you have	K*UF, K-/UF	carpal *(as wd)*	KARPL
can you have the	K*UFT, KUFT, K-/UFT	carpal tunnel	KARPLT
can you recall	K*URL	carpal tunnel syndrome	KARPLTS
can you recall the	K*URLT, KURLT	carpe diem	KARP/TKAOEPL
can you recollect	KURBG	carpet	KARPT
can you recollect the	KURBGT	carriage	KAEURPBLG
can you remember	KURPL	CART *(Communication Access Realtime Translation)*	
can you remember the	KURPLT		KR-RBGS/A*RBGS/R*T
can you think	KUPBG	CART	KR-RBGS/A*RT
can you think the	KUPBGT	casework	KAEURBG
can you understand	KUPBDZ	caseworker(s)	KAEURBG/ER(S)
can you want	KUPT	cashworthiness	KARB/WOR/TH*EUPBS
can't	K-PBT	casual	KARBL
canal	KAPBL	casually	KARBL/HREU

© 2004 *StenEd*® **Briefs & Phrases** (Excerpted from StenEd's Realtime Professional Dictionary)

casualty	KARBL/TEU	centralization	STRAL/SA*EUGS
CAT *(Computer-Aided Transcription)*		centralize	STRAL/AOEUZ
	KRAT	centrally	STRAL/HREU
CAT	KR-RBGS/A*T	CEO *(chief executive officer)*	KR-RBGS/KWRO*E
C.A.T.	KR-FPLT/A*T	ceremonial	SER/PHOEPBL
CAT scan *(computerized axial tomography scan)*		certain	SERPB
	KRAT/SKAPB	certainly	SERPB/HREU
CAT scan	KR-RBGS/A*T/SKAPB	certainty	SERPB/TEU
catastrophe	KA/TA*S/TPAOE	certainty	SERPBT
catastrophic	KAT/STROFBG	certiorari	SERB/RAEUR
catastrophic	KATS/TROFBG	certiorari	SERS/RAEUR
caught	KAUT	CFC *(chlorofluorocarbon)*	KR-RBGS/TP*BG
cauliflower	KAUL/TPHRO*UR	CFO *(chief financial officer)*	KR-RBGS/TPO*
cauliflower	KAUL/TPHROUR	CFR *(Code of Federal Regulations)*	
causa mortis	KAU/SA/PHORTS		KR-RBGS/TP*R
cause(s) *(as wd)*	KAUZ(/-S)	CFTC *(Commodity Futures Trading Commission)*	
cause celebre	KAUZ/SHREB		KR-RBGS/TP*RBGS/T*BG
cause of action	KAUBGS	THE CHAIR: *(colloquy)*	KHAEUR/KHAEUR
causes celebres	KAUZ/SHREBZ	chairman	KHAEURPL
causeway	KWAE	Chairman	KHA*EURPL
Causeway	KWA*E	THE CHAIRMAN: *(colloquy)*	
CBC *(Canadian Broadcasting Corporation)*			KHAEURPL/KHAEURPL
	KR-RBGS/PW*BG	chairmanship	KHAEURPL/SHEUP
CBS *(Columbia Broadcasting System)*		chairperson	KHAEURP
	KR-RBGS/PW*S	chairperson	KHAEUR/PERPB
cc *(cubic centimeter, carbon copy)*		Chairperson	KHA*EURP
	KR*BG	Chairperson	KHA*EUR/PERPB
CCA *(Circuit/County Court of Appeals)*		THE CHAIRPERSON: *(colloquy)*	
	KR-RBGS/KRA*		KHAEURPB/KHAEURPB
C.C.A.	KR-FPLT/KRA*	chairwoman	KWHAEURPL
CCP *(Code of Civil Procedure, Court of Common Pleas)*		chairwoman	KHAEUR/WOPL
	KR-RBGS/KR*P	Chairwoman	KWHA*EURPL
CCR *(Certified Court Reporter)*		Chairwoman	KHA*EUR/WOPL
	KR-RBGS/KR*R	THE CHAIRWOMAN: *(colloquy)*	
CCTV *(closed-circuit television)*			KWHAEURPL/KWHAEURPL
	KR-RBGS/KR*RBGS/T*F	chalkiness	KHAU/K*EUPBS
CCU *(critical/cardiac care unit)*		chalkiness	KHAUBG/K*EUPBS
	KR-RBGS/KR*U	challenge	KHAPBLG
cd	KR-D	challenger(s)	KHAPBLG/ER(S)
CD(s) *(compact disk, certificate of deposit)*		Challenger	KHA*PBLG/ER
	KR*D(Z)	chameleon	KPHAOEL/KWROPB
CD's	KR*D/AOES	chance *(as wd)*	KHAPBS
CDC *(Centers for Disease Control)*		chance of precipitation	KH*EUPGS
	KR*D/KR*RBGS	chanciness	KHAPB/S*EUPBS
CDC	KR-RBGS/TK*BG	change	KHAEUPBG
cDNA *(complementary DNA)*	KR*/TK*RBGS/TPHA*	changeability	KHAEUPBG/-BLT
CD-ROM *(compact disk read-only memory)*		changeable	KHAEUPBG/-BL
	KR-RBGS/TKRO*PL	changeably	KHAEUPBG/PWHREU
cease *(as wd)*	SAOES	changeless	KHAEUPBG/HRES
cease and desist	STK*S	changeling	KHAEUPBG/HREUPBG
ceiling	KRAOELG	changer(s)	KHAEUPBG/ER(S)
celeb	SHREB	character	KARBGT
celestial	SHR*ES/KWRAL	characteristic(s)	KARBGT/EUBG(S)
celestial	SHRES/KHAL	characteristically	KARBGT/KHREU
cell *(as wd)*	KREL	characterization	KARBGT/SA*EUGS
cell phone	KR-FPB	characterize	KARBGT/AOEUZ
cellular phone	KR*FPB	CHARGE OF THE COURT *(cap & center)*	
center *(as wd)*	SEPBT/ER		KH-PBLG/KH-PBLG
center lane	STPHRAEPB	charisma	KREUZ/PHA
center line	STPHRAOEUPB	charismatic	KREUZ/PHAT/EUBG
central *(as wd)*	STRAL	charity	KHAEURT
Central America	STRAL/PHERBG	chauffeur	SHOEFR
Central American	STRAL/PHERPB	check(ing) *(as wd)*	KHEBG(/-G)

checkup	KH*UP	cigarette	STKPWRET
check up	KHUP	circuit *(as wd)*	SEURBGT
checking account(s)	KH-BGT(S)	circuit court	SKOURT
cheekiness	KHAOE/K*EUPBS	Circuit Court	SKO*URT
cheekiness	KHAOEBG/K*EUPBS	circuitous	SEURBGT/OUS
cheeriness	KHAOE/R*EUPBS	circuitously	SEURBGT/OUS/HREU
cheeriness	KHAOER/R*EUPBS	circuitousness	SEURBGT/OUS/*PBS
(Cheering.)	KHAO*ERG	circuitry	SEURBGT/REU
(Cheers and applause.)	KHA*UZ	circuity	SEURBGT/TEU
cheesiness	KHAOE/S*EUPBS	circumstance	SEURBG
cheesiness	KHAOEZ/S*EUPBS	circumstances	SEURBGZ, SEURBG/-S
chemical *(as wd)*	KEPL/KAL	circumstantial *(as wd)*	SEURBLG
chemical warfare	KWAFR	circumstantial *(as wd)*	SEURBG/-RBL
chemical weapon(s)	KWEP(S)	circumstantial evidence	SK*EFD, SKEFD
chemotherapy	KAOEPL/THAEURP	circumstantiality	SEURBG/-RBL/TEU
Chevrolet	KH*EF/HRAEU	circumstantiality	SEURBLG/TEU
Chevrolet	SH*EF/HRAEU	circumstantially	SEURBG/-RBL/HREU
chewiness	KHAOU/W*EUPBS	circumstantially	SEURBLG/HREU
Chicago	KHEUG	circumstantiate	SEURBG/KHAEUT
chief *(as wd)*	KHAOEF	circumstantiate	SEURBG/SHAEUT
Chief *(as wd)*	KHAO*EF	circumstantiation	SEURBG/KHAEUGS
chief executive	KHAOEBGS	circumstantiation	SEURBG/SHAEUGS
Chief Executive	KHAO*EBGS	citify	STEU/TPEU
chief justice	KHAOEPBLGS	city *(as wd)*	STEU
Chief Justice	KHAO*EPBLGS	City *(as wd)*	ST*EU
child *(as wd)*	KHAOEULD	city council	SKOUPBS
child abuse	KHAOUS	civic	S*EUFBG
child support	KHORT	civil *(as wd)*	S*EUFL
children	KHEURPB	civil rights	SHR-RTS
chilliness	KHEUL/HR*EUPBS	claimant	KHRAEUPLT
chipmunk	KHEUP/PH*UPBG	clamminess	KHRAPL/PH*EUPBS
chiropractic	KPRABG/TEUBG	class *(as wd)*	KHRASZ
chiropractic	KPRABGT/EUBG	class action	KHRA*BGS
chiropractor	KPRABG/TOR	class action suit	KHRA*BGS/SAOUT
chloric	KHROERBG, KHRORBG	classifiable	KHR-FBL
cholesterol	KHR*ES/ROEL	classification	KHR-FGS
cholesterol	KHR*ES/ROL	classified	KHR-FD
cholesterol	KHRES/TROEL	classifier(s)	KHR-FR(S)
cholesterol	KHRES/TROL	classifies	KHR-FS
choosiness	KHAOZ/S*EUPBS	classify	KHR-F
choppiness	KHOP/P*EUPBS	classifying	KHR-FG
chorus	KHOERS	classroom	KHRAOPL
chose in possession	KHOEZ/TPH-/PEGS	clavicular	KHRA*FBG/HRAR
chose in possession	SHOEZ/TPH-/PEGS	clean *(as wd)*	KHRAOEPB
chubbiness	KHUB/PW*EUPBS	cleanup	KHR*UP
chumminess	KHUPL/PH*EUPBS	clean up	KHRUP
chunk	KH*UPBG	cleanliness	KHREPB/HR*EUPBS
chunkier	KH*UPBG/KWRER	clear *(as wd)*	KHRAOER
chunkiest	KH*UPBG/KWR*ES	clear and convincing	
chunkily	KH*UPBG/HREU	evidence	KHR*EFD, KHREFD
chunkiness	KH*UPBG/K*EUPBS	clearinghouse	KHRAOERG/HOUS
chunkiness	KH*UPBG/KEU/*PBS	clearness	KHRAO*ERPBS
chunkiness	KHUPB/K*EUPBS	cleavage	KHRAO*EFPBLG
chunky	KH*UPBG/KEU	clergyman	KHRERPBLG/PHAPB
CIA *(Central Intelligence Agency)*		clergymen	KHRERPBLG/PHEPB
	KR-RBGS/A*EU	clergywoman	KHRERPBLG/WOPL
C.I.A. *(Central Intelligence Agency)*		clergywomen	KHRERPBLG/WEUPL
	KR-FPLT/A*EU	clerk *(as wd)*	KHRERBG
CIC *(Computer Integrated Courtroom)*		THE CLERK: *(colloquy)*	KHRERBG/KHRERBG
	KR-RBGS/*EUBG	Clerk of the Circuit Court	KHROURBGT
CIF *(cost, insurance, and freight)*		Clerk of the Court	KHROURT
	KR-RBGS/*EUF	Cleveland	KHRAO*EFLD
cigar	STKPWAR	Cleveland	KHRAOEFLD

Clifford	KHREUFRD
clink	KHR*EUPBG
clinker(s)	KHR*EUPBG/ER(S)
Clinton	KHR*EUPBT
Clinton	KHR*PBT
Clinton Administration	KHR*EURGS
Clorox	KHROERBGS
close *(s snd)(as wd)*	KHROES
close *(z snd)(as wd)*	KHROEZ
close corporation	KHROEZ/KORPGS
close corporation	KHROES/KORPGS
close-up	KHRO*UP
close up	KHROUP
closed caption	KHROEPGS
closing argument(s)	KHRARGT(S), KHRARGT(/-S)
closing statement(s)	KHROEPLT(S), KHROEPLT(/-S)
clothes	KHRO*ETS
cloture	KHROEFP
cloud *(as wd)*	KHROUD
cloud cover	KHROUBG
cloudiness	KHROU/TK*EUPBS
cloudiness	KHROUD/TK*EUPBS
cloudy *(as wd)*	KHROU/TKEU
cloudy *(as wd)*	KHROUD/TKEU
cloudy skies	KHRAOEUZ
CLU *(Chartered Life Underwriter)*	KR-RBGS/HR*U
clumsiness	KHRUPL/S*EUPBS
CLVS *(Certified Legal Video Specialist)*	KR-RBGS/HR*FS
cm *(centimeter)*	KR*PL
CMA *(Certified Medical Assistant)*	KR-RBGS/PHA*
CMR *(Certified Merit Reporter)*	KR-RBGS/PH*R
CMRS *(Certified Manager of Reporter Services)*	KR-RBGS/PH*RBGS/R*S
CMRS	KR-RBGS/PH*RS
CNBC *(Cable National Broadcasting Company)*	KR-RBGS/ TPH*RBGS/PW*BG
CNN *(Cable Network News)*	KR-RBGS/TPH*PB
Co.	KOFPLT
coagency	KO/AGT/SEU
coagent	KO/AGT
coagulant	KWAG/HRAPBT
coagulate	KWAG/HRAEUT
coagulation	KWAG/HRAEUGS
co-chairman	KO/KHAEURPL
co-chairperson	KO/KHAEURP
co-chairperson	KO/KHAEUR/PERPB
cockiness	KOBG/K*EUPBS
cocounsel	KO/KOUPBL
co-counsel	KO/H-F/KOUPBL
COD *(cash/collect on delivery)*	KR-RBGS/O*D
COD	KROD
C.O.D.	KR-FPLT/*OD
C.O.D.	KRO*D
codefendant(s)	KO/TK-FT(S)
co-defendant(s)	KO/H-F/TK-FT(S)
coeducation	KO/EGS
coefficient	KO/TPEURBT
coffer	KOFR
coffin	KAUFPB
coffin	KOFPB
cohabit	KO/HABT
coincide(s)	KOEUPB/SAO*EUD(Z)
coincide(s)	KOEUPB/SAOEUD(Z)
coincidence	KOEUPBS/TKEPBS
coincident	KOEUPBS/TKEPBT
coincidental	KOEUPBS/TKEPB/TAL
coincidentally	KOEUPBS/TKEPBT/HREU
coinsurance	KO/STPHURPBS
coinsure	KO/STPHUR
coinsurer(s)	KO/STPHUR/ER(S)
colander(s)	KHRAPBD/ER(S)
cold *(as wd)*	KOELD, KOLD
cold front	KOEFRT
coldhearted	KOELD/HARTD
coldhearted	KOLD/HARTD
coldheartedly	KOELD/HARTD/HREU
coldheartedly	KOLD/HARTD/HREU
colicky	KOL/KEU
coliseum	KOL/SAOEPL
colitis	KHRAOEUTS
Colombia	KHROPL/KWRA
Colombo	KHROPL/PWOE
colonel	KURPBL
colonial	KHROEPB/KWRAL
colonial	KO/HROEPBL
colonialism	KHROEPB/KWRAL/EUFPL
colonialism	KO/HROEPBL/EUFPL
Colorado	KRO*/KRO*
colossal	KHROS/SAL
Columbia	KHRUPL/KWRA
Columbian	KHRUPL/KWRAPB
columbine	KHRUPL/PWAOEUPB
Columbus	KHRUPL/PWUS
columnar	KHRUPL/TPHAR
columnist	KHRUPL/TPH*EUS
com	KPHO
com	KR*/O*PL
.com *(suf)*	KPHOFPLT
COM	KPHO*
COM	KROPL
COM	KR-RBGS/O*PL
combat	KPWAT
combatant	KPWAT/TAPBT
combative	KPWAT/*EUF
combination	KPWEUPBGS
combination	KPWEU/TPHAEUGS
combinatorial	KPWEUPB/TOEURL
combine	KPWAOEUPB
combustibility	KPW*US/-BLT
combustible	KPW*US/-BL
combustion	KPW*UGS, KPWUGS
comedian	KPHAOED/KWRAPB
comedic	KPHAOED/EUBG
comedienne	KPHAOED/KWREPB
comet	KOPLT
comfort(s)	K-FRT(S)
comfortability	K-FRBLT
comfortability	K-FRT/-BLT

comfortable	K-FRBL	complacency	KPHRAEU/SEPB/SEU
comfortable	K-FRT/-BL	complacency	KPHRAEUS/EPB/SEU
comfortably	K-FRBL/HREU	complacent	KPHRAEU/SEPBT
comfortably	K-FRT/PWHREU	complacent	KPHRAEUS/EPBT
comforted	K-FRTD	complain	KPHRAEUPB
comforting	K-FRT/-G	complainant	KPHRAEU/TPHAPBT
commercial	KPHERBL	complaint	KPHRAEUPBT
common (as wd)	KPHOPB	complaisance	KPHRAEU/SAPBS
common sense	KPH-PBS	complaisant	KPHRAEU/SAPBT
communal	KPHAOUPBL	complete(ly) (as wd)	KPHRAOET(/HREU)
community (as wd)	KPHAOUPBT	complete and accurate	KHRABGT
community (as wd)	KPHUPBT	completely and accurately	KHRAEBGT
community college	KPHEPBLG	completeness	KPHRAOET/*PBS
Community College	KPH*EPBLG	completion	KPHRAOEGS
companion	KPAPB/KWROPB	complex	KPHREBGS
companionship	KPAPB/KWROPB/SHEUP	complexion	KPHR*EBGS
company	KPAEPB	complexity	KPHREBGS/TEU
Company	KPA*EPB	compliance	KPHRAOEUPBS
comparable	KPAEURBL	compliant	KPHRAOEUPBT
comparably	KPAEUR/PWHREU	complicate	KOFRP/KAEUT
comparably	KPAR/PWHREU	complicate	KPHREU/KAEUT
comparative	KPAEUR/T*EUF	complication	KOFRP/KAEUGS
comparative	KPAR/T*EUF	complication	KPHREU/KAEUGS
comparatively	KPAEUR/T*EUF/HREU	comply	KPHRAOEU
comparatively	KPAR/T*EUF/HREU	component	KPOEPBT
compare	KPAEUR	component	KOPL/POEPBT
comparison	KPAEUR/SOPB	compose	KPOEZ
comparison	KPAR/SOPB	composer(s)	KPOEZ/ER(S)
compartment(s)	KPART/-PLT(S)	composite	KPOZ/SEUT
compartmental	KPART/-PLT/TAL	composition	KOFRP/SEUGS
compassi	KPASZ	composition	KOPL/POGS
compassion	KPAGS	compost	KPO*ES
compassionate	KPAGS/TPHAT	composure	KPOE/SHUR
compatibility	KPAT/-BLT	composure	KPOEZ/KWRUR
compatible	KPAT/-BL	compound(s)	KPOUPBD(Z)
compatibly	KPAT/PWHREU	comprehend(s)	KOFRP/HEPBD(Z)
compensable	KPEPBS/-BL	comprehend(s)	KPRE/HEPBD(Z)
compensate	KPEPB/SAEUT	comprehensible	KOFRP/HEPBS/-BL
compensation	KPEPB/SAEUGS	comprehensible	KPRE/HEPBS/-BL
compensation	KOFRP/SAEUGS	comprehensibly	KOFRP/HEPBS/PWHREU
compensatory (as wd)	KPEPBS/TOEUR	comprehensibly	KPRE/HEPBS/PWHREU
compensatory damages	KPEPBLGS	comprehension	KOFRP/HEPBGS
compete	KPAOET	comprehension	KPRE/HEPBGS
competence	KOFRP/TEPBS	comprehensive(s)	KOFRP/HEPBS/*EUF(S)
competence	KPE/TEPBS	comprehensive(s)	KPRE/HEPBS/*EUF(S)
competency	KOFRP/TEPB/SEU	comprehensively	KOFRP/HEPBS/*EUF/HREU
competency	KPE/TEPB/SEU	comprehensively	KPRE/HEPBS/*EUF/HREU
competent (as wd)	KOFRP/TEPBT	compress	KPRESZ
competent (as wd)	KPE/TEPBT	compression	KPREGS
competent		compressor	KPRES/SOR
producing cause	KPRAUZ	comprise	KPRAOEUZ
competently	KOFRP/TEPBT/HREU	compromise	KOFRP/PHAOEUZ
competently	KPE/TEPBT/HREU	compulsion	KPULGS
competition	KOFRP/TEUGS	compulsive	KPULS/*EUF
competition	KPE/TEUGS	compulsively	KPULS/*EUF/HREU
competitive	KPET/T*EUF	compulsorily	KPULS/REU/HREU
competitively	KPET/T*EUF/HREU	compulsoriness	KPUL/SO*EURPBS
competitiveness	KPET/T*EUFPBS	compulsoriness	KPULS/R*EUPBS
competitiveness	KOPL/PET/T*EUFPBS	compulsoriness	KPULS/REU/*PBS
competitiveness	KPET/T*EUF/*PBS	compulsory	KPULS/REU
competitor	KPET/TOR	compunction	KPUPBGS
complacence	KPHRAEU/SEPBS	computation	KPAOU/TAEUGS
complacence	KPHRAEUS/EPBS	computation	KOFRP/TAEUGS

Term	Brief	Term	Brief
computational	KPAOU/TAEUGS/TPHAL	conformist	K-FRPL/*EUS
computational	KOFRP/TAEUGS/TPHAL	conformity	K-FRPL/TEU
compute	KPAOUT	congratulate	TKPWRAFP
computer(s) (as wd)	KPAOURT(/-S), KPAOURT(S)	congratulations	TKPWRAFPGS/-S
		congratulations	TKPWRAFPGSZ
computer(s) (as wd)	KPAOUT/ER(S)	congratulatory	TKPWRAFP/HRA/TOEUR
computer disk	KPAOURTD	congregate	KOPBG/TKPWAEUT
computerese	KPAOURT/RAOEZ	congregation	KOPBG/TKPWAEUGS
computerese	KPAOUT/RAOEZ	congregational	KOPBG/TKPWAEUGS/TPHAL
computerize	KPAOURT/AOEUZ		
computerize	KPAOUT/RAOEUZ	congress	KOPBG
computerphobe	KPAOURT/TPOEB	Congress	KO*PBG
computerphobia	KPAOURT/TPOEB/KWRA	congressional	KOPBGS/TPHAL
computerphobic	KPAOURT/TPOEB/EUBG	Congressional	KO*PBGS/TPHAL
concentrate	KOPBS/TRAEUT	Congressional Record	KOPBGS/TPHAL/RORD
concentration	KOPBS/TRAEUGS	congressman	KPHAPB
concern(s)	K-RPB(S)	congressman	KOPBG/PHAPB
concerned	K-RPBD	Congressman	KPHA*PB
concerning	K-RPBG	Congressman	KO*PBG/PHAPB
condescend(s)	KOPBD/SEPBD(Z)	congressmen	KPHEPB
condescendingly	KOPBD/SEPBD/TKPWHREU	congressmen	KOPBG/PHEPB
		Congressmen	KPH*EPB
condition(s)	K-PB(S)	Congressmen	KO*PBG/PHEPB
conditional	K-PBL	congressperson	KPERPB
conditional	K-PB/TPHAL	congressperson	KOPBG/PERPB
conditionally	K-PB/HREU	Congressperson	KP*ERPB
conditionally	K-PBL/HREU	Congressperson	KO*PBG/PERPB
conditioned	K-PBD	congresswoman	KWOPL
conditioner(s)	K-PB/ER(S)	congresswoman	KOPBG/WOPL
conditioning	K-PBG	Congresswoman	KWO*PL
conduct	KUBGT	Congresswoman	KO*PBG/WOPL
conductance	KUBGT/TAPBS	congresswomen	KWEUPL
conduction	K*UBGS	congresswomen	KOPBG/WEUPL
conductive	KUBGT/*EUF	Congresswomen	KW*EUPL
conductivity	KUBGT/*EUFT	Congresswomen	KO*PBG/WEUPL
conductivity	KUBG/T*EUFT	connect	KEBGT
conductivity	KUBGT/*EUF/TEU	connecter(s)	KEBGT/ER(S)
conductor	KUBGT/TOR	Connecticut	KEBGT/KUT
conductor	KUBG/TOR	Connecticut	KR*T/KR*T
Coney Island	KO/TPHAOE/AO*EULD	connection	K*EBGS
Coney Island	KO/TPHAOE/AOEULD	connective	KEBGT/*EUF
confederacy	KOPB/TPED/SEU	connector	KEBGT/TOR
confer(s)	K-FR(S)	connector	KEBG/TOR
conferee	K-FR/RAOE	connoisseur	KOPB/SAOUR
conference	K-FRPBS	connotation	KOPB/TAEUGS
conferment(s)	K-FRPLT(S)	conscientious	KERBS
conferral	K-FRL	conscientiously	KERBS/HREU
conferred	K-FRD	conscientiousness	KERBS/*PBS
conferrer(s)	K-FR/ER(S)	conscionability	KOPBGS/-BLT
conferring	K-FRG	conscionable	KOPBGS/-BL
confidence(s)	K-FD(Z)	conscious	KORBS
confident	K-FT	consciously	KORBS/HREU
confidential	K-FT/-RBL	consciousness	KORBS/*PBS
confidentiality	K-FT/-RBL/TEU	conservancy	KOPB/S*EFRB/SEU
confidentially	K-FT/-RBLT	conservancy	KOPB/SEFRB/SEU
confidentially	K-FT/-RBL/HREU	conservation	KOPBS/SRAEUGS
confidently	K-FT/HREU	conservationist	KOPBS/SRAEUGS/*EUS
conform(s)	K-FRPL(S)	consider(s)	K-R(S)
conformance	K-FRPL/PHAPBS	considerable	K-RBL
conformation	K-FRPL/PHAEUGS	considerable	K-R/-BL
conformation	K-FRPLGS	considerably	K-R/PWHREU
conformed	K-FRPLD	considerably	K-RBL/HREU
conforming	K-FRPLG	considerate	K-RT

considerate	K-R/RAT
considerately	K-R/RAT/HREU
considerately	K-RT/HREU
consideration	K-RGS
consideration	K-R/RAEUGS
considered	K-RD
considering	K-RG
conspiracy	SPAOERS
constitute	TAOUT
constitution	TAOUGS
Constitution	TAO*UGS
constitutional	TAOUGS/TPHAL
constitutional right	TAOURT
constitutional rights	TAOURTS, TAOURT/-S
constitutionality	TAOUGS/TPHAL/TEU
constitutionally	TAOUGS/HREU
construct	KRUBGT
construction	KR*UBGS
constructive	KRUBGT/*EUF
constructively	KRUBGT/*EUF/HREU
consultation	KOPBS/TAEUGS
contact	KABGT
contemplation	KOPBT/PHRAEUGS
contemporaneous	KEFRP/RAEUPBS
contemporaneous	KEPL/PRAEUPBS
contemporaneously	KEFRP/RAEUPBS/HREU
contemporaneously	KEPL/PRAEUPBS/HREU
contingency	KOPB/TEUPBG/SEU
contingent	KOPB/TEUPBG/EPBT
continual	KOPBT/KWRAL
continual	KOPBT/KWRAOUL
continual	KOPBT/KWRUL
continually	KOPBT/KWRAL/HREU
continually	KOPBT/KWRAOUL/HREU
continually	KOPBT/KWRUL/HREU
continuance	KOPBT/WAPBS
continuation	KOPBT/WAEUGS
continue	KOPBT
continuous	KOPBT/OUS
continuously	KOPBT/OUS/HREU
continuously	KOPBT/SHREU
continuum	KOPBT/UPL
contraband(s)	KPWAPBD(Z)
contract(s)	KR-T(S)
contracted	KR-TD
contracting	KR-T/-G
contraction	KR*BGS
contractor	KR-T/TOR
contractor(s)	KR-RT(S)
contractual	KR-T/KHUL
contractually	KR-T/KHUL/HREU
contracture	KR-T/KHUR
contractus	KR-T/TUS
contradict	KR*BGT
contradiction	KR*GS
contradictorily	KR*BGT/REU/HREU
contradictorily	KR*BGT/TOEUR/HREU
contradictoriness	KR*BGT/R*EUPBS
contradictoriness	KR*BGT/REU/*PBS
contradictoriness	KR*BGT/TO*EURPBS
contradictoriness	KR*BGT/TOEUR/*PBS
contradictory	KR*BGT/REU
contradictory	KR*BGT/TOEUR
contrasexual	KOPB/TRA/SWAUL
contribute	KREUBT
contribution	KREUBGS
contributor	KREUBT/TOR
contributorily (as wd)	KREUBT/TOEUR/HREU
contributorily negligent	KREUPBLGT
contributory (as wd)	KREUBT/TOEUR
contributory negligence	KREUPBLG
control	KROL
controllable	KROL/-BL
controlled substance	KRO*LS
controller(s)	KROL/ER(S)
controversial	TRO*EFRL
controversy	TRO*EFRS
controvert	TRO*EFRT
controvertibility	TRO*EFRT/-BLT
controvertible	TRO*EFRT/-BL
convenience	SRAOEPBS
convenient	SRAOEPBT
conveniently	SRAOEPBT/HREU
conversation	K-FRGS
conversational	K-FRGS/TPHAL
convict	KWEUBGT
convictability	KWEUBGT/-BLT
convictable	KWEUBGT/-BL
conviction	KW*EUBGS
cooperate	KAOPT
cooperate	KO/OERPT
cooperation	KAOPGS
cooperation	KO/OERPGS
cooperative(s)	KAOPT/*EUF(S)
cooperatively	KAOPT/*EUF/HREU
cooperator	KAOPT/TOR
cooperator	KO/OERPT/TOR
coordinate (n&j)	KAORD/TPHAT
coordinate (v)	KAORD/TPHAEUT
coordination	KAORD/TPHAEUGS
coordinator	KAORD/TPHAEU/TOR
co-president(s)	KO/P-T(S)
cordially	KORPBLG/HREU
corequisite	KO/REBG/S*EUT
corespondent	KO/SPOPBD/EPBT
corespondent	KO/SPOPBT
coroner	KOERPB
coronet	KORPBT
Corp.	KO*RP, KORP
corporate	KORPT
corporately	KORPT/HREU
corporation	KORPGS
Corporation	KO*RPGS
corporeal	KOR/POEURL
corpus juris	KORPS/SKWRAOURS
corral	KRAL
correct (as wd)	KREBGT
correct me if I am wrong	KRAOPBG
correct me if I'm wrong	KROPBG
correction	KR*EBGS
correlate	KOR/HRAEUT
correlate	KOR/RELT
correlation	KOR/HRAEUGS
correlation	KOR/RELGS
correlative	KOR/HRAEUT/*EUF
correlative	KOR/RELT/*EUF

correspond(s)	KOR/SPOPBD(Z)	counterargument	KO*UPBT/ARGT
correspondence	KOR/SPOPB/TKEPBS	counterbalance	KO*UPBT/PWHRA*PBS
correspondence	KOR/SPOPBD/EPBS	counterintelligence	KO*UPBT/SPWEPBLGS
correspondent	KOR/SPOPBD/TKEPBT	countermeasure(s)	KO*UPBT/PH-RB(S)
correspondent	KOR/SPOPBD/EPBT	counterproductive	KO*UPBT/PRUBGT/*EUF
correspondent	KOR/SPOPBT	counterproductive	KO*UPBT/PRUBG/T*EUF
corroborant	KROB/RAPBT	counterstatement	KO*UPBT/STAEUPLT
corroborate	KROB/RAEUT	coup d'etat	KAOUD/TA
corroboration	KROB/RAEUGS	coup de grace	KAOUD/TKPWRAS
corroborative	KROB/T*EUF	coup de grace	KAOUD/TKPWRAUS
corroboratory	KROB/TOEUR	coup de grace	KOUD/TKPWRAS
corrode(s)	KROED(Z)	coup de grace	KOUD/TKPWRAUS
corrosion	KROEGS	coup de grace	KOUP/TKPWRAS
corrupt	KRUPT	coup de grace	KOUP/TKPWRAUS
corruption	KRUPGS	courage	KURPBLG
could *(as wd)*	KOULD	courageous	KRAEUPBLG/OUS
couldn't	KO*PBT	courageously	KRAEUPBLG/OUS/HREU
could've	KO*UF	courageously	KRAEUPBLG/SHREU
could be	KOUB	course *(as wd)*	KOURS
could believe	KOUBL	course of action	KOURBGS
could feel	KOUFL	court *(as wd)*	KOURT
could find	KOUFPBD	Court *(as wd)*	KO*URT
could have	KOUF	court and jury	KORPBLG
could have been	KOUFB	Court and jury	KO*RPBLG
could have believed	KOUFBLD	courthouse	KROUS
could have had	KOUFD	Courthouse	KRO*US
could have recalled	KOUFRLD	Court instructs the jury	KEUPBLG
could have recollected	KOUFRBGD	court of appeals	KPAELS
could have remembered	KOUFRPLD	Court of Appeals	KPA*ELS
could he say	KOEBZ	court record	KRORD
could I approach the bench	KOEUFPT	court report	KRORT
could I please	KOEUPLS	court report	KOURT/RORT
could I say	KOEUBZ	court reporter	KROERT
could recall	KOURL	court reporter	KRORT/ER
could recollect	KOURBG	court reporter	KOURT/RORT/ER
could remember	KOURPL	courtroom	KRAOPL
could she say	SKOEBZ	Courtroom	KRAO*PL
could understand	KOUPBDZ	Court will come to order	KHRORD
could want	KOUPT	cousin	KUZ/-PB
could we approach the bench	KOEFPT	coverage	KO*FRPBLG
could you describe	KOUDZ	covert	KO*EFRT, KO*FRT
could you please	KOUPLS	covet	KO*FT
could you repeat	KOURPT	coward(s)	KOURD(Z)
could you repeat the question	KOURPGS	cowardice	KOUR/TKEUS
could you rephrase	KOUFRS	cowardly	KOURD/HREU
could you rephrase the question	KOUFRGS	cower	KO*UR
could you say	KOUBZ	coziness	KOE/S*EUPBS
could you tell me	KOUPLT	coziness	KOEZ/*PBS
could you tell us	KOUTS	coziness	KOEZ/S*EUPBS
could your Honor	KOURPB	CP/M *(Control Program/Microprocessors)*	KR-RBGS/P*PL
could your Honor please	KOURPBLS	CPA *(Certified Public Accountant)*	KR-RBGS/PA*
councilman	KOUPBS/PHAPB	C.P.A.	KR-FPLT/PA*
councilmen	KOUPBS/PHEPB	CPE *(Certified Program Evaluator)*	KR-RBGS/P*E
councilwoman	KOUPBS/WOPL	cpi *(characters per inch)*	KR*/P*EU
councilwomen	KOUPBS/WEUPL	CPI *(consumer price index)*	KR-RBGS/P*EU
counsel	KOUPBL	CPL *(Combined Programming Language)*	KR-RBGS/P*L
Counsel	KO*UPBL	CPO *(chief petty officer)*	KR-RBGS/PO*
counselor	KOURPBL	CPR *(cardiopulmonary resuscitation)*	KR-RBGS/P*R
Counselor	KO*URPBL		

cps *(characters/cycles per second)*	KR*/P*S
CPU *(central processing unit)*	KR-RBGS/P*U
crabbiness	KRAB/PW*EUPBS
craftiness	KRAF/T*EUPBS
cranial	KRAEUPBL
crank	KRA*PBG
crankier	KRA*PBG/KWRER
crankiest	KRA*PBG/KWR*ES
crankily	KRA*PBG/HREU
crankiness	KRA*PBG/K*EUPBS
crankiness	KRAPB/K*EUPBS
crankshaft	KRA*PBG/SHAFT
cranky	KRA*PBG/KEU
crashworthiness	KRARB/WO*RT/*PBS
crashworthiness	KRARB/WOR/TH*EUPBS
craziness	KRAEU/S*EUPBS
craziness	KRAEUZ/*PBS
craziness	KRAEUZ/S*EUPBS
creaminess	KRAOE/PH*EUPBS
creaminess	KRAOEPL/PH*EUPBS
create	KRAET
creation	KRAEGS
creative	KRAET/*EUF
creatively	KRAET/*EUF/HREU
creativity	KRAET/*EUF/TEU
creativity	KRAET/*EUFT
creativity	KRAE/T*EUFT
creator	KRAET/TOR
creature	KRAOEFP
credibility	KREBLT
credible *(as wd)*	KREBL
credible evidence	KR*EFD, KREFD
credibly	KREBL/HREU
credibly	KRED/PWHREU
credit	KRET
creditability	KRET/-BLT
creditable	KRET/-BL
creditably	KRET/PWHREU
creditor	KRED/TOR
creditor	KRET/TOR
creepiness	KRAOE/P*EUPBS
creepiness	KRAOEP/P*EUPBS
crematorium	KRAOEPL/TOEURPL
CRI *(Certified Reporting Instructor)*	KR-RBGS/R*EU
cricket	KREUBGT
cried	KRAOEUD
crime *(as wd)*	KRAOEUPL
crime of passion	KROFPGS
criminal(s) *(as wd)*	KR-L(S)
criminal informant	KREUFRPLT
criminal information	KREUFGS
criminal intent	KREUPBT
criminalist	KR-L/*EUS
criminality	KR-L/TEU
criminalization	KR-L/SA*EUGS
criminally	KR-L/HREU
criminate	KREUPLT
crimination	KREUPLGS
criminative	KREUPLT/*EUF
criminator	KREUPLT/TOR
criminatory	KREUPLT/TOEUR
criminologist	KR-L/O*LGS
criminology	KR-L/OLG
cringe	KREUPBG
crispiness	KREUS/P*EUPBS
criterion	KRAOEU/TAOERPB
cross *(as wd)*	KROSZ
cross-appeal	KRAEL
cross-claim	KRAEUPL
cross-complaint	KRAEUPBT
cross-examination	KR-BGS
CROSS-EXAMINATION *(cap & center)*	KR-BGS/KR-BGS
cross-examine	KROEBGS
cross-interrogatory	KROEUG
cross-motion	KR-PLGS
cross-petition	KR-PGS
cross-question	KR-GS
cross-suit	KRAOUT
crosswalk	KRAUBG
CRR *(Certified Realtime Reporter)*	KR-RBGS/R*R
CRT *(cathode-ray tube)*	KR-RBGS/R*T
crumminess	KRUPL/PH*EUPBS
crumple	KRUFRPL
crustiness	KRUS/T*EUPBS
CSC *(Civil Service Commission)*	KR-RBGS/S*BG
C-SPAN *(Cable Satellite Public Affairs Network)*	KR-RBGS/SPAPB
CSR *(Certified Shorthand Reporter)*	KR-RBGS/S*R
c.t.a. *(cum testamento annexo [with the will annexed])*	KR*PD/TA*
cul-de-sac	KULD/SABG
cumulative	KAOUPL/T*EUF
cumulatively	KAOUPL/T*EUF/HREU
curiously	KAOUR/SHREU
curliness	KUR/HR*EUPBS
current *(as wd)*	KURPBT
current weather conditions	KWEBGS
curricula	KREUBG/HRA
curricular	KREUBG/HRAR
curriculum	KREUBG/HRUPL
curriculum vitae	KREUBG/HRUPL/SRAOET
curriculum vitae	KREUBG/HRUPL/SRAOEUT
cursoriness	KUR/SO*EURPBS
cursoriness	KURS/R*EUPBS
cybercriminal	SAO*EUB/KR-L
cylinder(s)	SHREUPBD/ER(S)
cylindrical	SHREUPB/TKREU/KAL

daffiness	TKAF/TP*EUPBS
dailiness	TKAEU/HR*EUPBS
dailiness	TKAEUL/HR*EUPBS
Dallas	TKHRAS
damage	TKAPBLG
Damascus	TKPHAS/KUS
dammit	TKAPLT
damn	TKA*PL
damned	TKA*PLD
damnedest	TKA*PLD/*ES
danger	TKAEUPBLG
danger	TKAEUPBG/ER
dangerous *(as wd)*	TKAEUPBLGS
dangerous *(as wd)*	TKAEUPBG/ROUS
dangerous *(as wd)*	TKAEUPBLG/OUS
dangerous weapon(s)	TKWREP(S)
dangerously	TKAEUPBLG/SHREU
dangerously	TKAEUPBLGS/HREU
dangerously	TKAEUPBG/ER/SHREU
dangerously	TKAEUPBG/ROUS/HREU
dangerousness	TKAEUPBLGS/*PBS
dangerousness	TKAEUPBG/ROUS/*PBS
dangerousness	TKAEUPBLG/OUS/*PBS
dank	TKA*PBG
darling	TKARLG
Darvocet	TKAFRB/SET
database	TKAEUBS
date *(as wd)*	TKAEUT
date of birth	TK*EURT
date of the accident	TKAFBGS
daughter(s) *(as wd)*	TKAUR(/-S), TKAUR(S)
daughter and son	TKRAS
daughters and sons	TKRASZ, TKRAS/-S
daughter or son	TKROS
daughters or sons	TKROSZ, TKROS/-S
daughter-in-law	TKAURPBL
daughters-in-law	TKAURPBLS
daughter-in-laws	TKAURPBL/-S
DAV *(Disabled American Veterans)*	TK-RBGS/A*F
David	TKA*EUFD
Davis	TKA*EUFS
day *(as wd)*	TKAEU
day-by-day	TKAEUBD
day care	TKAEUBG
daylight	TKAEULGT
day of the accident	TKAEUFBGS
day or night	TKAORPBT
daytime	TKAEUPLT
day-to-day	TKAEUTD
dba *(doing business as)*	TK*/PWA*
d.b.a.	TK*/PD/PWA*
d/b/a	TK*/SHR-RB/PWA*
d/b/a	TKAOEB/KWRAEU
DBA	TK-RBGS/PWA*
DBE *(de bene esse)*	TK-RBGS/PW*E
DBN *(de bonis non)*	TK-RBGS/PW*PB
dc *(direct current)*	TK-BG
DC *(District of Columbia, direct current)*	TK*BG
DDS *(Doctor of Dental Surgery/Science)*	TK-RBGS/TK*S
D.D.S.	TK-FPLT/TK*S
DDT *(dichlorodiphenyltrichloroethane)*	TK-RBGS/TK*T
DEA *(Drug Enforcement Administration)*	TK-RBGS/A*E
deadly *(as wd)*	TKED/HREU
deadly weapon	TKWEP
deadly weapons	TKWEPS, TKWEP/-S
deaf *(as wd)*	TKEF
deaf or hard-of-hearing	TKHOFRG
deaf or hearing-impaired	TKHAERPD
de-Americanize	TKE/PHERPB/AOEUZ
death *(as wd)*	TK*ET
death penalty	TK*EPLT
death sentence	TK*EPBS
debit	TKEBT
decedent	TKE/SAOEPBT
decelerate	TKHRERT
deceleration	TKHRERGS
December	TKES
decentralization	TKE/STRAL/SA*EUGS
decentralize	TKE/STRAL/AOEUZ
decide(s)	TK-DZ(/-S)
decidedly	TK-DZ/TKHREU
declassify	TKE/KHR-F
decomposition	TKE/KOFRP/SEUGS
decomposition	TKE/KOPL/POGS
decompress	TKE/KPRESZ
decompression	TKE/KPREGS
decontrol	TKE/KROL
decorum	TKE/KOERPL
decorum	TKE/KORPL
decreed	TKE/KRAOED
decriminalization	TKE/KR-L/SA*EUGS
decriminalize	TKE/KR-L/AOEUZ
deed *(as wd)*	TKAOED
deed of trust	TKR*US
defect	TKEFBGT
defection	TK*EFBGS
defective	TKEFBGT/*EUF
defectively	TKEFBGT/*EUF/HREU
defector	TKEFBG/TOR
defector	TKEFBGT/TOR
defederalize	TKE/TPRAL/AOEUZ
defend(s)	TKEFD(Z)
defend(s)	TKEFPBD(Z)
defendable	TKEFD/-BL
defendable	TKEFPBD/-BL
defendant(s) *(as wd)*	TK-FT(S)
THE DEFENDANT: *(colloquy)*	TK-FT/TK-FT
Defendant's Exhibit	TK-FBGS
Defendant's Exhibit No.	TK*FBGS
defender(s)	TKEFD/ER(S)
defender(s)	TKEFPBD/ER(S)
defense *(as wd)*	TKEFS
defense *(as wd)*	TKEFPBS

defense attorney	TKOERPB	delimitation	TKHREUPL/TAEUGS
Defense Attorney	TKO*ERPB	delimiter(s)	TKHREUPLT/ER(S)
defenseless	TKEFS/HRES	delineate	TKHREUPB/KWRAEUT
defenseless	TKEFPBS/HRES	delineation	TKHREUPB/KWRAEUGS
defensible	TKEFS/-BL	delineator	TKHREUPB/KWRAEU/TOR
defensible	TKEFPBS/-BL	delinquency	TKHREUPB/KWEPBS/SEU
defensive	TKEFS/*EUF	delinquent	TKHREUPB/KWEPBT
defensive	TKEFPBS/*EUF	delirious	TKHRAOER/KWROUS
defensively	TKEFS/*EUF/HREU	delirium (as wd)	TKHRAOERPL
defensively	TKEFPBS/*EUF/HREU	delirium (as wd)	TKHRAOER/KWRUPL
deference	TKEFRPBS	delirium tremens	TK-TS
deferens	TKEFRPBZ	deliver	TKHR*EUFR
deferent	TKEFRPBT	deliver	TKHR*EUF/ER
deferential	TKEFRPB/-RBL	deliverable	TKHR*EUFRBL
deferentially	TKEFRPB/-RBL/HREU	deliverable	TKHR*EUF/ERBL
deferment	TKEFRPLT	deliverable	TKHR*EUF/RABL
deferral	TKEFRL	deliverance	TKHR*EUFRPBS
deficient	TKE/TPEURBT	deliverance	TKHR*EUF/ERPBS
definite	TKEFPBT	deliverance	TKHR*EUF/RAPBS
definitely	TKEFPBT/HREU	delivery (as wd)	TKHR*EUF/REU
deflower	TKE/TPHRO*UR	delivery (as wd)	TKHR*EUFR/REU
deform(s)	TK-FRPL(S)	delivery room	TKHR*RPL
deformation	TK-FRPLGS	delude(s)	TKHRAOUD(Z)
deformation	TK-FRPL/PHAEUGS	deluge	TKHRAOUPBLG
deformed	TK-FRPLD	delusion	TKHRAOUGS
deforming	TK-FRPLG	delusional	TKHRAOUGS/TPHAL
deformity	TK-FRPL/TEU	delusive	TKHRAOUS/*EUF
defrayal	TKE/TPRAEUL	demand(s)	TKPHAPBD(Z)
degradation	TKEG/TKAEUGS	demean	TKPHAOEPB
dehumanize	TKE/HAOUPL/AOEUZ	demeanor	TKPHAOERPB
deification	TKAOEF/KAEUGS	demeanor	TKPHAOE/TPHOR
deja vu	TKAEUPBLG/SRAOU	demented	TKPHEPBT/-D
Delaware	TK*E/TK*E	dementia	TKEPLT/SHA
delay	TKHRAEU	dementia	TKPHEPB/SHA
delayed	TKHRAEUD	demerit	TKPHERT
delayed	TKE/HRAEUD	demerit	TKE/PHERT
delectable	TKHREBGT/-BL	demise	TKPHAOEUZ
delegable	TKELG/-BL	demit	TKPHEUT
delegacy	TKELG/SEU	demobilization	TKE/PHOEBL/SA*EUGS
delegalize	TKE/HRAOEL/AOEUZ	democracy	TKPHOBG/SEU
delegatee	TKELG/TAOE	democracy	TKPHOBG/RA/SEU
delegatory	TKELG/TOEUR	democratize	TKPHOBG/TAOEUZ
delete	TKHRAOET	democratize	TKPHOBG/RA/TAOEUZ
deletion	TKHRAOEGS	demodulation	TKPHOPBLG/HRAEUGS
deliberate (j&v)	TKHREUBT	demographer	TKPHOG/TPER
deliberate (j)	TKHREUB/RAT	demographic	TKEPL/TKPWRAFBG
deliberate (v)	TKHREUB/RAEUT	demographically	TKEPL/TKPWRAFBG/HREU
deliberately	TKHREUB/RAT/HREU	demography	TKPHOG/TPEU
deliberately	TKHREUBT/HREU	demolish	TKPHOL/EURB
deliberation	TKHREUB/RAEUGS	demonstrable	TKPHOPB/STRABL
deliberation	TKHREUBGS	demonstrable	TKPHOPBS/TRABL
deliberative	TKHREUBT/*EUF	demonstrate	TKEPL/STRAEUT
delicious	TKHREURBS	demonstrate	TKPHOPB/STRAEUT
deliciously	TKHREURBS/HREU	demonstration	TKEPL/STRAEUGS
deliciousness	TKHREURBS/*PBS	demonstration	TKPHOPB/STRAEUGS
delict	TKHREUBGT	demonstrative	TKPHOPB/STRA/T*EUF
delictual	TKHREUBG/KHUL	demonstrative	TKPHOPB/STRAT/*EUF
delictum	TKHREUBG/TUPL	demonstrative	TKPHOPBS/TRA/T*EUF
delictum	TKHREUBGT/UPL	demonstrator	TKEPL/STRAEU/TOR
delight	TKHRAOEUGT	demonstrator	TKPHOPB/STRAEU/TOR
delightful	TKHRAOEUGT/-FL	demote	TKPHOET
delightfully	TKHRAOEUGT/TPHREU	demotion	TKPHOEGS
delimit	TKHREUPLT	demurrage	TKE/PHURPBLG

denationalization	TKE/TPHARBL/SA*EUGS	depreciation	TKE/PRAOERBGS
denial	TKE/TPHAOEUL	depreciation	TKPRAOE/SHAEUGS
dentistry	TKEPBT/STREU	depreciation	TKPRAOERB/KWRAEUGS
deodorant	TKOED/RAPBT	depress	TKPRESZ
deodorize	TKOED/RAOEUZ	depressant	TKPRES/SAPBT
deodorizer(s)	TKOED/RAOEUZ/ER(S)	depression	TKPREGS
depart	TKPART	depressive	TKPRESZ/*EUF
department(s)	TK-PT(S)	depressive	TKPRES/S*EUF
department(s)	TKPART/-PLT(S)	deprive	TKPRAO*EUF
departmental	TK-PT/TAL	deprogram	TKE/PRAPL
departmental	TKPART/-PLT/TAL	deputation	TKEP/TAEUGS
departmentalize	TK-PT/HRAOEUZ	deputization	TKEPT/SA*EUGS
departmentalize	TKPART/-PLT/HRAOEUZ	deputize	TKEP/TAOEUZ
departmentally	TK-PT/HREU	deputy	TKEP/TEU
departmentally	TKPART/-PLT/HREU	derange	TKE/RAEUPBG
departure(s)	TKPAR/KHUR(S)	derangement	TKE/RAEUPBG/-PLT
depend(s)	TKPEPBD(Z)	derivative	TKR*EUF/T*EUF
dependability	TKPEPBD/-BLT	derogative	TKROG/T*EUF
dependable	TKPEPBD/-BL	derogatorily	TKROG/TOEUR/HREU
dependably	TKPEPBD/PWHREU	derogatoriness	TKROG/TO*EURPBS
dependence	TKPEPBS	derogatoriness	TKROG/TOEUR/*PBS
dependence	TKPEPB/TKEPBS	derogatory	TKROG/TOEUR
dependence	TKPEPBD/EPBS	derringer(s)	TKERPBG/ER(S)
dependency	TKPEPB/SEU	describable	TKRAOEUBL
dependency	TKPEPB/TKEPB/SEU	describable	TKRAOEUB/-BL
dependency	TKPEPBD/EPB/SEU	describably	TKRAOEUB/PWHREU
dependent	TKPEPBT	describe	TKRAOEUB
dependent	TKPEPB/TKEPBT	description	TKREUPGS
dependent	TKPEPBD/EPBT	descriptive	TKREUPT/*EUF
depersonalization	TKE/PERPBL/SA*EUGS	descriptively	TKREUPT/*EUF/HREU
depict	TKPEUBGT	descriptor	TKREUPT/TOR
depiction	TKP*EUBGS	desegregate	TKE/SEG/TKPWAEUT
deplane	TKPHRAEPB	desegregation	TKE/SEG/TKPWAEUGS
deplete	TKPHRAOET	deselect	TKE/SHREBGT
depletion	TKPHRAOEGS	designate (n)	TKES/TPHAT
deplorable	TKPHROERBL	designate (n)	TKEZ/TPHAT
deplorably	TKPHROER/PWHREU	designate (v)	TKES/TPHAEUT
deplore	TKPHROER	designate (v)	TKEZ/TPHAEUT
deploy	TKPHROEU	designation	TKES/TPHAEUGS
deployment	TKPHROEUPLT	designation	TKEZ/TPHAEUGS
depolarization	TKE/POEL/SA*EUGS	designator	TKES/TPHAEU/TOR
deponent	TKPOEPBT	designator	TKEZ/TPHAEU/TOR
deport	TKPORT	destruct	TKRUBGT
deportation	TKPOR/TAEUGS	destructibility	TKRUBGT/-BLT
deportment	TKPORT/-PLT	destructible	TKRUBGT/-BL
depose	TKPOEZ	destruction	TKR*UBGS
deposit	TKPOZ/SEUT	destructive	TKRUBGT/*EUF
depositary	TKPOZ/TAEUR	destructively	TKRUBGT/*EUF/HREU
deposition (as wd)	TKEPGS	destructiveness	TKRUBGT/*EUFPBS
deposition (as wd)	TKEP/POGS	destructiveness	TKRUBGT/*EUF/*PBS
deposition (as wd)	TKEP/SEUGS	detective(s)	TK-BGT(S)
Deposition Exhibit	TK-BGS	determinable	TKERPL/-BL
Deposition Exhibit No.	TK*BGS	determinably	TKERPL/PWHREU
depositor	TKPOZ/TOR	determinant	TKERPL/TPHAPBT
depository	TKPOZ/TOEUR	determinate	TKERPL/TPHAT
deprave	TKPRA*EUF	determination	TKERPLGS
depravity	TKPRA*F/TEU	determination	TKERPL/TPHAEUGS
depreciable	TKPRAOERB/-BL	determinative	TKERPL/T*EUF
depreciate	TKPRAOERBT	determine	TKERPL
depreciate	TKE/PRAOERBT	Detroit	TKROEUT
depreciate	TKPRAOE/SHAEUT	devaluate	TK*EFLT
depreciate	TKPRAOERB/KWRAEUT	devaluation	TK*EFLGS
depreciation	TKPRAOERBGS	devalue	TKE/SRAL

develop	TKWOP	dimension	TKPHEPBGS
developer(s)	TKWOP/ER(S)	dimensional	TKPHEPBGS/TPHAL
development(s)	TKWOPLT(S), TKWOPLT(/-S)	diminish	TKPHEUPB/EURB
		diminishment	TKPHEUPB/SH-PLT
development(s)	TKWOP/-PLT(S)	diminutive	TKPHEUPB/T*EUF
developmental	TKWOPLT/TAL	dimple	TKEUFRPL
developmental	TKWOP/-PLT/TAL	dining room	TK*EURPL
device	TKWAOEUS	diploid	TKPHROEUD
devisable	TKWAOEUZ/-BL	diploma	TKPHROE/PHA
devise	TKWAOEUZ	diplomacy	TKPHROEPL/SEU
devisee	TKWAOEU/SAO*E	direct(ing) *(as wd)*	TKREBGT(/-G)
devisee	TKWAOEU/SAOE	direct cause	TKRAUZ
devisor	TKWAOEU/SO*R	direct evidence	TKR*EFD, TKREFD
devisor	TKWAOEU/SOR	direct examination	TKR-BGS
diabetes	TKAOEUBTS	DIRECT EXAMINATION *(cap & center)*	
diabetic(s)	TKAOEUBT(/-S)		TKR-BGS/TKR-BGS
diagnose	TKAOEUG	direct your attention	TKRURPBGS
diagnoses	TKAOEUGZ	directing your attention	TKRURPBGSZ
diagnosis	TKAOEUGS	direction	TKR*EBGS
diagnostic	TKAOEUGT	directional	TKR*EBGS/TPHAL
diamond(s)	TKAOEUPLD(Z)	directive(s)	TKREBGT/*EUF(S)
diarrheal	TKAOEU/RAOEL	directly	TKREBGT/HREU
dibs	TKEUBS	directness	TKREBGT/*PBS
did *(as wd)*	TKEUD	director	TKREBG/TOR
didn't	TK-PBT	director	TKREBGT/TOR
did he believe	TKEBL	directorship	TKREBG/TOR/SHEUP
did he feel	TKEFL	directorship	TKREBGT/TOR/SHEUP
did he recall	TKERL	directory	TKREBG/TOEUR
did he recollect	TKERBG	directory	TKREBGT/TOEUR
did he say	TKEBZ	directory	TKREBG/TREU
did he understand	TKEPBDZ	directory	TKREBGT/REU
did I believe	TKEUBL	dirtiness	TKEUR/T*EUPBS
did I feel	TKEUFL	disabilities	TKAEUBLTS, TKAEUBLT/-S
did I have	TKEUF		
did I recall	TKEURL	disability	TKAEUBLT
did I recollect	TKEURBG	disable	TKAEUBL
did I remember	TKEURPL	disabled	TKAEUBLD, TKAEUBL/-D
did I say	TKEUBZ		
did I understand	TKEUPBDZ	disables	TKAEUBLS, TKAEUBL/-S
did I want	TKEUPT		
did she say	STKEBZ	disabling	TKAEUBLG, TKAEUBL/-G
did you find	TKUFPBD		
did you have	TKEUD/UF	disaccredit	TKEUS/AEU/KRET
did you recall	TKURL	disadvantage	TKEUS/SRAPBG
did you recollect	TKURBG	disaffect	TKEUS/AFBGT
did you remember	TKURPL	disaffection	TKEUS/A*FBGS
did you say	TKUBZ	disaffirmation	TKEUS/AFR/PHAEUGS
did you understand	TKUPBDZ	disagree	TKEUS/TKPWRAOE
did you want	TKUPT	disagreeable	TKEUS/TKPWRAOEBL
diet	TKAOEUT	disagreed	TKEUS/TKPWRAOED
differ	TKEUFR	disagreeing	TKEUS/TKPWRAOEG
difference	TKEUFRPBS	disagreement	TKEUS/TKPWRAOEPLT
different	TKEUFRPBT	disagrees	TKEUS/TKPWRAOES
differential(s)	TKEUFRPB/-RBL(S)	disappear	TKEUS/PAOER
differentiate	TKEUFRPB/SHAEUT	disappearance	TKEUS/PAOERPBS
differentiation	TKEUFRPB/SHAEUGS	disassociate	TKEUS/SOERBT
differently	TKEUFRPBT/HREU	disassociation	TKEUS/SOERBGS
difficult	TKEUFLT	disbelief	TKEUS/PWHRAOEF
difficulty	TKEUFLT/TEU	disbelieve	TKEUS/PWHRAO*EF
digit	TKEUPBLGT	disbelievingly	TKEUS/PWHRAO*EF/ TKPWHREU
dilapidate	TKHRAP/TKAEUT		
dilapidation	TKHRAP/TKAEUGS	discharge	TKARPBLG
dilemma	TKHREPL/PHA	discomfort(s)	TKEUS/K-FRT(S)

disconnect	TKEUS/KEBGT	displeasure	TKEUS/PHR-RB
disconnectedly	TKEUS/KEBGT/TKHREU	disposition	TKEUS/POGS
disconnection	TKEUS/K*EBGS	dispossess	TKEUS/PESZ
discontinuance	TKEUS/KOPBT/WAPBS	dispossession	TKEUS/PEGS
discontinuation	TKEUS/KOPBT/WAEUGS	disprove	TKEUS/PRO*F
discontinue	TKEUS/KOPBT	disqualification	TKEUS/KW-FGS
discourage	TKEUS/KURPBLG	disqualified	TKEUS/KW-FD
discouragement	TKEUS/KURPBLG/-PLT	disqualifies	TKEUS/KW-FS
discredit	TKEUS/KRET	disqualify	TKEUS/KW-F
discrepancy	TKEUS/KREP/SEU	disqualifying	TKEUS/KW-FG
discriminate	TKEUS/KREUPLT	disquiet	TKEUS/KWAO*EUT
discrimination	TKEUS/KREUPLGS	disregard(s)	TKRARD(Z)
discriminative	TKEUS/KREUPLT/*EUF	disregard(s)	TKEUS/RARD(Z)
discriminator	TKEUS/KREUPLT/TOR	disreputable	TKEUS/REPT/-BL
discriminatorily	TKEUS/KREUPLT/ TOEUR/HREU	disreputably	TKEUS/REPT/PWHREU
		disrespect	TKEUS/R-PT
discriminatorily	TKEUS/KREUPL/ TOEUR/HREU	disrespectful	TKEUS/R-PT/-FL
		disrespectfully	TKEUS/R-PT/TPHREU
discriminatory	TKEUS/KREUPLT/ TOEUR	dissatisfaction	TKEUS/STPA*BGS
		dissatisfy	TKEUS/STPAOEU
discriminatory	TKEUS/KREUPL/ TOEUR	disservice	TKEUS/S-FS
		dissidence	TKEUSZ/TKEPBS
discussion (as wd)	TKEUS/KUGS	dissident	TKEUSZ/TKEPBT
discussion off the record	TKAUFR	dissimilar	TKEUS/SHRAR
(Discussion off the record.)	TKA*UFR	dissimilarity	TKEUS/SHRART
discwriter	TKEUS/*BG/WREUR	dissimilarity	TKEUS/SHRAR/TEU
disease	TK-Z	dissipate	TKEUSZ/PAEUT
disfavor	TKEUS/TPA*EUFR	dissipation	TKEUSZ/PAEUGS
disherit	TKEUS/HERT	dissolute	TKEUS/SHRAOUT
dishonest	TKEUS/HO*PBS	dissolute	TKEUSZ/HRAOUT
dishonestly	TKEUS/HO*PBLS	dissolution	TKEUS/SHRAOUGS
dishonestly	TKEUS/HO*PBS/HREU	dissolution	TKEUSZ/HRAOUGS
dishonesty	TKEUS/HO*PBTS	dissolve	TKEUS/SO*F
dishonesty	TKEUS/HO*PBS/TEU	dissonance	TKEUSZ/TPHAPBS
dishonesty	TKEUS/HOPBS/TEU	dissonant	TKEUSZ/TPHAPBT
disillusion	TKEUS/HRAOUGS	distinct	TKWEUPBGT
disimmune	TKEUS/PHAOUPB	distinction	TKWEUPBGS
disimprison	TKEUS/EUPL/PREUZ	distinctive	TKWEUPBGT/*EUF
disincorporate	TKEUS/EUPB/KORPT	distinctively	TKWEUPBGT/*EUF/ HREU
disincorporation	TKEUS/EUPB/KORPGS		
disinformation	TKEUS/TPH-F/PHAEUGS	distinctly	TKWEUPBGT/HREU
disinformation	TKEUS/TPH-FGS	distinguish	TKWEURB
disinherit	TKEUS/EUPB/HERT	distinguishable	TKWEURB/-BL
disinterest	TKEUS/SPWR*ES	distinguishably	TKWEURB/PWHREU
disinterested	TKEUS/SPWR*ES/-D	distraught	TKEUS/TRAUT
disinvest	TKEUS/TPH*FS	distributable	TKREUBT/-BL
disinvestment	TKEUS/TPH*FS/-PLT	distribute	TKREUBT
disloyal	TKEUS/HROEUL	distributee	TKREUBT/TAOE
disloyalty	TKEUS/HROEUL/TEU	distribution	TKREUBGS
dismember	TKEUS/PHEB	distributive	TKREUBT/*EUF
dismortgage	TKEUS/PHORPBLG	distributor	TKREUBT/TOR
disorderly (as wd)	TKEUS/ORD/HREU	district (as wd)	TKREUBGT
disorderly conduct	TKORBGT	district attorney	TKROERPB
disorganization	TKEUS/ORG/SA*EUGS	District Attorney	TKRO*ERPB
disorganization	TKEUS/ORGS	district attorney general	TKROERPBG
disorganize	TKEUS/ORG	District Attorney General	TKRO*ERPBG
disorient	TKEUS/OEURPBT	district attorney's office	TKROEFRPBS
disorientation	TKEUS/OEURPB/TAEUGS	district court	TKROURT
disparage	TKEUS/PAEURPBLG	District Court	TKRO*URT
disparage	TKEUS/PARPBLG	District of Columbia	TK*BG/TK*BG
disparagement	TKEUS/PAEURPBLG/-PLT	District of Columbia	TKREUBGT/ KHRUPL/KWRA
disparagement	TKEUS/PARPBLG/-PLT		
disparate	TKEUS/PRAT	disturb	TKURB

disturbance	TKURPBS	do you understand	TKAOUPBDZ
disunite	TKEUS/KWRAOEUPBT	do you want	TKAOUPT
divers *(j)*	TKAO*EUFRZ	DOA *(dead on arrival)*	TK-RBGS/AO*
diverse	TKAO*EUFRS	DOB *(date of birth)*	TK-RBGS/O*B
divide(s)	TKWAOEUD(Z)	D.O.B.	TK-FPLT/O*B
divider(s)	TKWAOEUD/ER(S)	DOC *(Department of Commerce)*	
division	TKWEUGS		TK-RBGS/O*BG
divisional	TKWEUGS/TPHAL	docket	TKOBGT
divorce *(as wd)*	TKWORS	Docket	TKO*BGT
divorce agreement(s)	TKWORPLT(/-S)	doctor(s)	TKR-(S)
divorce settlement(s)	TKWORPLTS(/-S)	Doctor	TKR*
divorcee	TKWOR/SAOE	Doctor,	TKR*RBGS
divorcee	TKWOR/SAEU	doctor's office	TKRAUFS
divulge	TKEU/SRULG	doctored	TKR-D
dizziness	TKEUZ/*PBS	doctoring	TKR-G
dizziness	TKEUZ/S*EUPBS	DOD *(Department of Defense)*	
DJI *(Dow-Jones Industrials)*	TK-RBGS/SKWR*EU		TK-RBGS/O*D
DJIA *(Dow-Jones Industrial Average)*		DOE *(Department of Energy)*	
	TK-RBGS/SKWR*EU/A*RBGS		TK-RBGS/O*E
		does *(as wd)*	TKUZ
DLO *(dead letter office)*	TK-RBGS/HRO*	doesn't	TKUPBT
DMT *(dimethyltryptamine)*	TK-RBGS/PH*T	does he believe	TKAOEBL
DMV *(Department of Motor Vehicles)*		does he feel	TKAOEFL
	TK-RBGS/PH*F	does he have	TKAOEF
DMZ *(demilitarized zone)*	TK-RBGS/PH*Z	does he recall	TKAOERL
DNA *(deoxyribonucleic acid)*	TK-RBGS/TPHA*	does he recollect	TKAOERBG
DNR *(do not resuscitate)*	TK-RBGS/TPH*R	does he remember	TKAOERPL
do *(as wd)*	TKO	does he think	TKAOEPBG
don't	TKOPBT, TKOEPBT	does he think so	TKAOEPBGS
do I believe	TKAOEUBL	does he think the	TKAOEPBGT
do I feel	TKAOEUFL	does he understand	TKAOEPBDZ
do I have	TKAOEUF	does he want	TKAOEPT
do I recall	TKAOEURL	does she believe	STKAOEBL
do I recollect	TKAOEURBG	does she feel	STKAOEFL
do I remember	TKAOEURPL	does she have	STKAOEF
do I think	TKAOEUPBG	does she recall	STKAOERL
do I think so	TKAOEUPBGS	does she recollect	STKAOERBG
do I think the	TKAOEUPBGT	does she remember	STKAOERPL
do I understand	TKAOEUPBDZ	does she think	STKAOEPBG
do I want	TKAOEUPT	does she think so	STKAOEPBGS
do-it-myself(er)	TKOEUT/PHAO*EUS(/ER)	does she think the	STKAOEPBGT
		does she understand	STKAOEPBDZ
do-it-myselfer(s)	TKOEUT/PHAO*EUS/ER(S)	does she want	STKAOEPT
		doh!	TKHOE
do-it-yourself(er)	TKOEUT/KWRO*URS(/ER)	D'oh!	TKHO*E
		DOI *(Department of Interior)*	
do-it-yourselfer(s)	TKOEUT/KWRO*URS/ER(S)		TK-RBGS/O*EU
		doing(s)	TKOEUPBG(/-S)
do you believe	TKAOUBL	DOJ *(Department of Justice)*	TK-RBGS/O*PBLG
do you ever	TKAOUFR	DOL *(Department of Labor)*	TK-RBGS/O*L
do you feel	TKAOUFL	doldrums	TKOEL/TKRUPLS
do you find	TKAOUFPBD	doldrums	TKOL/TKRUPLS
do you have	TKAOUF	dollar(s)	TKHRAR(/-S),
do you have the	TKAOUFT		TKHRAR(S)
do you know	TKAO*UPB	domain	TKPHAEUPB
do you mean	TKAOUPL	domestic(s) *(as wd)*	TKPH*ES/EUBG(S)
do you mind	TKAOUPLD	domestic abuse	TKPHAOUS
do you recall	TKAO*URL	domestic dispute	TKPHAOUT
do you recollect	TKAOURBG	domestic partner	TKPHART
do you remember	TKAOURPL	domestic violence	TKPHAOEULS
do you think	TKAOUPBG	domesticate	TKPH*ES/KAEUT
do you think so	TKAOUPBGS	domestication	TKPH*ES/KAEUGS
do you think the	TKAOUPBGT	domesticity	TKPHES/TEUS/TEU

© 2004 *StenEd*® Briefs & Phrases (Excerpted from StenEd's Realtime Professional Dictionary)

Dominica	TKPHEUPB/KA	drug and intoxicant	TKRAPBGT
dominion	TKPHEUPB/KWROPB	drugs and intoxicants	TKRAPBGTS
dominium *(legal)*	TKPHEUPB/KWRUPL	drug enforcement	TKROERPLT
donald	TKOPBLD	drug or alcohol	TKRORL
Donald	TKO*PBLD	drugs or alcohol	TKRORLS
dopiness	TKOE/P*EUPBS	drug or intoxicant	TKRORBGT
dopiness	TKOEP/P*EUPBS	drugs or intoxicants	TKRORBGTS
DOS *(Department of State, disk operating system)*		drunk	TKR*UPBG
	TK-RBGS/O*S	drunkard(s)	TKR*UPBG/ARD(Z)
DOS	TKO*S	drunken	TKR*UPBG/-PB
dot *(as wd)*	TKOT	drunkenly	TKR*UPBG/-PB/HREU
DOT *(Department of Transportation)*		drunkenness	TKR*UPBG/-PB/*PBS
	TK-RBGS/O*T	drunker	TKR*UPBG/ER
dot.com	TKPHOFPLT	drunkest	TKR*UPBG/*ES
dot-com	TKPHOF	DSL *(digital subscriber line)*	TK-RBGS/S*L
dot com	TKPHO	d.t.'s *(delirium tremens)*	TKE/TAOEZ
dowager	TKOUPBLG/ER	dubitable	TKAOUBT/-BL
dowel	TKOUL	duces tecum	TKAOUS/TAOEBG
dower	TKO*UR	duel	TKAO*UL
Dow-Jones average	TKOUFRPBLG	duet	TKAOUT
Dow-Jones average	TK-PBLGS/A*FRPBLG	duh	TKU
downgoing	TKOUPB/TKPWOEUPBG	DUI *(driving under the influence)*	
downhearted	TKOUPB/HARTD		TKW*EU
downside	TKOUPBDZ	DUI	TKAOE/KWRAOEU
downside	TKOUDZ	dungarees	TKUPBG/RAOES
dpi *(dots per inch)*	TK*/P*EU	dungarees	TKUPBG/RAOEZ
Dr.	TKR-FPLT	dunk	TK*UPBG
Dr.	TK-R	duo	TKWOE
dramatization	TKRAPLT/SA*EUGS	duplicate *(n&j)*	TKAOUP/KAT
drank	TKRA*PBG	duplicate *(v)*	TKAOUP/KAEUT
drawer	TKRAUR	duplication	TKAOUP/KAEUGS
drayage	TKRAEUPBLG	duration	TKRAEUGS
dreaminess	TKRAOE/PH*EUPBS	during *(as wd)*	TKURG, TKUR/-G
dreaminess	TKRAOEPL/PH*EUPBS	during the	TKURGT
dreariness	TKRAOE/R*EUPBS	duskiness	TKUS/K*EUPBS
dreariness	TKRAOER/R*EUPBS	dustiness	TKUS/T*EUPBS
dressiness	TKRES/S*EUPBS	duties *(as wd)*	TKAOU/TEU/-S
drink	TKR*EUPBG	duties and responsibilities	TKAOUBLTS
drinkable	TKR*EUPBG/-BL	duties or responsibilities	TKAOURBLTS
drinker(s)	TKR*EUPBG/ER(S)	DVD *(digital video disc)*	TK-RBGS/SR*D
drivable	TKRAO*EUFBL	DVM *(Doctor of Veterinary Medicine)*	
driver('s) *(as wd)*	TKRAO*EUFR(/AOES)		TK-RBGS/SR*PL
driver side	TKR-DZ	dwelling	TKWELG
driver's side	TKR-DZ/AOE	DWI *(driving while intoxicated)*	
driver's license	TKR-LS		TK-RBGS/W*EU
driveway	TKRAE	DWI	TKWEU
driving *(as wd)*	TKRAO*EUF/-G	dyspnea	TKEUS/TPHA
driving on a revoked license	TKR-RL	dystrophy	TK*EUS/TPEU
driving under the influence *(DUI)*	TKRUFL		
driving while impaired	TKREUPLD		
driving while intoxicated *(DWI)*	TKROBGS		
droopiness	TKRAOP/P*EUPBS		
drought	TKROUT		
drowsiness	TKROU/S*EUPBS		
drowsiness	TKROUZ/S*EUPBS		
Drs.	TKR-FPLTS		
Drs.	TK-RS		
drug(s) *(as wd)*	TKRUG(/-S)		
drug and alcohol	TKRAPBL		
drugs and alcohol	TKRAPBLS		

e- *(pre w/hyphen)*	H*EF
ea.	AEFPLT
each *(as wd)*	AOEFP
each and every	KHA*EFR, KHAEFR
earliness	*ER/HR*EUPBS
earliness	ERL/HR*EUPBS
early *(as wd)*	*ER/HREU
early *(as wd)*	ERL/HREU
early morning	ERPBLG
earning(s)	ERPBG(S), ERPBG(/-S)
earthiness	*ER/TH*EUPBS
earwitness	AOER/W-PBS
easiness	E/S*EUPBS
easiness	AOEZ/S*EUPBS
east *(as wd)*	AO*ES
East *(as wd)*	K-P/AO*ES
East Africa	AO*ES/AFR/KA
east side	*EDZ
eastbound *(as wd)*	*EB
eastbound lane	*EBL
eastbound traffic	*EBT
Easter Island	AO*ES/ER/AO*EULD
Easter Island	AO*ES/ER/AOEULD
easterly	AO*ERL
eastern	AO*ERPB
Eastern	K-P/AO*ERPB
easterner(s)	AO*ERPB/ER(S)
easterner(s)	AO*ES/TPHER(/-S)
Easterner(s)	K-P/AO*ERPB/ER(S)
Easterner(s)	K-P/AO*ES/TPHER(/-S)
EBCDIC *(extended binary-coded decimal interchange code)*	EBS/TKEUBG
e-book	H*EF/PWAOBG
e-business	H*EF/PWEUZ
e-commerce	H*EF/KPHERS
economic	KPHEUBG
economical	KPHEUBG/KAL
economically	KPHEUBG/HREU
economist	KPH*EUS
economize	KPHAOEUZ
economy	KPHEU
ecosystem	E/KO/S-PL, EBG/KO/S-PL
ecstasy	*EBGS/SEU
Ecuadoran	EBG/WA/TKORPB
ecumenical	EBG/PHEPB/KAL
EDA *(Economic Development Administration)*	ERBGS/TKA*
EDP *(electronic data processing)*	ERBGS/TK*P
EDT *(Eastern daylight time)*	ERBGS/TK*T
educate	EGT
education	EGS
educational *(as wd)*	ELGS
educational *(as wd)*	EGS/TPHAL
educational background	EBGD
educationally	ELGS/HREU
educationally	EGS/TPHAL/HREU
educator	ERGT
EEC *(European Economic Community)*	ERBGS/*EBG
EEOC *(Equal Employment Opportunity Commission)*	ERBGS/*ERBGS/O*BG
EEOC	ERBGS/O*EBG
effect	EFBGT
effective	EFBGT/*EUF
effectively	EFBGT/*EUF/HREU
effectiveness	EFBGT/*EUF/*PBS
effectiveness	EFBGT/*EUFPBS
effectual	EFBG/KHUL
effectually	EFBG/KHUL/HREU
effectuate	EFBG/KHAEUT
effectuate	EFBG/SHAEUT
efferent	EFRPBT
efficiency	TPEURBT/SEU
efficient	TPEURBT
efficiently	TPEURBT/HREU
effort	EFRT
effortless	EFRT/HRES
effortlessly	EFRT/HRES/HREU
effortlessness	EFRT/HRES/*PBS
EFT *(electronic funds transfer)*	ERBGS/TP*T
EFTS *(electronic funds transfer system)*	ERBGS/TP*RBGS/T*S
EFTS	ERBGS/TP*TS
e.g. *(exempli gratia [for example])*	*EG
eighty	AEUBGT
EIN *(employer identification number)*	ERBGS/*EUPB
either	AOERT
EKG *(electrocardiogram/graph)*	ERBGS/K*G
elect	HREBGT
election	HR*EBGS
electioneer	HR*EBGS/AOER
elective(s)	HREBGT/*EUF(S)
elector	HREBGT/TOR
elector	HREBG/TOR
electoral	HREBG/TOERL
electoral	HREBG/TORL
electorate	HREBG/TRAT
Electra	HREBG/TRA
electric	HREBGT/REUBG
electric	HREBG/TREUBG
electrical	HREBGT/REU/KAL
electrical	HREBG/TREU/KAL
electrically	HREBG/TREUBG/HREU
electrically	HREBGT/REUBG/HREU
electrically	HREBGT/REU/KHREU
electrically	HREBG/TREU/KHREU
electrician	HREBG/TREUGS
electricity	HREBG/TREUS/TEU
electrify	HREBGT/TPEU
electrify	HREBGT/REU/TPEU
electrify	HREBG/TREU/TPEU
electrocardiogram	HREBGT/KARD/TKPWRAPL

electrocardiograph	HREBGT/ KARD/TKPWRAF	EMT *(emergency medical technician)*	ERBGS/PH*T
electrocute	HREBGT/KAOUT	encompass	EPB/KPASZ
electrocution	HREBGT/KAOUGS	encourage	EPB/KURPBLG
electrode(s)	HREBG/TROED(Z)	encouragement	EPB/KURPBLG/-PLT
electrolysis	HREBG/TROL/SEUS	endanger	EPB/TKAEUPBLG
electrolyte	HREBG/TRO/HRAOEUT	endanger	EPB/TKAEUPBG/ER
electrolytic	HREBG/TRO/ HREUT/EUBG	endangerment	EPB/TKAEUPBLG/-PLT
		endangerment	EPB/TKAEUPBG/ERPLT
electromagnet	HREBG/TRO/ PHAG/TPHET	energies	TPH-RPBLGS
		energize	TPH-RPBLGZ
electromagnetic	HREBG/TRO/ PHAG/TPHET/EUBG	energizer	TPH-RPBLGZ/ER
		energy	TPH-RPBLG
electron	HREBG/TROPB	enforcement	EPB/TPORPLT
electronic(s)	HREBG/TROPB/EUBG(S)	enforcement	EPB/TPOERPLT
electronically	HREBG/TROPB/KHREU	engine(s)	EPBG/-PB(S)
electroshock	HREBG/TRO/SHOBG	engineer	EPBG/TPHAOER
electrostatic	HREBG/TRO/STAT/EUBG	enough	TPHUF
element(s)	HR-PLT(S)	enter(s)	SPWR-(S)
elemental	HR-PLT/TAL	entered	SPWR-D
elementariness	HR-PLT/R*EUPBS	entering	SPWR-G
elementariness	HR-PLT/REU/*PBS	enthrall	SPWRAUL
elementariness	HR-PLT/TA*EURPBS	enthrone	SPWROEPB
elementariness	HR-PLT/TAEUR/*PBS	enthuse	SPWAOUZ
elementary	HR-PLT/REU	entourage	SPWAOURPBLG
elementary	HR-PLT/TAEUR	entourage	SPWOURPBLG
eleven	HR*EFPB	entrench	SPWREFRPBLG
eleventh	HR*EFPBT	entrepreneur	SPWREP/TPHUR
eleventh	HR*EF/*PBT	entrepreneur	SPWREP/TPHAOUR
Ellis Island	EL/HREUS/AO*EULD	entrepreneurial	SPWREP/TPHURL
Ellis Island	EL/HREUS/AOEULD	entrepreneurial	SPWREP/TPHAOURL
elsewhere	ELS/WR-	envious	EPB/SROUS
emaciate	E/PHAEURBT	enviously	EPB/SROUS/HREU
emaciation	E/PHAEURBGS	environment	SRAOEURPLT
e-mail	H*EF/PHAEUL	environmental	SRAOEURPLT/TAL
embankment	EPL/PWA*PBG/-PLT	environmentalist	SRAOEURPLT/HR*EUS
embarrass	EPL/PWARS	environmentally	SRAOEURPLT/HREU
embarrassment	EPL/PWARS/-PLT	EOE *(equal opportunity employer)*	ERBGS/O*E
embolism	EPL/PWHREUFPL		
embolus	EPL/PWHRUS	EPA *(Environmental Protection Agency)*	ERBGS/PA*
embryo	EPL/PWROE		
embryology	EPL/PWROLG	epicurean	EP/KAOURPB
embryonic	EPL/PWROPB/EUBG	EPROM *(erasable programmable read-only memory)*	E/PROPL
emergencies	PH-RPBLGS		
emergency *(as wd)*	PH-RPBLG	EPS *(earnings per share)*	ERBGS/P*S
emergency room	PH*RPL	equality	E/KWALT, E/KWAULT
emergency room	PH-RPBLG/RAOPL	equestrian	E/KW*ES/RAPB
emotivity	E/PHOE/T*EUFT	equestrian	E/KWES/TRAPB
emotivity	E/PHOET/*EUFT	equipment	KWEUPLT
employability	PHROEUBLT	equipment	E/KWEUPLT
employable	PHROEUBL	ERA *(Equal Rights Amendment)*	ERBGS/RA*
employee	PHROE		
employer	PHROEUR	ERT *(estrogen replacement therapy)*	ERBGS/R*T
employment	PHROEUPLT		
emporium	EPL/POEURPL	escapable	E/SKAEUPBL
empower	EPL/PO*UR	escapable	ES/KAEUPBL
empowerment	EPL/POURPLT	ESOP *(employee stock ownership plan)*	E/SOP
empowerment	EPL/PO*URPLT		
emptiness	EFRP/T*EUPBS	esoteric	ES/TERBG
emptiness	EPL/T*EUPBS	ESP *(extrasensory perception)*	ERBGS/S*P
EMS *(emergency medical service)*	ERBGS/PH*S	ESPN *(Entertainment Sports Network)*	ERBGS/S*RBGS/P*PB
		ESPN	ERBGS/SP*PB

Esq.	ES/KW-FPLT	examination	KP-PLGS
Esq.	ES/KW-SERBL	EXAMINATION *(cap & center)*	KP-GS/KP-GS
essential	SERBL	examine	KP-PL
essentially	SERBL/HREU	examines	KP-PLS
EST *(Eastern standard time)*	ERBGS/S*T	examined	KP-PLD
establish	PWHREURB	examinee	KP-PL/TPHAOE
establishment(s)	PWHREUPLT(/-S), PWHREUPLT(S)	examiner	KP-RPL
establishment(s)	PWHREURB/-PLT(S)	examiner	KP-PL/ER
estrange	ES/TRAEUPBG	examiners	KP-RPLS
estrangement(s)	ES/TRAEUPBG/-PLT(S)	examiners	KP-PL/ERS
estuary	ES/KHAEUR	examining	KP-PLG
ETA *(estimated time of arrival)*	ERBGS/TA*	example	KPAFRPL
e-tail	H*EF/TAEUL	excellence	KPHREPBS
e-tailer(s)	H*EF/TAEUL/ER(S)	excellent	KPHREPBT
etc.	ETS	excellently	KPHREPBT/HREU
ethereal	E/THAOERL	exchange	EBGS/KHAEUPBG
euphoric	KWRAOU/TPORBG	excitement	KPAOEUPLT
euphoric	KWRAOU/TPOERBG	exclusivity	EBGS/KHRAOUS/*EUFT
Europe	KWRAOURP	ex contractu	EBGS/KR-T/TAOU
evaluate	*EFLT	excusable	KPAOUZ/-BL
evaluation	*EFLGS	excuse *(n)*	KPAOUS
evaluator	*EFLT/TOR	excuse *(v)*	KPAOUZ
evangelism	E/SRAPBG/HREUFPL	excuse me	KPUPL
evangelist	E/SRAPBG/HR*EUS	ex delicto	EBGS/TKHREUBG/TOE
evangelistic	E/SRAPBG/HR*EUS/EUBG	exemplify	KPEFRP/TPEU
evangelize	E/SRAPBG/HRAOEUZ	exercise	KPERZ
even	*EFPB, EFPB	exerciser(s)	KPERZ/ER(S)
evening	*EFPB/-G, EFPB/-G	exhale	KPAEUL
evening	AO*EF/-PBG, AO*EFPB/-G	exhaust	KPA*US
evening of the accident	EFPBGS	exhaustion	KPA*UGS, KPAUGS
evenly	*EFPB/HREU, EFPB/HREU	exhibit	KPEUBT
evenness	*EFPB/*PBS, EFPB/*PBS	Exhibit	KP*EUBT
event	*EFPBT	exhibition	KPEUBGS
event	EFPBT	exhibitionism	KPEUBGS/EUFPL
eventful	*EFPBT/-FL	exhibitionist	KPEUBGS/*EUS
eventful	EFPBT/-FL	exhibitor	KPEUB/TOR
eventual	*EFPB/KHUL	exhibitor	KPHEUB/TOR
eventual	*EFPBT/KHUL	exhort	KPORT
eventuality	*EFPB/KHAL/TEU	exhume	KPAOUPL
eventuality	*EFPB/KHUL/TEU	ex-husband	*EBGS/HUZ, EBGS/HUZ
eventually	*EFPB/KHUL/HREU	ex officio	EBGS/TPEURB/KWROE
ever	*FR, -FR	expect(s)	KP-PT(S)
every	*EFR, EFR	expectable	KP-PT/-BL
everybody	*EFRB, EFRB	expectancy	KP-PT/APB/SEU
everyday	*EFRD, EFRD	expectancy	KP-PT/TAPB/SEU
everyone	*EFRPB, EFRPB	expectant	KP-PT/TAPBT
everything	*EFRG, EFRG	expectation	KP-PT/TAEUGS
everywhere	*EFR/WR-, EFR/WR-	expected	KP-PTD
Evidence Code *(Section)*	*EFD/KOED	expecting	KP-PT/-G
evidence	*EFD	expectorant	KP-PT/RAPBT
evident	*EFT	expert *(as wd)*	EBGS/PERT
evidential	*EFT/-RBL	expert witness	KP-PBS
evidentiary	*EFT/SHAEUR	exposition	EBGS/POGS
evidently	*EFT/HREU	ex-president(s)	*EBGS/P-T(S)
exacerbate	KPAS/PWAEUT	ex-President	KP*T
exacerbation	KPAS/PWAEUGS	ex-President	*EBGS/P*T
examination	KP-GS	ex-President Bush	KP*T/PW*URB
		ex-President Carter	KP*T/KA*RT/ER
		ex-President Clinton	KP*T/KHR*EUPBT
		ex-President Clinton	KP*T/KHR*PBT
		ex-President Clinton	KP*T/KHREUPB/TOPB
		ex-President Ford	KP*T/TPO*RD

ex-President Johnson	KP*T/SKWROPB/SOPB
ex-President Kennedy	KP*T/KEPB/TKEU
ex-President Nixon	KP*T/TPHEUBG/SOPB
ex-President Reagan	KP*T/RAOE/TKPWAPB
ex-President Reagan	KP*T/RAEU/TKPWAPB
expressivity	EBGS/PRES/S*EUFT
expressivity	EBGS/PRESZ/*EUFT
expressway	KPRAE
Expressway	KPRA*E
expunge	EBGS/PUPBG
expungement	EBGS/PUPBG/-PLT
extenuating *(as wd)*	EBGS/TEPB/ KWRAEUT/-G
extenuating circumstance	KPERBG
extenuating circumstances	KPERBGZ, KPERBG/-S
extracurricular	KPRA/KREUBG/HRAR
extraditable	KPRA/TKAOEUT/-BL
extradite	KPRA/TKAOEUT
extradition	KPRA/TKEUGS
extrajudicial	KPRA/SKWRAOU/ TKEURBL
extralegal	KPRA/HRAOEL
extramarital	KPRA/PHAEUR/TAL
extramarital	KPRA/PHAR/TAL
extramural	KPRA/PHAOURL
extranational	KPRA/TPHARBL
extraordinarily	STRAORD/HREU
extraordinariness	STRAORD/*PBS
extraordinary	STRAORD
extraordinary	KPRA/ORD/TPHAEUR
extrasensory	KPRA/SEPB/SOEUR
extrasensory	KPRA/SEPBS/REU
extraterrestrial	KPRA/TR*ES/RAL
extraterrestrial	KPRA/TR*ES/RAOEL
extraterrestrial	KPRA/TR*ES/REUL
extraterrestrial	KPRA/TRES/TRAL
extraterrestrial	KPRA/TRES/TRAOEL
extraterrestrial	KPRA/TRES/TREUL
extraterritorial	KPRA/TER/TOEURL
extrovert	EBGS/TRO*EFRT
eyeball	KWRAOEUBL
eyes	KWRAOEUZ, KWRAOEU/-S
eyewitness	KWRAOEU/W*PBS
eyewitness	KWRAOEU/W-PBS
e-zine	H*EF/SAO*EPB

fabricate	TPAB/KAEUT
fabrication	TPAB/KAEUGS
fabricator	TPAB/KAEU/TOR
face *(as wd)*	TPAEUS
face-to-face	TPAEUF
fact(s) *(as wd)*	TPABGT(/-S)
facts and circumstances	TPARBGZ
fair(ly) *(as wd)*	TPAEUR(/HREU)
fair and accurate	TPA*RBG
fair and impartial	TPA*RBL
fair preponderance	TPAEURPDZ
fair to say	TPAEURTS
fairly and accurately	TPA*ERBG
fairly and impartially	TPA*ERBL
fairness	TPA*EURPBS
fallacious	TPHRAEURBS
fallaciously	TPHRAEURBS/HREU
fallopian	TPHROEP/KWRAPB
familiar	TPHRAR
familiarity	TPHRAR/TEU
familiarity	TPHRART
familiarization	TPHRAR/SA*EUGS
familiarize	TPHRAR/AOEUZ
familiarly	TPHRAR/HREU
family *(as wd)*	TPHAPL/HREU
family court	TPHROURT
Family Court	TPHRO*URT
famous	TPAEUPLS
famously	TPAEUPL/SHREU
famously	TPAEUPLS/HREU
fanciness	TPAPB/S*EUPBS
farfetched	TPAR/TPEFPD
farsighted	TPAR/SAOEUGTD
father(s) *(as wd)*	TPAUR(/-S)
father and mother	TPAPL
fathers and mothers	TPAPLS, TPAPL/-S
father-in-law	TPAURPBL
fathers-in-law	TPAURPBLS,
father-in-laws	TPAURPBL/-S
fatherly	TPAUR/HREU
father or mother	TPOPL
fathers or mothers	TPOPLS, TPOPL/-S
faultiness	TPAL/T*EUPBS
faultiness	TPAUL/T*EUPBS
favor	TPA*EUFR
favorable	TPA*EUFRBL
favorite	TPA*EUFRT
FBI *(Federal Bureau of Investigation)*	TP-RBGS/PW*EU
F.B.I.	TP-FPLT/PW*EU
FCA *(Farm Credit Administration)*	TP-RBGS/KRA*
FCC *(Federal Communications Commission)*	TP-RBGS/KR*BG
FCIC *(Federal Crop Insurance Corporation)*	TP-RBGS/KR*EUBG

FDA *(Food and Drug Administration)*	TP-RBGS/TKA*
FDIC *(Federal Deposit Insurance Corporation)*	TP-RBGS/TK*EUBG
FDR *(Franklin Delano Roosevelt)*	TP-RBGS/TK*R
featherbrained	TP*ET/ER/PWRAEUPBD
feature	TPAOEFP
February	TPEB
federal *(as wd)*	TPRAL
Federal *(as wd)*	TPRA*L
federal court	TPROURT
Federal Court	TPRO*URT
federal government	TPROFT
Federal Government	TPRO*FT
federal judge	TPRUPBLG
federalism	TPRAL/EUFPL
federalist	TPRAL/*EUS
federalize	TPRAL/AOEUZ
federally	TPRAL/HREU
felicitate	TPHREUS/TAEUT
felicitation	TPHREUS/TAEUGS
felicity	TPHREUS/TEU
fellatio	TPHRAEU/SHOE
fellatio	TPHRAEURB/KWROE
felon	TPHROPB
felonious	TPHROEPB/KWROUS
felonious	TPHROPB/KWROUS
feloniously	TPHROEPB/SHREU
feloniously	TPHROPB/SHREU
feloniously	TPHROEPB/KWROUS/HREU
feloniously	TPHROPB/KWROUS/HREU
felonry	TPHROPB/REU
felony	TPHROPB/TPH*EU
FEMA *(Federal Emergency Management Agency)*	TPAO*E/PHA
FEMA	TP-RBGS/*ERBGS/PHA*
female	TPAEL
ferocious	TPROERBS
ferociously	TPROERBS/HREU
ferociousness	TPROERBS/*PBS
fertilization	TPERT/SA*EUGS
festivity	TP*ES/*EUFT
festivity	TPES/T*EUFT
fetishism	TPET/SHEUFPL
few	TPU
fewer	TPU/ER
fewest	TPU/*ES
FHA *(Federal Housing Administration)*	TP-RBGS/HA*
FHMA *(Federal Home Mortgage Corp. [Freddie Mac])*	TP-RBGS/H*RBGS/PHA*
FI. FA. *(fieri facias [cause to be made])*	TPAOEU/TPAEU
fibrillation	TPEUB/HRAEUGS
fibula	TPEUB/HRA
fibular	TPEUB/HRAR
FICA *(Federal Insurance Contributions Act)*	TPAOEU/KA
FICA	TP-RBGS/*EURBGS/KRA*
fictionally	TP*EUBGS/HREU
fidget	TPEUPBLGT
fidgety	TPEUPBLG/TEU
fidgety	TPEUPBLGT/TEU
fieri facias	TPAOEUR/TPAEURBS
fieriness	TPAOEU/R*EUPBS
fieriness	TPAOEUR/R*EUPBS
FIFO *(first-in, first-out)*	TPAOEU/TPOE
FIFO	TP-RBGS/*EURBGS/TPO*
fifty	TPEUFT
finance	TP-PBS
financial(s)	TP-PBL(S)
financial(s)	TP-PBS/-RBL(S)
financially	TP-PBL/HREU
financially	TP-PBS/-RBL/HREU
financier	TP-PBS/SAOER
f-ing	TP*G
fingerprint	TPREUPBT
fink	TP*EUPBG
fire *(as wd)*	TPAOEUR
firearm	TPAOEURPL
firebomb	TPAOEURB
fire department	TPAOEURD
fire truck	TPAOEURBG
first *(as wd)*	TP*EURS
first-degree	TP-D
first degree	TP*D
first-degree murder	TP-PLD
First Lady	TPEURLD
first name	TPEURPB
first of all	TPEUFRL
first thing	TPEURPBG
first time	TPEURT
flabbiness	TPHRAB/PW*EUPBS
flakiness	TPHRAEU/K*EUPBS
flakiness	TPHRAEUBG/K*EUPBS
flange	TPHRAPBG
flank	TPHRA*PBG
flashiness	TPHRARB/SH*EUPBS
flashlight(s)	TPHR-LT(S)
floodlight(s)	TPHRAOLT(/-S), TPHRAOLT(S)
floodplain	TPHRAEUPB
floppiness	TPHROP/P*EUPBS
Florida	TPHR*/TPHR*
Florida	TPHRAFPLT
floterial	TPHROE/TAOERL
flowage	TPHROEPBLG
flower	TPHRO*UR
floweriness	TPHRO*UR/R*EUPBS
floweriness	TPHRO*UR/REU/*PBS
flowery	TPHRO*UR/REU
flu	TPHRU
fluffiness	TPHRUF/TP*EUPBS
flunk	TPHR*UPBG
fluvial	TPHRAO*UFL
fly-by-night	TPHRAOEUPBT
FMC *(Federal Maritime Commission)*	TP-RBGS/PH*BG
FNMA *(Federal National Mortgage Association [Fannie Mae])*	TP-RBGS/TPH*RBGS/PHA*
foaminess	TPOEPL/PH*EUPBS

foaminess	TPOE/PH*EUPBS	forty	TPOURT
f.o.b. *(free on board)*	TP*PD/O*B	forum contractus	TPOR/UPL/KR-T/TUS
FOB	TP-RBGS/O*B	forward(s)	TPWARD(Z)
fogginess	TPOG/TKPW*EUPBS	forwarder	TPWARD/ER
follow-up	TPHRO*UP	fought	TPAUT
follow up	TPHROUP	FOX	TPO*BGS
follow(ing) *(as wd)*	TPOL/HROE(/-G)	FOX	TP-RBGS/O*BGS
following the accident	TPEBGS	foxiness	TPOBG/S*EUPBS
foolhardiness	TPAOL/HAR/TK*EUPBS	foxiness	TPOBGS/S*EUPBS
football	TPAOBL	FPC *(Federal Power Commission)*	
footprint	TPAOPBT		TP-RBGS/P*BG
for *(as wd)*	TP-R	fragmentariness	TPRAG/PHEPB/
for a minute	TPEUPLT		TA*EURPBS
for a moment	TPOPLT	fragmentariness	TPRAG/-PLT/
for example	TPREBGS		TA*EURPBS
for identification	TPOEUD	frank	TPRA*PBG
for instance	TPREUPBS	Frank	K-P/TPRA*PBG
for instance	TPREUPB/STAPBS	frankly	TPRA*PBG/HREU
for instance	TPREUPBS/TAPBS	frankness	TPRA*PBG/*PBS
for me to say	TPORPLTS	fraudulence	TPRAUPBS
for or against	TPO*RPBS	fraudulent	TPRAUPBT
for the	TP-RT	fraudulently	TPRAUPBT/HREU
for the record	TPRORD	fraught	TPRAUT
for the record	TP-RT/RORD	FRB *(Federal Reserve Board)*	TP-RBGS/R*B
forefather	TPOER/TPAUR	freakiness	TPRAOE/K*EUPBS
foregoing	TPOER/TKPWOEUPBG	freakiness	TPRAOEBG/K*EUPBS
forejudgment	TPOER/SKWRUPLT	free *(as wd)*	TPRAOE
foreknowledge	TPOER/TPHOPBLG	free and voluntary	TPRA*F
THE FOREMAN: *(colloquy)*		freely and voluntarily	TPRA*EF
	TPORPL/TPORPL	freeway	TPRAE
foremother	TPOER/PHOER	Freeway	TPRA*E
forensic	TPREPBS/EUBG	freight	TPRAEUT
foreperson	TPOER/PERPB	freighter(s)	TPRAEUT/ER(S)
Foreperson	TPO*ER/PERPB	frequency	TPRAOEBGT/SEU
THE FOREPERSON: *(colloquy)*		frequent	TPRAOEBGT
	TPORPB/TPORPB	frequently	TPRAOEBGT/HREU
forest	TPO*RS	Friday(s)	TPREUD(Z)
forester(s)	TPO*RS/ER(S)	friendliness	TPREPBD/HR*EUPBS
forestland	TPO*RS/HRAPBD	fright	TPRAOEUT
forestry	TPO*RS/REU	frighten(s)	TPRAOEUT/-PB(S)
forethought	TPOER/THAUT	frightened	TPRAOEUT/-PBD
forever	TPR*FR, TPR-FR	frightening	TPRAOEUT/-PBG
forevermore	TPR*FR/PHOR,	frightful	TPRAOEUT/-FL
	TPR-FR/PHOR	frightfully	TPRAOEUT/TPHREU
foreverness	TPR*FR/*PBS,	frigid	TPREUPBLGD
	TPR-FR/*PBS	frigidity	TPREUPBLGD/TEU
forevers	TPR*FRS, TPR-FRS	frilliness	TPREUL/HR*EUPBS
forewoman	TPOER/WOPL	fringe	TPREUPBG
Forewoman	TPO*ER/WOPL	friskiness	TPREUS/K*EUPBS
THE FOREWOMAN: *(colloquy)*		frizziness	TPREUZ/S*EUPBS
	TPWOPL/TPWOPL	FRM *(fixed-rate mortgage)*	TP-RBGS/R*PL
forewomen	TPOER/WEUPL	from *(as wd)*	TPR-
forget	TPERGT	from the	TPR-T
forgetful	TPERGT/-FL	from the evidence	TPR*EFD, TPREFD
forgetfulness	TPERGT/TPHR*PBS	from the record	TPRERBGD
forgettable	TPERGT/-BL	from this point	TPR*EUPT
forgot	TPORGT	from time to time	TPREUPLT
forgotten	TPORGT/-PB	front *(as wd)*	TPROPBT
formally	TPORPL/HREU	front-end	TPRO*EPBD
fortunate	TP-RPBT	front end	TPROEPBD
fortunately	TP-RPBLT	front seat	TPROPBTS
fortunately	TP-RPBT/HREU	frostiness	TPROS/T*EUPBS
fortune(s)	TP-RPB(S)		

FRS *(Federal Reserve System)*
                              TP-RBGS/R*S
FTC *(Federal Trade Commission)*
                              TP-RBGS/T*BG
FTD *(Florists' Transworld Delivery)*
                              TP-RBGS/T*D
FTP *(file transfer protocol)* TP-RBGS/T*P
FTS *(Federal Telecommunications System)*
                              TP-RBGS/T*S
full *(as wd)*   TPUL
full-time   TPAOEUPL
fungibility   TPUPBG/-BLT
fungible(s)   TPUPBG/-BL(S)
funk   TP*UPBG
funniness   TPUPB/TPH*EUPBS
furriness   TPUR/R*EUPBS
further   TPURT
furtherance   TPURT/RAPBS
furthermore   TPURT/PHOR
furthest   TPURT/*ES
fussiness   TPUS/S*EUPBS
FUTA *(Federal Unemployment Tax Act)*
                              TPAOU/TA
FUTA   TP-RBGS/*URBGS/TA*
future   TPAOUFP
futurist   TPAOUFP/*EUS
futuristic   TPAOUFP/*EUS/EUBG
fuzziness   TPUZ/*PBS
fuzziness   TPUZ/S*EUPBS
FYI *(for your information)* TP-RBGS/KWR*EU

G

gabbiness   TKPWAB/PW*EUPBS
gadget   TKPWAPBLGT
galactic   TKPWHRABGT/EUBG
galactic   TKPWHRABG/TEUBG
galactose   TKPWHRABG/TOES
gallon   TKPWHROPB
gangplank   TKPWAPBG/PHRA*PBG
GAO *(General Accounting Office)*
                              TKPW-RBGS/AO*
garage   TKPWRAPBLG
garnishee   TKPWARPB/SHAOE
gaseous   TKPWARBS
gassiness   TKPWAS/S*EUPBS
GATT   TKPWA*T
gaudiness   TKPWAU/TK*EUPBS
gaudiness   TKPWAUD/TK*EUPBS
gazillion   TKPWA/S*L
GED *(general equivalency diploma)*
                              TKPW-RBGS/*ED
general *(as wd)*   SKWREPB
General *(as wd)*   SKWR*EPB
General Electric   SKWR*BGT
general manager   SKWR-PLG
General Motors   SKWR*PLTS
generality   SKWREPB/TEU
generalization   SKWREPB/SA*EUGS
generalize   SKWREPB/AOEUZ
generally   SKWREPB/HREU
generic   SKWRE/TPHERBG
generic   SKWRE/TPHAEURBG
generically   SKWRE/TPHERBG/HREU
generically   SKWRE/TPHAEURBG/HREU
Geneva *(as wd)*   SKWRE/TPHAOE/SRA
Geneva Convention   SKWR*EFGS
gentleman   SKWRE/PHAPB
gentlemen   SKWRE/PHEPB
gentlemen of the jury   SKWRAERPBLG
gentlemen of the jury   SKWRERPBLG
Gentlemen of the Jury   SKWR*ERPBLG
Gentlemen of the Jury   SKWRA*ERPBLG
gentlewoman   SKWRE/WOPL
gentlewomen   SKWRE/WEUPL
geographic   SKWRAOE/TKPWRAFBG
geographically   SKWRAOE/TKPWRAFBG/HREU
geophysical   SKWRAOE/TP-L
geophysical   SKWRAOE/KWRO/TP-L
Georgia   TKPWA*/TKPWA*
Gerald   SKWRERLD
gerund(s)   SKWRERPBD(Z)
Gettysburg   TKPWETS/PWURG
ghastliness   TKPWA*S/HR*EUPBS
ghostwrite   TKPWO*ES/WREU
ghostwriter(s)   TKPWO*ES/WREUR(/-S)
ghostwritten   TKPWO*ES/WREUPB

giddiness	TKPWEUD/TK*EUPBS		TKPWO*FPLT
GIF *(graphics interchange format)*		govern	TKPWO*FRPB
	TKPW-RBGS/*EUF	governess	TKPWO*FRPBS
GIGO *(garbage in, garbage out)*		government *(as wd)*	TKPWO*FT, TKPWOFT
	TKPWAOEU/TKPWOE	Government *(as wd)*	K-P/TKPWO*FT,
girlfriend	TKPWOEUF		K-P/TKPWOFT
give *(as wd)*	TKPW*EUF	Government's Exhibit	TKPW-BGS
give up	TKPWUP	Government's Exhibit No.	TKPW*BGS
glassiness	TKPWHRAS/S*EUPBS	governmental	TKPWO*FT/TAL
gloominess	TKPWHRAO/PH*EUPBS	governmental	TKPWOFT/TAL
gloominess	TKPWHRAOPL/PH*EUPBS	governor	TKPWO*F/TPHOR
glossiness	TKPWHROS/S*EUPBS	Governor	K-P/TKPWO*F/TPHOR
glove *(as wd)*	TKPWHR*UF	GPA *(grade point average)*	TKPW-RBGS/PA*
glove *(as wd)*	TKPWHRO*F	GPO *(Government Printing Office)*	
glove compartment	TKPWHR-PT		TKPW-RBGS/PO*
gm *(gram)*	TKPW*PL	grade *(as wd)*	TKPWRAEUD
GMAC *(General Motors Acceptance Corp.)*		grade school	TKPWAOL
	TKPW-RBGS/	Grade School	TKPWA*OL
	PH*RBGS/A*BG	graduate *(as wd, n)*	TKPWRAPBLG/WAT
GMAC	TKPW-RBGS/PHA*BG	graduate school	TKPWRAOL
G-man *(government man)*	TKPW-/PHAPB	Graduate School	TKPWRA*OL
GMC *(General Motors Corp.)*		gram(s) *(as wd)*	TKPWRAPL(/-S)
	TKPW-RBGS/PH*BG	gram(s) of cocaine	TKPWRABG(S),
G-men *(government men)*	TKPW-/PHEPB		TKPWRABG(/-S)
GNMA *(Government National Mortgage Association*		gramps	TKPWRAFRPS
[Ginnie Mae])	TKPW-RBGS/	grand *(as wd)*	TKPWRAPBD
	TPH*RBGS/PHA*	grandchild	TKPWR-FP
GNP *(gross national product)*		grandchildren	TKPWR-PB
	TKPW-RBGS/TPH*P	granddaughter(s)	TKPWR-D(Z)
go	TKPWO	grandfather(s)	TKPWR-F(S)
goddamnit	TKPWOD/TKAPLT	grandfathered	TKPWR-FD
godfather(s)	TKPWOD/TPAUR(/-S)	grandfathering	TKPWR-FG
godliness	TKPWOD/HR*EUPBS	grand juror	TKPWR-RPBLG
godmother(s)	TKPWOD/PHOER(/-S)	Grand Juror	TKPWR*RPBLG
goes	TKPWOES, TKPWOEZ	grand jury	TKPWR-PBLG
going *(as wd)*	TKPWO/-G,	Grand Jury	TKPWR*PBLG
	TKPWOEUPBG	grand larceny	TKPWHRARS
going to object	TKPWOBT	grandmother(s)	TKPWR-PL(S)
golf	TKPWOF	grandparent(s)	TKPWR-PT(/-S),
golfer	TKPWOFR		TKPWR-PT(S)
good *(as wd)*	TKPWAOD	grandson(s)	TKPWR-S(/-S),
good afternoon	TKPWAOFRPB		TKPWR-S(Z)
good-bye	TKPWAOB	grange	TKPWRAEUPBG
good day	TKPWAEUD	Grange	TKPWRA*EUPBG
good enough	TKPWUF	graphic	TKPWRAFBG
good evening	TKPWAOPBG	graphically	TKPWRAFBG/HREU
good faith	TKPWA*EUT	grassiness	TKPWRAS/S*EUPBS
good luck	TKPWHRUBG	grassroot(s) *(j)*	TKPWRAOT(/-S),
good many	TKPW-PL		TKPWRAOTS
good many days	TKPW-PLDZ	gravid	TKPWRA*FD
good many times	TKPW-PLTS	GRE *(Graduate Record Examination)*	
good morning	TKPWAORPBG		TKPW-RBGS/R*E
good night	TKPWAOPBT	greasiness	TKPWRAE/S*EUPBS
goofball	TKPWAOFBL	greasiness	TKPWRAES/S*EUPBS
goofiness	TKPWAO/TP*EUPBS	greasiness	TKPWRAEZ/S*EUPBS
goofiness	TKPWAOF/TP*EUPBS	great *(as wd)*	TKPWRAET
GOP *(Grand Old Party [Republican])*		great bodily harm	TKPWRORPL
	TKPW-RBGS/O*P	great bodily injury	TKPWROPBLG
GOP	TKPWO*P	great deal	TKPWRAEL
G.O.P.	TKPW-FPLT/O*P	great extent	TKPWRAEBGS
gorilla	TKPWREUL/HRA	Great Lakes	TKPWRAEUBGS
goriness	TKPWOER/R*EUPBS	great many	TKPWRAEPL
.gov *(suf)*	TKPWOFPLT,	great many days	TKPWRAEPLDZ

great many times	TKPWRAEPLTS		
greater (as wd)	TKPWRAET/ER		
greater number of witnesses	TKPWREUTS		
greater weight of the evidence	TKPWRA*EUFD		
greater weight of the evidence	TKPWRAEUFD		
greediness	TKPWRAOE/TK*EUPBS		
greediness	TKPWRAOED/TK*EUPBS		
green (as wd)	TKPWRAOEPB		
green light(s)	TKPWR-LT(S), TKPWR-LT(/-S)		
grogginess	TKPWROG/TKPW*EUPBS		
grouchiness	TKPWROU/KH*EUPBS		
grouchiness	TKPWROUFP/KH*EUPBS		
group (as wd)	TKPWRAOUP		
group (as wd)	TKPWROUP		
group insurance	TKPWRURPBS		
grower	TKPWRO*UR		
grown (as wd)	TKPWROUPB		
grown-up	TKPWR*UP		
grown up	TKPWRUP		
grubbiness	TKPWRUB/PW*EUPBS		
grumpiness	TKPWRUFRP/P*EUPBS		
grumpiness	TKPWRUPL/P*EUPBS		
GSA (General Services Administration)	TKPW-RBGS/SA*		
GTE (General Telephone & Electronics)	TKPW-RBGS/T*E		
GTO (Gran Turismo Omologato, grand touring)	TKPW-RBGS/TO*		
guaranteed	TKPWARPB/TAOED		
gubernatorial	TKPWAOUB/TOEURL		
guidance	TKPWAOEUPBDZ		
guidance	TKPWAOEUPBS		
guideline	TKPWHRAOEUPB		
guilt (as wd)	TKPWEULT		
guilt or innocence	TKPWORPBS		
guiltily	TKPW-LT/HREU		
guiltily	TKPWEULT/HREU		
guiltiness	TKPW-LT/*PBS		
guiltiness	TKPWEUL/T*EUPBS		
guilty (as wd)	TKPW-LT		
guilty or innocent	TKPWORPBT		
guilty or not guilty	TKPWORPBG		
guilty verdict	TKPW-RBGT		
Gulf of Mexico	TKPWUFPL		
gumminess	TKPWUPL/PH*EUPBS		
gun (as wd)	TKPWUPB		
gunfight	TKPWUFT		
gunfire	TKPWUFR		
gunman	TKPWA*PL		
gunmen	TKPW*EPL		
gunpoint	TKPWUPT		
gunshot	TKPWURBT		
gunshot wound	TKPWOUPBD		
gunk	TKPW*UPBG		
gustiness	TKPWUS/T*EUPBS		

habeas corpus	HAEUBS/KORPS
habilitate	HABLT
habilitation	HABLGS
habilitative	HABLT/*EUF
habit	HABT
habitability	HABT/-BLT
habitable	HABT/-BL
habitual	HABT/KHUL
habitually	HABT/KHUL/HREU
habituate	HABT/KHAEUT
habituation	HABT/KHAEUGS
had (as wd)	HAD
hadn't	H-PBT
had been	H-B
had believed	H-BLD
had felt	H-FLT
had had	H-D
had recalled	H-RLD
had recollected	H-RBGD
had remembered	H-RPLD
had the	H-T
hairball	HAEURBL
hairiness	HAEU/R*EUPBS
hairiness	HAEUR/R*EUPBS
half	HAF
1/2 (half symbol)(suf)	HAFS
halfhearted	HAF/HARTD
halfheartedly	HAF/HARTD/HREU
hand (as wd)	HAPBD
handgun	H-G
handicap	HAPBD/KAP
handiness	HAPB/TK*EUPBS
H & R Block	H-R/PWHROBG
handwrite	HAPBD/WREU
handwriting	HAPBD/WREUG
handwriting	HAPBD/WREU/-G
handwritten	HAPBD/WREUPB
handwritten	HAPBD/WREU/-PB
hank	HA*PBG
Hank	K-P/HA*PBG
hanker(s)	HA*PBG/ER(S)
Hanukkah	HAPB/KA
Hanukkah	HAUPB/KA
happen	HAP
happening(s)	HAP/-G(S)
happenstance	HAP/STAPBS
happiness	HAP/P*EUPBS
harass	HARS
harassment	HARPLT, HARS/-PLT
hard (as wd)	HARD
hardball	HARBL
hardhearted	HARD/HARTD
hardiness	HAR/TK*EUPBS
hard-of-hearing	HOFRG
harebrained	HA*ER/PWRAEUPBD
harebrained	HAEUR/PWRAEUPBD

harem	HAEURPL	he believes	HEBLS
harness	HA*RPBS	he can	HE/K-
Harold	HARLD	he could	HEBGD
harum-scarum	HAEURPL/SKAEURPL	he couldn't	HEBGD/-PBT
has *(as wd)*	HAZ	he feel	HEFL
hasn't	HAPBT	he feels	HEFLS
has been	HAB	he felt	HEFLT
has felt	HAFLT	he has	HEZ
hatchet	HAFPT	he have	HE/SR-
haughtier	HAUT/KWRER	he is	HES
haughtiest	HAUT/KWR*ES	he just want	HEFPT
haughtily	HAUT/HREU	he just wanted	HEFPTD
haughtiness	HAU/T*EUPBS	he just wants	HEFPTS
haughtiness	HAUT/T*EUPBS	he knows	H*EPBS
haughtiness	HAU/TEU/*PBS	he recalled	HERLD
haughtiness	HAUG/T*EUPBS	he recalls	HERLS
haughtiness	HAUGT/T*EUPBS	he recollected	HERBGD
haughtiness	HAUT/TEU/*PBS	he recollects	HERBGS
haughty	HAU/TEU, HAUT/TEU	he remembered	HERPLD
have *(as wd)*	SR-	he remembers	HERPLS
haves	SR-S	he said	HEBS
have been	SR-B	he say	HEBZ
have been had	SR-BD	he says	HEBSZ
have felt	SR-FLT	he/she	HAOERBS
have had	SR-D	he/she	HE/SH*E
having	SR-G	he should	HERBD
have I said	SREUBS	he think	HEPBG
have not	SR-/TPHOT	he thinks	HEPBGS
haven't	SR-PBT	he understand(s)	HEPBDZ(/-S)
have recalled	SR-RLD	he understood	H*EPBDZ
have recollected	SR-RBGD	he want	HEPT
have remembered	SR-RPLD	he wanted	HEPTD
have said	SR-BS	he wants	HEPTS
have the	SR-T	he was	HEFS
have you been	SRUB	he will	HE/HR-
have you ever	SRUFR	head(s) *(as wd)*	HED(Z)
have you ever been	SRUFRB	headache	HAEUBG
have you ever had	SRUFRD	headlight(s)	H-LT(S)
have you ever wanted	SRUFRPTD	health *(as wd)*	H*ELT
have you had	SRUD	healthcare	H*BG
have you said	SRUBS	health care	H-BG
have you wanted	SRUPTD	health department	H*ELTD
havoc	HA*FBG	health insurance	HURPBS
Hawaii	H*EU/H*EU	healthiness	HEL/TH*EUPBS
Hawaii	HAFPLT	hearing *(as wd)*	HAERG
Hawaii	HA/WAOEU	hearing-impaired	HAERPD
Hawaiian	H*EU/H*EU/KWRAPB	hearsay	HAERBZ
Hawaiian	HA/WAOEUPB	heartbroken	HART/PWROEPB
Hawaiian	HAFPLT/KWRAPB	heartiness	HAR/T*EUPBS
hazardous	HAZ/TKOUS	heavyhearted	H*EF/SREU/HARTD
haziness	HAEU/S*EUPBS	heebie-jeebies	HAOEB/SKWRAOEB/-S
haziness	HAEUZ/S*EUPBS	heftiness	HEF/T*EUPBS
HBO *(Home Box Office)*	H-RBGS/PWO*	help	H*EP
HDL *(high-density lipoprotein)*		helper(s)	H*EP/ER(S)
	H-RBGS/TK*L	helpful	H*EP/-FL
HDTV *(high-definition television)*		helpfully	H*EP/TPHREU
	H-RBGS/TK*RBGS/T*F	helpfulness	H*EP/TPHR*PBS
he *(as wd)*	HE	helping(s)	H*EP/-G(S)
he'd	HAO*ED	helpless	H*EP/HRES
he'll	HAO*EL	helplessly	H*EP/HRES/HREU
he's	HAO*ES	helplessness	H*EP/HRES/*PBS
he believe	HEBL	hemispheric	HEPLS/TPAOERBG
he believed	HEBLD	hemispheric	HEPLS/TPERBG

her *(as wd)*	HER
her Honor	HERPB
herculean	HERBG/HRAOEPB
here *(as wd)*	HAOER
here's	HAO*ERS
hereabout(s)	HAOERBT(S), HAOERBT(/-S)
here about	HAOER/ABT
hereafter	HAOER/AFR
here after	HAOER/AF
hereby	HAOERB
here by	HAOER/PWEU
herein	HAOERPB
here in	HAOER/TPH-
hereinabove	HAOERPB/PWO*F
hereinafter	HAOERPB/AFR
hereinbefore	HAOERPB/PW-FR
hereto	HAOERT
here to	HAOER/TO
heretofore	HAOERT/TPOER
hereunder	HAOERPBD
here under	HAOER/URPBD
herewith	HAOER/W*EUT
here with	HAOER/W-
hereditariness	HE/RED/TA*EURPBS
hermetic	HERPLT/EUBG
hermetical	HERPLT/KAL
hermetically	HERPLT/KHREU
hermit	HERPLT
heroic	HAOE/ROEUBG
heroin	HAEURPB
heroism	HER/WEUFPL
herself	H*ERS
heterosexual	HET/RO/SWAUL
HHS *(Health and Human Services)*	H-RBGS/H*S
hibernate	HAOEUB/TPHAEUT
hibernation	HAOEUB/TPHAEUGS
hieroglyphic	HAOEUR/TKPWHREUFBG
high *(as wd)*	HAOEU
highball	HAOEUBL
high school	HAOL
High School	HA*OL
highway	HAE
Highway	HA*E
hijack	HAOEUPBLG
hillside(s)	HEULD(Z)
hilliness	HEUL/HR*EUPBS
him/her	HEURPL
him/her	HEUPL/H*ER
himself	H*EUPLS
hinge	HEUPBG
his *(as wd)*	HEUZ
his/her	HEURZ
his/her	HEUZ/H*ER
his Honor	HEURPB
historic	HEUS/TOERBG
historic	HEUS/TORBG
historically	HEUS/TOERBG/HREU
historically	HEUS/TORBG/HREU
hit *(as wd)*	HEUT
hit-and-miss	H-PLS
hit-and-run	H-RPB
hit-or-miss	HORPLS
HIV *(human immunodeficiency virus)*	H*EUF
HIV	H-RBGS/*EUF
HMO *(health maintenance organization)*	H-RBGS/PHO*
hoi polloi	HOEU/PHROEU
hold *(as wd)*	HOELD, HOLD
holdup	HO*UP
hold up	HOUP
holiness	HOE/HR*EUPBS
holiness	HOEL/HR*EUPBS
holographic	HOEL/TKPWRAFBG
holographic	HOL/TKPWRAFBG
homework	HOERBG
homicidal	H-DZ/TKAL
homicide(s)	H-DZ(/-S)
Homo sapiens	HOEPL/SAEUP/KWREPBS
Homo sapiens	HOEPL/SAEUP/KWREPBZ
homosexual	HOE/PHO/SWAUL
homosexuality	HOE/PHO/SWAUL/TEU
honest	HO*PBS
honestly	HO*PBLS
honestly	HO*PBS/HREU
honesty	HO*PBTS
honesty	HO*PBS/TEU
honk	HO*PBG
honky tonk	HO*PBG/KEU/TO*PBG
honorarium	HOPB/RAEURPL
honoris respectum	HOPB/REUS/R-PT/UPL
hoodwink	HAOD/W*EUPBG
hornet	HORPBT
horniness	HOR/TPH*EUPBS
horrendous	HORPBD/OUS
horrendously	HORPBD/SHREU
horrendously	HORPBD/OUS/HREU
hors d'oeuvre(s)	O*R/TK/*EFRB(Z)
hors d'oeuvre(s)	O*R/TKEFRB(Z)
horsepower	HOERS/PO*UR
horsepower	HORS/PO*UR
hospitable	HOPT/-BL
hospitably	HOPT/PWHREU
hospital	HOPT
Hospital	HO*PT
hospitality	HOPT/TEU
hospitalization	HOPGS
hospitalization	HOPT/SA*EUGS
hospitalize	HOPT/AOEUZ
House *(as wd) (Congress)*	HO*US
House of Representatives	HOURPTS
housebroken	HOUS/PWROEPB
househusband	HOUS/HUZ
housework	HOURBG
how *(as wd)*	HOU
how about	HOUBT
how can	HOUBG
how could	HOUBGD
however	HO*UFR, HOUFR
how ever	HOU/-FR, HOU/*FR
how fast	HOUFZ
how in the world	HOUPBT/WORLD
how large	HOURPBLG
how late	HOULT

how long	HOUPBG	hydropower	HAOEU/TKRO/PO*UR
how many	HOUPL	hymn	H*EUPL
how many days	HOUPLDZ	hyperactivity	HAO*EUP/ABG/T*EUFT
how many times	HOUPLTS	hyperactivity	HAO*EUP/ABGT/*EUFT
how much	HOUFP	hyperphysical	HAO*EUP/TP-L
how often	HOUFPB	hypersensitivity	HAO*EUP/ SEPBS/T*EUFT
how old	HOULD		
how shall	HOURB	hypochondria	HO*EUP/KOPB/TKRA
how should	HOURBD	hypochondriac	HO*EUP/KOPB/TKRABG
how was	HOUFS		
how were	HOURP		
hr.	H*R		
hrs.	H*RS		
H. Rept *(House report)*	H-FPLT/REPT		
H. Rept.	H-FPLT/R*EPT		
H. Res *(House resolution)*	H-FPLT/REZ		
H. Res.	H-FPLT/R*EZ		
HRT *(hormone replacement therapy)*	H-RBGS/R*T		
HTML *(HyperText Markup Language)*	H-RBGS/T*RBGS/PH*L		
http *(hypertext transfer protocol)*	H*/T*BGZ/T*P		
HTTP	H-RBGS/T*RBGS/T*P		
HUAC *(House Un-American Activities Committee)*	HAOU/A*BG		
HUAC	H-RBGS/*URBGS/A*BG		
HUD *(Housing and Urban Development)*	H*UD		
HUD	H-RBGS/*UD		
huffiness	HUF/TP*EUPBS		
huh	HU		
huh-uh *(negative)*	HU/U		
human *(as wd)*	HAOUPL		
human being	HAOUB		
humanism	HAOUPL/EUFPL		
humanist	HAOUPL/*EUS		
humanistic	HAOUPL/*EUS/EUBG		
humanitarian	HAOUPL/TAEURPB		
humanitarianism	HAOUPL/ TAEURPB/EUFPL		
humanity	HAOUPL/TEU		
humanization	HAOUPL/SA*EUGS		
humanize	HAOUPL/AOEUZ		
humankind	HAOUPL/KAOEUPBD		
humanly	HAOUPL/HREU		
humanoid	HAOUPL/OEUD		
humid	HAOUPLD		
humidifier(s)	HAOUPLD/TPEU/ER(S)		
humidify	HAOUPLD/TPEU		
humidity	HAOUPLD/TEU		
hundred(s) *(as wd)*	HUPB(S), HUPB(/-S)		
hundred dollar(s)	HUPBD(Z)		
hundredth	H*UPBT		
hunk	H*UPBG		
husband	HUZ		
husbandman	HUZ/PHAPB		
husbandry	HUZ/REU		
huskiness	HUS/K*EUPBS		
hydrochloric	HAOEU/TKRO/ KHROERBG		
hydrochloric	HAOEU/TKRO/ KHRORBG		

I (Roman numeral)	1R
I (as wd)	EU
I'd	AO*EUD
I'll	*EUL
I'm	AO*EUPL
I've	AO*EUF
I believe	EUBL
I believe so	EUBLS
I believed	EUBLD
I can	EU/K-
I cannot	EU/K-/TPHOT
I can't	KWRAPBT, EU/K-PBT
I can't be	KWRAB
I can't believe	KWRABL
I can't feel	KWRAFL
I can't go	KWRAG
I can't have	KWRAF
I can't have been	KWRAFB
I can't have had	KWRAFD
I can't imagine	KWRAPBLG
I can't recall	KWRARL
I can't recollect	KWRARBG
I can't remember	KWRARPL
I can't say	KWRABZ
I can't think	KWRAPBG
I can't understand	KWRAPBDZ
I can't want	KWRAPT
I could	EUBGD
I could not	EUBGD/TPHOT
I couldn't	EUBGD/-PBT
I didn't	KWREUPBT, EU/TK-PBT
I didn't believe	KWREUBL
I didn't believe so	KWREUBLS
I didn't do	KWREUD
I didn't feel	KWREUFL
I didn't go	KWREUG
I didn't have	KWREUF
I didn't imagine	KWREUPBLG
I didn't know	KWR*EUPB
I didn't mean	KWREUPL
I didn't mean to	KWREUPLT
I didn't mean to say	KWREUPLTS
I didn't recall	KWREURL
I didn't recollect	KWREURBG
I didn't remember	KWREURPL
I didn't say	KWREUBZ
I didn't think	KWREUPBG
I didn't think so	KWREUPBGS
I didn't understand	KWREUPBDZ
I didn't want	KWREUPT
I don't	KWROPBT
I don't believe	KWROBL
I don't believe so	KWROBLS
I don't care	KWROBG
I don't ever	KWROFR
I don't feel	KWROFL
I don't find	KWROFPBD
I don't go	KWROG
I don't have	KWROF
I don't have the	KWROFT
I don't imagine	KWROPBLG
I don't know	KWRO*PB
I don't mean	KWROPL
I don't mean to	KWROPLT
I don't mean to say	KWROPLTS
I don't mind	KWROPLD
I don't recall	KWRORL
I don't recollect	KWRORBG
I don't remember	KWRORPL
I don't say	KWROBZ
I don't think	KWROPBG
I don't think so	KWROPBGS
I don't understand	KWROPBDZ
I don't want	KWROPT
I feel	EUFL
I felt	EUFLT
I have	EUF
I have been	EUFB
I have believed	EUFBLD
I have had	EUFD
I haven't	EUFPBT
I just want	EUFPT
I just wanted	EUFPTD
I know	KWR*PB
I object	EUBT
I recall	EURL
I recalled	EURLD
I recollect	EU/REBGT
I remember	EURPL
I remembered	EURPLD
I said	EUBS
I say	EUBZ
I says	EUBSZ
I shall	EURBL
I should	EURBD
I think	EUPBG
I think the	EUPBGT
I understand	EUPBDZ
I understood	*EUPBDZ
I want	EUPT
I wanted	EUPTD
I was	EUFS
I were	EURP
I will	EU/HR-
I would	EULD
I would say	EULDZ
IBM (International Business Machines)	EURBGS/PW*PL
ibuprofen	AOEUB/PROEFPB
ICBM (intercontinental ballistic missile)	EURBGS/KR*RBGS/PW*PL
ICBM	EURBGS/KR*PBL
ICC (Interstate Commerce Commission)	EURBGS/KR*BG
iconography	AOEUBG/TPHOG/TPEU
ICU (intensive care unit)	EURBGS/KR*U
ID (identification)	*EUD
Idaho	*EUD/*EUD

idea(s)	KWR-D(Z)	if I recall	TPEURL
ideal(s)	KWR-L(S)	if I recollect	TPEURBG
idealism	KWR-L/EUFPL	if I remember	TP*EURPL, TP-/EURPL
idealist	KWR-L/*EUS	if I said	TPEUBS
idealistic	KWR-L/*EUS/EUBG	if I say	TPEUBZ
idealistically	KWR-L/*EUS/KHREU	if I says	TPEUBSZ
idealization	KWR-L/SA*EUGS	if I should	TPEURBD
idealize	KWR-L/AOEUZ	if I think	TPEUPBG
ideally	KWR-L/HREU	if I think the	TPEUPBGT
identical	AOEUFL	if I understand	TPEUPBDZ
identical	AOEUD/KAL	if I understood	TP*EUPBDZ
identically	AOEUFL/HREU	if I want	TPEUPT
identically	AOEUD/KHREU	if I wanted	TPEUPTD
identifiability	AOEUFBLT	if I was	TPEUFS
identifiability	AOEUD/TPEUBLT	if I were	TPEURP
identifiability	AOEUD/TPAOEUBLT	if I were the	TPEURPT
identifiable	AOEUFBL	if I would	TPEULD
identifiable	AOEUD/TPEUBL	if she believed	STPEBLD
identifiable	AOEUD/TPAOEUBL	if she believes	STPEBLS
identification	AOEUFGS	if she can	STPEBG
identification	AOEUD/TPEU/KAEUGS	if she cannot	STPEBG/TPHOT
identifier(s)	AOEUF/ER(S)	if she can't	STPEBG/-PBT
identifier(s)	AOEUD/TPEU/ER(S)	if she could	STPEBGD
identify	AOEUF	if she could not	STPEBGD/TPHOT
identify	AOEUD/TPEU	if she couldn't	STPEBGD/-PBT
identity	AOEUT	if she feels	STPEFLS
identity	AOEUD/TEU	if she felt	STPEFLT
i.e. *(id est [that is])*	AOEU/KWRAOE	if she recalled	STPERLD
if *(as wd)*	TP-	if she recalls	STPERLS
if he believed	TPEBLD	if she recollected	STPERBGD
if he believes	TPEBLS	if she recollects	STPERBGS
if he can	TPEBG	if she remembered	STPERPLD
if he cannot	TPEBG/TPHOT	if she remembers	STPERPLS
if he can't	TPEBG/-PBT	if she said	STPEBS
if he could	TPEBGD	if she say	STPEBZ
if he could not	TPEBGD/TPHOT	if she says	STPEBSZ
if he couldn't	TPEBGD/-PBT	if she should	STPERBD
if he feels	TPEFLS	if she should not	STPERBD/TPHOT
if he felt	TPEFLT	if she shouldn't	STPERBD/-PBT
if he recalled	TPERLD	if she thinks	STPEPBGS
if he recalls	TPERLS	if she wanted	STPEPTD
if he recollected	TPERBGD	if she wants	STPEPTS
if he recollects	TPERBGS	if she was	STPEFS
if he remembered	TPERPLD	if she were	STPERP
if he remembers	TPERPLS	if she were the	STPERPT
if he said	TPEBS	if the	TP-T
if he say	TPEBZ	if the Court please	TPOURPLTS
if he says	TPEBSZ	if the Court pleases	TPOURPLTSZ
if he should	TPERBD	if you believe	TPUBL
if he should not	TPERBD/TPHOT	if you believed	TPUBLD
if he shouldn't	TPERBD/-PBT	if you can	TP-/UBG
if he thinks	TPEPBGS	if you cannot	TP-/UBG/TPHOT
if he wanted	TPEPTD	if you can't	TP-/KWROU/K-PBT
if he wants	TPEPTS	if you could	TPUBGD
if he was	TPEFS	if you feel	TPUFL
if he were	TPERP	if you felt	TPUFLT
if he were the	TPERPT	if you find	TPUFPBD
if I believe	TPEUBL	if you have	TPUF
if I believed	TPEUBLD	if you have had	TPUFD
if I can	TPEUBG	if you know	TP*UPB
if I could	TPEUBGD	if you recall	TP*URL, TP-/URL
if I feel	TPEUFL	if you recollect	TPURBG, TP-/URBG
if I felt	TPEUFLT	if you remember	TPURPL, TP-/URPL

if you said	TPUBS	impingement	EUPL/PEUPBG/-PLT
if you say	TPUBZ	implication	EUFRPL/KAEUGS
if you says	TPUBSZ	importance	PORPBS
if you should	TPURBD	important	PORPBT
if you think	TPUPBG	importantly	PORPBT/HREU
if you think the	TPUPBGT	imposition	EUPL/POGS
if you want	TPUPT	impossibility	EUPL/POBLT
if you wanted	TPUPTD	impossible	EUPL/POBL
if you were	TPURP	impossibly	EUPL/POEBL
if you were the	TPURPT	imprison	EUPL/PREUZ
if you will	TP*UL	imprisonment	EUPL/PREUZ/-PLT
if you would	TPULD	improbability	EUPL/PROBLT
if your Honor	TPURPB	improbable	EUPL/PROBL
if your Honor please	TPURPBLS	improbably	EUPL/PROEBL
IFO *(identified flying object)*	EURBGS/TPO*	improve	EUPL/PRO*F
ifs	TP-S	improvement	EUPL/PRO*FPLT
II *(Roman numeral)*	2R	in *(as wd)*	TPH-
III *(Roman numeral)*	3R	in a minute	TPHEUPLT, TPHAPLT
illegal	EUL/HRAOEL	in a minute, please	TPHEUPLTS, TPHAPLTS
illegality	EUL/HRAOEL/TEU		
illegalize	EUL/HRAOEL/AOEUZ	in a moment	TPHOEPLT, TPHOPLT
illegally	EUL/HRAOEL/HREU	in a moment, please	TPHOEPLTS, TPHOPLTS
Illinois	*EUL/*EUL		
illiteracy	EUL/HREUT/SEU	in addition	TPHEUGS
imaginable	PHAPBLG/-BL	in addition to	TPHEUGS/TO
imaginably	PHAPBLG/PWHREU	in an effort	TPHAEFRT
imaginary	PHAPBLG/TPHAEUR	in and about	TPHABT
imagination	PHAPBLG/TPHAEUGS	in and of itself	TPHAFTS
imaginative	PHAPBLG/T*EUF	in and out	TPHOUT
imaginatively	PHAPBLG/T*EUF/HREU	in any event	TPHEUPBT
imagine	PHAPBLG	in as much	TPH-/S-FP
imbalance	EUPL/PWHRA*PBS	in delicto	TPH-/TKHREUBG/TOE
IMF *(International Monetary Fund)*		in each	TPHAOEFP
	EURBGS/PH*F	in effect	TPHEFBGT
imitable	EUPLT/-BL	in evidence	TPH*EFD, TPHEFD
immaterial	EUPL/TERL	in fact	TPH-FT
immaterial	EUPLT	in initio	TPH-/TPHEURB/KWROE
immature	EUPL/KHUR	in lieu of	TPH-/HRAOUF
immaturity	EUPL/KHUR/TEU	in memoriam	TPH-/PHE/PHOEURPL
immeasurable	EUPL/PH-RB/-BL	in my humble opinion	TPH-/PHUP
immediacy	PHAOED/SEU	in my opinion	TPH-/PHEUP
immediate	PHAOED	in order	TPHORD
immediately	PHAOED/HREU	in order to	TPHORD/TO
immovable	EUPL/PHO*FBL	in other words	TPHORDZ
impassivity	EUPL/PASZ/*EUFT	in our opinion	TPHOURP
impassivity	EUPL/PAS/S*EUFT	in re	TPHR*E
impatience	EUPL/PAEURBS	in reference	TPHREFRPBS
impatient	EUPL/PAEURBT	in regard	TPHRARD
impatiently	EUPL/PAEURBT/HREU	in respect	TPH-RPT
imperfect	EUPL/PEFRT	in spite of	TPH-/SPAOEUF
imperfection	EUPL/P*EFRGS	in the	TPH-T
imperial	EUPL/PAOERL	in the event	TPH*EFPBT
imperialism	EUPL/PAOERL/EUFPL	in the event	TPHEFPBT
imperialist	EUPL/PAOERL/*EUS	in the hospital	TPHOPT
imperil	EUPL/PERL	in the meantime	TPHEPLT
imperil	EUPL/P*ERL	in the morning	TPHERPBG
imperium	EUPL/PAOERPL	in view of	TPH-/SRAOUF
impersonal	EUPL/PERPBL	in your opinion	TPHURP
impersonally	EUPL/PERPB/HREU	in your own words	TPHURPBDZ
impersonally	EUPL/PERPBL/HREU	in your words	TPHURDZ
impersonate	EUPL/PERPB/TPHAEUT	inaccuracy	EUPB/ABG/SEU
impersonation	EUPL/PERPB/TPHAEUGS	inaccurate	EUPB/ABG/RAT
impinge	EUPL/PEUPBG	inadmissible	EUPB/PHEUBL

inapplicable	EUPB/PHREUBL	indefinite	EUPB/TKEFPBT
inappropriate	EUPB/PROEPT	indefinitely	EUPB/TKEFPBT/HREU
inappropriately	EUPB/PROEPT/HREU	indemnify	EUPB/TKEPL/TPEU
inasmuch *(as wd)*	EUPB/S-FP	indemnitee	EUPB/TKEPL/TAOE
inasmuch as	EUPB/S-FPS	indemnitor	EUPB/TKEPL/TOR
Inc.	EUPB/*BG	indemnity	EUPB/TKEPL/TEU
Inc.	EUPB/KR-FPLT	independence	EUPB/TKPEPBS
incapability	EUPB/KAEUPBLT	independent	EUPB/TKPEPBT
incapable	EUPB/KAEUPBL	independently	EUPB/TKPEPBT/HREU
incapacitate	EUPB/KPAS/TAEUT	indescribable	EUPB/TKRAOEUBL
incapacitation	EUPB/KPAS/TAEUGS	indescribable	EUPB/TKRAOEUB/-BL
incapacity	EUPB/KPAS/TEU	indestructible	EUPB/TKRUBGT/-BL
inchoate	EUPB/KOET	indestructibly	EUPB/TKRUBGT/
inchoative	EUPB/KOET/*EUF		PWHREU
incidence	EUPB/STKEPBS	indeterminate	EUPB/TKERPL/TPHAT
incident	EUPB/STKEPBT	Indiana	*EUPB/*EUPB
incidental	EUPB/STKEPB/TAL	indicant	EUPB/KAPBT
incidentally	EUPB/STKEPBT/HREU	indicate	EUPBD/KAEUT
income(s)	TPH-BG(S)	(Indicating.)	KA*EUGT
incoming	TPH-BG/-G	indication	EUPBD/KAEUGS
incomparable	EUPB/KPAEURBL	indicator	EUPBD/KAEU/TOR
incompatibility	EUPB/KPAT/-BLT	indices	EUPBD/SAOEZ
incompatible	EUPB/KPAT/-BL	indict	TKAO*EUT
incompetence	EUBGTS	indictable	TKAO*EUT/-BL
incompetence	EUPB/KPE/TEPBS	indictee	TKAO*EUT/TAOE
incompetency	EUBGSZ	indictment	TKAO*EUPLT
incompetency	EUBGT/SEU	indictment	TKAOEUPLT
incompetency	EUPB/KPE/TEPB/SEU	indictment	TKAO*EUT/-PLT
incompetent	EUBGT	indictor	TKAO*EUT/TOR
incompetent	EUPB/KPE/TEPBT	indifference	EUPB/TKEUFRPBS
incompetent, irrelevant,		indifferent	EUPB/TKEUFRPBT
and immaterial	EUBGT/EURT/AEUPLT	indigence	EUPBD/SKWREPBS
incompetent, irrelevant,		indigent	EUPBD/SKWREPBT
immaterial	EUBGT/EURT/EUPLT	indigestible	EUPBD/SKWR*ES/-BL
incomplete	EUPB/KPHRAOET	indigestion	EUPBD/SKWR*EGS
incompletely	EUPB/KPHRAOET/HREU	indigestion	EUPBD/SKWREGS
incompleteness	EUPB/KPHRAOET/*PBS	indigo	EUPBD/TKPWOE
incomprehensible	EUPB/KPRE/HEPBS/-BL	indirect	EUPB/TKREBGT
inconsiderable	EUPB/K-RBL	indirectly	EUPB/TKREBGT/HREU
inconsiderate	EUPB/K-RT	indiscriminate	EUPB/TKEUS/KREUPLT
inconsiderate	EUPB/K-R/RAT	indiscriminately	EUPB/TKEUS/
incontrovertible	EUPB/TRO*EFRT/-BL		KREUPLT/HREU
incontrovertibly	EUPB/TRO*EFRT/	indiscrimination	EUPB/TKEUS/
	PWHREU		KREUPLGS
inconvenience	EUPB/SRAOEPBS	indisputable	EUPBD/SPAOUT/-BL
inconvenient	EUPB/SRAOEPBT	indisputably	EUPBD/SPAOUT/
inconveniently	EUPB/SRAOEPBT/HREU		PWHREU
incorporate	EUPB/KORPT	indistinct	EUPB/TKWEUPBGT
incorporation	EUPB/KORPGS	indistinguishable	EUPB/TKWEURB/-BL
incorporator	EUPB/KORPT/TOR	individual	SREUPBLG
incorrect	EUPB/KREBGT	individualism	SREUPBLG/EUFPL
incorrectly	EUPB/KREBGT/HREU	individualist	SREUPBLG/*EUS
incorrupt	EUPB/KRUPT	individualistic	SREUPBLG/*EUS/EUBG
incorruptible	EUPB/KRUPT/-BL	individuality	SREUPBLG/TEU
incredibility	EUPB/KREBLT	individuality	SREUPBLG
incredible	EUPB/KREBL	individualization	SREUPBLG/SA*EUGS
incredibly	EUPB/KREBL/HREU	individualize	SREUPBLG/AOEUZ
incriminate	EUPB/KREUPLT	individually	SREUPBLG/HREU
incrimination	EUPB/KREUPLGS	indivisible	EUPBD/SREUZ/-BL
incriminator	EUPB/KREUPLT/TOR	indolence	EUPBD/HREPBS
incriminatory	EUPB/KREUPLT/TOEUR	indolent	EUPBD/HREPBT
indefensible	EUPB/TKEFPBS/-BL	indulge	EUPB/TKULG
indefensible	EUPB/TKEFS/-BL	indulgence	EUPB/TKULG/EPBS

indulgent	EUPB/TKULG/EPBT	inhuman	EUPB/HAOUPL
indulger(s)	EUPB/TKULG/ER(S)	initial	TPHEURBL
industrial	STREUL	initialize	TPHEURBL/AOEUZ
industrialism	STREUL/EUFPL	initially	TPHEURBL/HREU
industrialist	STREUL/*EUS	initiate	TPHEURBT
industrialization	STREUL/SA*EUGS	initiate	TPHEURB/KWRAEUT
industrialize	STREUL/AOEUZ	initiate	TPHEURB/SHAEUT
industrious	STREU/OUS	initiation	TPHEURBGS
industrious	STREUL/OUS	initiation	TPHEURB/KWRAEUGS
industry	STREU	initiation	TPHEURB/SHAEUGS
inebriant	TPHAOEB/RAOEPBT	initiative	TPHEURB/T*EUF
inebriate	TPHAOEB/RAEUT	initiative(s)	TPHEURBT/*EUF(S)
inebriation	TPHAOEB/RAEUGS	initiator	TPHEURBT/TOR
inebriety	EUPB/PWRAOEU/TEU	initiator	TPHEURB/KWRAEU/TOR
ineffective	EUPB/EFBGT/*EUF	initio	TPHEURB/KWROE
ineffectiveness	EUPB/EFBGT/*EUFPBS	injure	SKWREUR
ineffectual	EUPB/EFBG/KHUL	injurious	SKWREUR/KWROUS
inefficiency	EUPB/TPEURBT/SEU	injurious	SKWREUR/OUS
inefficient	EUPB/TPEURBT	injury	SKWRAOUR
inefficiently	EUPB/TPEURBT/HREU	injury	SKWREUR/REU
inequality	EUPB/E/KWALT	ink	*EUPBG
inequality	EUPB/E/KWAULT	inkblot	*EUPBG/PWHROT
inescapable	EUPB/E/SKAEUPBL	inkling	*EUPBG/-LG
inescapable	EUPB/ES/KAEUPBL	inkling	*EUPBG/HREUPBG
inestimable	EUPB/*ES/PHABL	innocence	TPHEPBS
inexcusable	EUPB/KPAOUZ/-BL	innocent	TPHEPBT
inexpiable	EUPB/EBGS/PEUBL	innocently	TPHEPBT/HREU
infomercial	EUPB/TPO/PHERBL	innovate	TPHO*FT
inform(s)	TPH-F(S)	innovation	TPHO*FGS
informal	TPH-FL	innovative	TPHO*FT/*EUF
informal	TPH-F/PHAL	innovator	TPHO*FT/TOR
informality	TPH-FL/TEU	inoperative	EUPB/OERPT/*EUF
informally	TPH-FL/HREU	inopportune	EUPB/OP/TAOUPB
informant	TPH-F/PHAPBT	inpatient	EUPB/PAEURBT
information	TPH-FGS	INS *(Immigration and Naturalization Service)*	
information	TPH-F/PHAEUGS		EURBGS/TPH*S
informational	TPH-FGS/TPHAL	ins	TPH-S
informational	TPH-F/PHAEUGS/TPHAL	insecure	EUPB/SKUR
informative	TPH-F/T*EUF	insecurity	EUPB/SKURT
informatory	TPH-F/TOEUR	insecurity	EUPB/SKUR/TEU
informed	TPH-FD	insensitivity	EUPB/SEPBS/T*EUFT
informer(s)	TPH-FR(S), TPH-F/ER(S)	inside	TPH-DZ
informing	TPH-FG	insider(s)	TPH-DZ/ER(S)
infrequent	EUPB/TPRAOEBGT	insignia	EUPB/SEUG/TPHA
infrequently	EUPB/TPRAOEBGT/HREU	insignificance	EUPB/SEUG/KAPBS
		insignificant	EUPB/SEUG/KAPBT
infringe	EUPB/TPREUPBG	insipid	EUPB/SEUPD
infringement(s)	EUPB/TPREUPBG/-PLT(S)	insobriety	EUPB/SPWRAOEU/TEU
		insofar *(as wd)*	EUPB/SOFR
ingenue	APBG/TPHAOU	insofar as	EUPB/SOFRS
ingenue	EUPBG/TPHAOU	insolence	EUPB/SHREPBS
ingenuity	EUPBG/TPHAOU/TEU	insolence	EUPBS/HREPBS
inhabit	EUPB/HABT	insolent	EUPB/SHREPBT
inherit	EUPB/HERT	insolent	EUPBS/HREPBT
inheritable	EUPB/HERT/-BL	insomnia	EUPB/SOPL/KWRA
inhibit	EUPB/HEUBT	insomnia	EUPB/SOPL/TPHA
inhibition	EUPB/HEUBGS	insomniac	EUPB/SOPL/KWRABG
inhibition	EUPB/PWEUGS	insomniac	EUPB/SOPL/TPHABG
inhibitor	EUPB/HEUBT/TOR	inspect(s)	TPH-PT(S)
inhibitory	EUPB/HEUBT/TOEUR	inspected	TPH-PTD
inhospitable	EUPB/HOPT/-BL	inspecting	TPH-PT/-G
in-house	EUPB/HOUS	inspection	TPH-PGS
		inspector	TPH-PT/TOR

inspiration	EUPB/SPRAEUGS	insurable	STPHURBL
inspiration	EUPBS/PRAEUGS	insurance *(as wd)*	STPHURPBS
inspirational	EUPB/SPRAEUGS/TPHAL	insurance agent	STPHURGT
inspirational	EUPBS/PRAEUGS/TPHAL	insurance company	STPHURBG
installation	*EUPBS/HRAEUGS	Insurance Company	STPH*URBG
instigate	*EUPBS/TKPWAEUT	insurance policy	STPHURPS
instigation	*EUPBS/TKPWAEUGS	insure	STPHUR
instigator	*EUPBS/TKPWAEU/TOR	insurer(s)	STPHUR/ER(S)
institute	STAOUT	insurrection	EUPBS/R*EBGS
institution	STAOUGS	intact	SPWABGT
institutional	STAOUGS/TPHAL	intake	SPWAEUBG
institutionalization	STAOUGS/SA*EUGS	intangible	SPWAPBG/-BL
institutionalize	STAOUGS/HRAOEUZ	integrity	SPWEG/TEU
instruct *(as wd)*	STRUBGT	intel	SPWEL
instruct her not to answer	STHER/TPHAOPBS	Intel	SPW*EL
		intellect	SPWHREBGT
instruct her not to answer the question	STHER/TPHAOPBGS	intellectual	SPWHREBG/KHUL
		intellectualization	SPWHREBG/KHUL/SA*EUGS
instruct him not to answer	STHEUPL/TPHAOPBS	intellectualize	SPWHREBG/KHUL/AOEUZ
instruct him not to answer the question	STHEUPL/TPHAOPBGS	intellectually	SPWHREBGT/KHUL/HREU
instruct the witness not to answer	STWEUT/TPHAOPBS	intelligence	SPWEPBLGS
		intelligent	SPWEPBLGT
instruct the witness not to answer the question	STWEUT/TPHAOPBGS	intelligently	SPWEPBLGT/HREU
		intelligentsia	SPWEPBLGTS/KWRA
instructing her not to answer	STHERG/TPHAOPBS	intend(s)	SPWEPBD(Z)
		intense	SPWEPBS
		intent	SPWEPBT
instructing her not to answer the question	STHERG/TPHAOPBGS	intention	SPWEPBGS
		interact	SPWRABGT
instructing him not to answer	STHEUPLG/TPHAOPBS	interaction	SPWRA*BGS
		interagency	SPWER/AGT/SEU
instructing him not to answer the question	STHEUPLG/TPHAOPBGS	inter-American	SPWER/PHERPB
		interchange	SPWER/KHAEUPBG
instructing the witness not to answer	STWEUGT/TPHAOPBS	interchangeable	SPWER/KHAEUPBG/-BL
instructing the witness not to answer the question	STWEUGT/TPHAOPBGS	interchangeably	SPWER/KHAEUPBG/PWHREU
instruction	STR*UBGS	intercity	SPWER/STEU
instructional	STR*UBGS/TPHAL	interconnect	SPWER/KEBGT
instructor	STRUBG/TOR	interconnection	SPWER/K*EBGS
instructor	STRUBGT/TOR	intercourse	SPWROURS
instrument	STRUPLT	interdependence	SPWER/TKPEPBS
instrumental	STRUPLT/TAL	interdependence	SPWER/TKPEPB/TKEPBS
instrumentality	STRUPLT/TAL/TEU		
instrumentally	STRUPLT/HREU	interdependence	SPWER/TKPEPBD/EPBS
instrumentation	STRUPLT/TAEUGS		
insubordinate	EUPB/SPWORD/TPHAT	interdependent	SPWER/TKPEPBT
		interdependent	SPWER/TKPEPB/TKEPBT
insubordinate	EUPBS/PWORD/TPHAT		
insubordination	EUPB/SPWORD/TPHAEUGS	interdependent	SPWER/TKPEPBD/EPBT
		interest *(as wd)*	SPWR*ES
		interest account	SPWR-BGT
insubordination	EUPBS/PWORD/TPHAEUGS	interest of justice	SPWROFPBLGS
		interest rate(s)	SPWR-RT(S)
insubstantial	EUPB/STAPBL	interestingly	SPWR*ES/TKPWHREU
insubstantiality	EUPB/STAPBL/TEU	intergovernmental	SPWER/TKPWOFT/TAL
insufficiency	EUPB/SUF/SEU	intergovernmental	SPWER/TKPWO*FT/TAL
insufficient	EUPB/SUF	interim	SPWERPL
insufficiently	EUPB/SUF/HREU		
insupportable	EUPB/SPO*RT/-BL		

intermarriage	SPWER/PHAEURPBLG	investigation	TPH*FGS
interment	SPWERPLT	investigation	TPH*FS/TKPWAEUGS
intern	SPWERPB	investigative	TPH*FGT/*EUF
internal *(as wd)*	SPWERPBL	investigative	TPH*FS/TKPWAEUT/*EUF
Internal Revenue	SPWEFRB	investigator	TPH*FRGT
Internal Revenue		investigator	TPH*FGT/TOR
Service *(IRS)*	SPWEFRBS	investigator	TPH*FS/TKPWAEU/TOR
internalize	SPWERPBL/AOEUZ	investigatory	TPH*FGT/TOEUR
internally	SPWERPB/HREU	investigatory	TPH*FS/TKPWA/TOEUR
international *(as wd)*	SPWRARBL	investitive	TPH*FS/T*EUF
international *(as wd)*	SPWER/TPHARBL	investiture(s)	TPH*FS/KHUR(S)
International	SPWRA*RBL	investment(s)	TPH*FS/-PLT(S)
International	SPW*ER/TPHARBL	investor	TPH*FS/TOR
international airport	TPHAEUPT	inviolate	EUPB/SRAOEULT
International Airport	TPHA*EUPT	involuntary *(as wd)*	EUPB/SROL/TAEUR
internationally	SPWRARBL/HREU	involuntary manslaughter	TPHO*PLS
internationally	SPWER/TPHARBL/HREU	involve	SRO*F, SROF
internationally	SPWER/TPHAGS/HREU	involvement	SRO*FPLT, SROFPLT
internationally	SPWER/TPHARB/HREU	i.o.u. *(I owe you)*	*EUPD/O*U
internet	SPWERPBT	IOU	EURBGS/*OU
Internet	SPW*ERPBT	Iowa	A*EU/A*EU
interoffice	SPWER/AUFS	IPO *(initial public offering)*	EURBGS/PO*
interpolate	SPWERP/HRAEUT	IRA *(Individual Retirement Account, Irish Republican Army)*	
interpolate	SPWER/PHRAEUT		EURBGS/RA*
interpolation	SPWERP/HRAEUGS	Iraq	RAUBG
interpolation	SPWER/PHRAEUGS	Iraqi	RAUBG/KAOE
interposition	SPWER/POGS	IRC *(Internal Revenue Code)*	EURBGS/R*BG
interpret	SPWERPT	irrebuttable	EUR/PWUT/-BL
interpretation	SPWERPGS	irreconcilable *(as wd)*	EUR/REBG/SAOEUBL
interpretation	SPWERP/TAEUGS	irreconcilable	
interpreter(s)	SPWERPT/ER(S)	difference(s)	EURBGD(Z)
interrelate	SPWER/RELT	irregardless	EUR/RARD/HRES
interrog.	SPWROG	irregular	EUR/REG
interrogate	SPWERGT	irregularity	EUR/REG/TEU
interrogation	SPWERGS	irregularly	EUR/REG/HREU
interrogative	SPWROG/T*EUF	irrelevant	EURLT
interrogator	SPWERGT/TOR	irrepleviable	EUR/RE/PHR*EFBL
interrogatory	SPWROEUG	irresolvable	EUR/RE/SO*FBL
interrogatory	SPWROG/TOEUR	irrespective	EUR/R-PT/*EUF
interrupt	SPWRUPT	irrespectively	EUR/R-PT/*EUF/HREU
interruption	SPWRUPGS	irresponsibility	EUR/SPOPBLT
intersect	SPWREBGT	irresponsibility	EUR/SPOPBS/-BLT
intersection	SPWR*EBGS	irresponsible	EUR/SPOPBL
into *(as wd)*	SPWAO	irresponsible	EUR/SPOPBS/-BL
into account	SPWAOBGT	irresponsibly	EUR/SPOEPBL
into effect	SPWAOEFBGT	irresponsibly	EUR/SPOPBS/PWHREU
into the	SPWAOT	irreverent	EUR/R*EFRPBT
intone	SPWOEPB	irreversibility	EUR/SRERS/-BLT
intra-airport	SPWRA/AEURPT	irreversible	EUR/SRERS/-BL
intracranial	SPWRA/KRAEUPBL	irreversibly	EUR/SRERS/PWHREU
intrepid	SPWREPD	IRS *(Internal Revenue Service)*	
intrigue	SPWRAOEG		EURBGS/R*S
intro (wd)	SPWROE	is *(as wd)*	S-
introvert	SPWRO*EFRT	is also	S-LS
intrude(s)	SPWRAOUD(Z)	is fair to say	S-FRTS
intruder(s)	SPWRAOUD/ER(S)	is it a fact	STAFT
intrusion	SPWRAOUGS	is it fact	ST-FT
invalid(s)	EUPB/SRALD(Z)	is it fair to say	ST-FRTS
invalidity	EUPB/SRALD/TEU	is it true	STU
invaluable	EUPB/SRAL/-BL	is it your opinion	STURP
invest	TPH*FS	is not	STPHO*T, S-/TPHOT
investigate	TPH*FGT	is not fair to say	STPHOFRTS
investigate	TPH*FS/TKPWAEUT	is that	STHA

is that a fact	STHAFT
is that all	STHAUL
is that correct	STHABGT
is that correct?	STHARBGT
is that not	STHAPBT
is that right	STHART
is that right?	STHARGT
is that the	STHAT
is that true	STHAU
is that your	STHAUR
is the	S-T
is there	STHR-
is there any	STHREU
is there anybody	STHREUB
is there anybody else	STHREUBLS
is there anyone	STHREUPB
is there anyone else	STHREUPBLS
is there any reason	STHREURPB
is this	STH-
is this correct	STH-BGT
is this correct?	STH-RBGT
is this right	STH-RT
is this right?	STH-RGT
is to be	STOB
is whether or not	SWHRORPBT
is your Honor	SURPB
ISBN *(International Standard Book Number)*	
	EURBGS/S*RBGS/PW*PB
ISBN	EURBGS/SPW*PB
island(s)	AOEULD(Z)
Island(s)	AO*EULD(Z)
islander(s)	AOEULD/ER(S)
isn't *(as wd)*	S-PBT
isn't it a fact	STPHEUFT
isn't it correct	STPHEUBGT
isn't it fair to say	STPH-FRTS
isn't it true	STPHU
isn't that correct	STPHABGT
isn't that true	STPHAU
isn't the	STPH-T
isn't this correct	STPH-BGT
ISP *(Internet service provider)*	
	EURBGS/S*P
issue *(as wd)*	EURB/KWRAOU
issue *(as wd)*	EURB/SHAOU
issue of fact	SHAOUFT
issue of facts	SHAOUFT/-S
issues of fact	SHAOUFTS
it *(as wd)*	EUT
it'd	T*D
it'll	T*L
it's	T*S
its	EUTS
itself	*EUTS
it can	T-BG
it cannot	T-BG/TPHOT
it can't	EUT/K-PBT
it could	T-BGD
it feels	T-FLS
it felt	T-FLT
it had	T-D
it happened	T-PD
it happens	T-PS
it has	T-Z
it have	T-F
it is	T-S
it recalled	T-RLD
it recalls	T-RLS
it seems to me	SPHE
it shall	T-RB
it should	T-RBD
it was	T-FS, TWUZ
it was not	T-FS/TPHOT
it was not	TWUZ/TPHOT
it wasn't	T-FS/-PBT, TWUZ/-PBT
it wasn't	TWUPBT, TWAEPBT
it were	T-RP
it will	T-L
it will be	T-L/PW-, EUT/HR-B
it would	T-LD, TWOULD
it would be	TWOUB
it would be	T-LD/PW-, EUT/WOUB
it would have	TWOUF
it would have been	TWOUFB
it would have had	TWOUFD
IUD *(intrauterine device)*	EU-RBGS/*UD
IV *(Roman numeral)*	4R
IX *(Roman numeral)*	R9

jacket	SKWRABGT
Jacksonville	SKWRABGS/SREUL
January	SKWRAPB
jauntiness	SKWRAUPB/T*EUPBS
jazziness	SKWRAZ/S*EUPBS
JCR *(Journal of Court Reporting)*	SKWR-RBGS/KR*R
jealously	SKWREL/SHREU
jealousy	SKWREL/SEU
jeans	SKWRAEPBS
jeopardize	SKWREP/TKAOEUZ
jeopardy	SKWREP/TKEU
jerkiness	SKWRER/K*EUPBS
JFK *(John Fitzgerald Kennedy)*	SKWR-RBGS/TP*BG
jillion	SKWR-L
jinx	SKWREUPBGS
jitteriness	SKWREUT/R*EUPBS
joint *(as wd)*	SKWROEUPBT
joint venture	SKWRO*EUF
joint venture	SKWROEUF
JPL *(Jet Propulsion Laboratory)*	SKWR-RBGS/P*L
Jr.	SKWR-R
judgment	SKWRUPLT
judgmental	SKWRUPLT/TAL
juiciness	SKWRAOU/S*EUPBS
juiciness	SKWRAOUS/S*EUPBS
July	SKWRUL
junction	SKWRUPBGS
June	SKWRUPB
junior *(as wd)*	SKWRAOUPB/KWROR
Junior *(as wd)*	SKWRAO*UPB/KWROR
junior college	SKWREPBLG
Junior College	SKWR*EPBLG
junior high school	SKWRAOL
Junior High School	SKWRA*OL
junk	SKWR*UPBG
junker(s)	SKWR*UPBG/ER(S)
junket	SKWR*UPBGT
jurat	SKWRAOURT
juris	SKWRAOURS
jurisprudence	SKWRAOURS/PRAOUPBS
jurisprudence	SKWRURS/PRAOUPBS
jurisprudent	SKWRAOURS/PRAOUPBT
jurisprudent	SKWRURS/PRAOUPBT
jurist	SKWRAO*URS
juristic	SKWRAO*URS/*EUBG
juror	SKWRAOR
jury *(as wd)*	SKWRUR
Jury *(as wd)*	SKWR*UR
jury box	SKWROBGS
jury charge	SKWR-FP
Jury Charge	SKWR*FP
JURY CHARGE *(cap & center)*	SKWR-FP/SKWR-FP
Jury excused	SKWREBGS
(Jury excused.)	SKWR*EBGS
juryman	SKWRUR/PHAPB
jurymen	SKWRUR/PHEPB
Jury not present	SKWROUT
(Jury not present.)	SKWRO*UT
Jury present	SKWR-PT
(Jury present.)	SKWR*PT
jury-rig	SKWRUR/H-F/REUG
jury room	SKWR-RPL, SKWRURPL
jury trial	SKWR-T, SKWRURT
Jury was duly sworn	SKWRURPB
(Jury was duly sworn.)	SKWR*URPB
Jury was duly sworn and impaneled	SKWRURPBLD
(Jury was duly sworn and impaneled.)	SKWR*URPBLD
jurywoman	SKWRUR/WOPL
jurywomen	SKWRUR/WEUPL
jus *(as wd)*	SKWRUS
jus in re	SKWRUS/TPHR*E
jus in rem	SKWRUS/TPHREPL
jus rerum	SKWRUS/RAOERPL
just *(as wd)*	SKWR*US
just a minute	SKWREUPLT
just a minute	SKWRAPLT
just a minute, please	SKWREUPLTS
just a minute, please	SKWRAPLTS
just a moment	SKWROEPLT
just a moment	SKWROPLT
just a moment, please	SKWROEPLTS
just a moment, please	SKWROPLTS
just a second	SKWREBGD
just a second, please	SKWREBGDZ
just about	SKWRABT
justice *(as wd)*	SKWRUS/TEUS
justice of the peace	SKWR-P
justifiable	SKWRUF/-BL
justifiable	SKWRUFBL
justifiably	SKWRUF/PWHREU
justifiably	SKWRUFBL/HREU
justification	SKWRUFGS
justify	SKWRUF
juvenile *(as wd)*	SKWRAO*UFL
juvenile *(as wd)*	SKWRAO*UFPBL
juvenile court	SKWROURT
Juvenile Court	SKWRO*URT
juvenile delinquent	SKWRAO*UFLD
juvenility	SKWRAO*UFL/TEU
juxtaposition	SKWR*UBGS/POGS

kaleidoscope	KHRAOEUD/SKOEP
Kansas	K*S/K*S
Karachi	KRAUFP/KHAOE
karate	KRA/TAOE
keep *(as wd)*	KAOEP
keep in mind	KAOEPLD
Kennedy	KEPB/TKEU
Kentucky	KAO*EU/KAO*EU
Kentucky	KEFPLT
KFC *(Kentucky Fried Chicken)*	
	K-RBGS/TP*BG
kg *(kilogram)*	K*G
KGB *(Komitet gosudarstvennoi bezopasnosti)*	
	K-RBGS/TKPW*B
kilometer	KHROPL/TER
kilometer	KHROPLT/ER
kindergarten	KEUPBD/TKPWART/-PB
kindhearted	KAOEUPBD/HARTD
kindliness	KAOEUPBD/HR*EUPBS
kinkiness	KEUPB/K*EUPBS
kitchen	KEUFPB
KKK *(Ku Klux Klan)*	K-RBGS/K*BG
knighthood	TPHAO*EUGTD
knobbiness	TPHOB/PW*EUPBS
knowledge	TPHOPBLG
knowledgeable	TPHOPBLG/-BL
knowledgeably	TPHOPBLG/PWHREU
Korea	KRAOE/KWRA
Korean	KRAOE/KWRAPB
kudos	KAOU/TKOES
kudos	KAOU/TKOS
Kuwait	KWAEUT
Kuwait City	KWAEUT/ST*EU
Kuwait City	KWAEUT/STEU
Kuwaiti	KWAEUT/TAOE

L.A. *(Los Angeles)*	HRA*FPLT
LA	HRA*RBGS
laboratory	HRAB/TOEUR
laciness	HRAEUS/S*EUPBS
ladies *(as wd)*	HRAEU/TKEU/-S
ladies *(as wd)*	HRAEUD/TKEU/-S
ladies and gentlemen	HRAEUPBLG
Ladies and Gentlemen	HRA*EUPBLG
ladies and gentlemen of the jury	HRAEURPBLG
Ladies and Gentlemen of the Jury	HRA*EURPBLG
lamb	HRA*PL
LAN *(local area network)*	HRA*PB
LAN	HR-RBGS/A*PB
lank	HRA*PBG
lankier	HRA*PBG/KWRER
lankiest	HRA*PBG/KWR*ES
lankily	HRA*PBG/HREU
lankily	HRAPB/KHREU
lankiness	HRA*PBG/K*EUPBS
lankiness	HRAPB/K*EUPBS
lanky	HRA*PBG/KEU
LAPD *(Los Angeles Police Department)*	
	HRA*PD
LAPD	HR-RBGS/A*RBGS/P*D
larceny	HRARS
laughter *(as wd)*	HRAFT/ER
(Laughter.)	HRA*UFR
(Laughter and applause.)	HRA*UFRZ
lavender	HRA*FPBD/ER
law *(as wd)*	HRAU
law clerk	HRAURBG
law enforcement	HRAEURPLT
law enforcement officer	HRAEUFR
law enforcement officers	HRAEUFRS
law firm	HRAUFRPL
law office	HRAUFS
law officer	HRAUFR
law officers	HRAUFRS
law school	HRAOL
Law School	HRA*OL
lawsuit	HRAUT
lawyer	HRAUR
layoff	HRAUF
layperson	HRAEU/PERPB
laywoman	HRAEU/WOPL
laywomen	HRAEU/WEUPL
laziness	HRAEUZ/*PBS
laziness	HRAEUZ/S*EUPBS
lb(s).	HR*/PW*PLD(Z)
lb(s). *(pound[s])*	HR*B(S)
LBJ *(Lyndon Baines Johnson)*	
	HR-RBGS/PW*PBLG
LBO *(leveraged buyout)*	HR-RBGS/PWO*
LCD *(liquid crystal display)*	HR-RBGS/KR*D

LDL *(low-density lipoprotein)*	HR-RBGS/TK*L	let the record further indicate	HRAEUFRBGT
leafiness	HRAOE/TP*EUPBS	let the record further reflect	HREFRBGT
leafiness	HRAOEF/TP*EUPBS	let the record further show	HROEFRS
leakiness	HRAEBG/K*EUPBS	let the record indicate	HRAEURBGT
leatheriness	HR*ET/R*EUPBS	let the record reflect	HRERBGT
LED *(light-emitting diode)*	HR-RBGS/*ED	let the record show	HROERS
leeriness	HRAOE/R*EUPBS	leverage	HR*EFRPBLG
leeriness	HRAOER/R*EUPBS	liar	HRAOEUR
left *(as wd)*	HREFT	libertarian	HREUB/TAEURPB
left arm	HR*RPL	libertarianism	HREUB/TAEURPB/EUFPL
left fender	HR*FPBD	license	HRAOEUPBS
left foot	HR*FT	lieutenant	HRAOUPBT
left hand	HREFT/HAPBD	life *(as wd)*	HRAOEUF
left-hand *(j)*	HR*PBD	life insurance	HRURPBS
left-hand lane	HR*PBLD	life-support	HRORT
left-hand side	HR*PBDZ	LIFO *(last in, first out)*	HRAOEU/TPOE
left-hand turn	HR*PBTD	limit	HREUPLT
left-handed	HR*PBD/-D	limitless	HREUPLT/HRES
left lane	HR*L	line *(as wd)*	HRAOEUPB
left leg	HR*LG	lineup	HR*UP
left side	HR*DZ	line up	HRUP
left turn	HR*T	lingerie	HRAUPBG/RAEU
legal *(as wd)*	HRAOEL	link	HR*EUPBG
legal cause	HRAUZ	linkage	HR*EUPBG/APBLG
legal conclusion	HRELGS	lipid(s)	HREUPD(Z)
legalese	HRAOEL/AOEZ	listen(s)	HR-PB(S)
legalese	HRAOEL/HRAOEZ	listened	HR-PBD
legal ease	HRAOEL/SP-S/AOEZ	listener(s)	HR-PB/ER(S)
legalism	HRAOEL/EUFPL	listening	HR-PBG
legality	HRAOEL/TEU	literature	HREUT/KHUR
legalization	HRAOEL/SA*EUGS	lithographic	HR*EUT/TKPWRAFBG
legalize	HRAOEL/AOEUZ	little *(as wd)*	HREUL
legally	HRAOEL/HREU	little bit	HREUBT
legend(s)	HREPBLGD(Z)	Little Rock	K-P/HREUL/ROBG
legendarily	HREPBLGD/ TKAEUR/HREU	littler	HREUL/ER
legendary	HREPBLGD/TKAEUR	littlest	HREUL/*ES
legginess	HREG/TKPW*EUPBS	livid	HR*EUFD
legislate	HREGT	lividity	HR*EUFD/TEU
legislation	HREGS	living *(as wd)*	HR*EUF/-G
legislative	HREGT/*EUF	living room	HR*EUFRPL
legislatively	HREGT/*EUF/HREU	lock *(as wd)*	HROBG
legislator	HREGT/TOR	lockup	HRO*UP
legislatorial	HREGT/TOEURL	lock up	HROUP
legislature(s)	HREGT/KHUR(S)	locket	HROBGT
length *(as wd)*	HR*EPBT, HR*EPBGT	locus contractus	HROE/KUS/KR-T/TUS
length of time	HR-FT	locus delicti	HROE/KUS/ TKHREUBG/TAOEU
lengthen	HR*EPBT/-PB		
lengthily	HR*EPBT/HREU	loftiness	HROF/T*EUPBS
lengthiness	HR*EPBT/TH*EUPBS	long range	HROPBG/RAEUPBG
lengthwise	HR*EPBT/WAO*EUZ	longitude(s)	HROPBG/TAOUD(Z)
lengthy	HR*EPBT/TH*EU	longitudinal	HROPBG/TAOUD/TPHAL
lengthy	HREPB/TH*EU	long-range	HROPBG/H-F/RAEUPBG
lesbian	HREZ/PWAOEPB	long-term	HRERPL
let *(as wd)*	HRET	looniness	HRAO/TPH*EUPBS
let's	HR*ETS	looniness	HRAOPB/TPH*EUPBS
let the record also indicate	HRAEURBLGT	lopsided	HROPDZ/-D
let the record also reflect	HRERBLGT	Louis XIV	HRAOU/WAOE/14
		Louis	HRAOUS
let the record also show	HROERLS	Louisiana	HRA*/HRA*
		Louisiana	HRAFPLT

Louisville	HRAOU/SREUL
lounge	HROUPBG
lounger(s)	HROUPBG/ER(S)
lousiness	HROU/S*EUPBS
lousiness	HROUZ/S*EUPBS
loveliness	HR*UF/HR*EUPBS
lowball	HROEBL
loyal	HROEUL
loyalty	HROEUL/TEU
lozenge	HROZ/EPBG
LPM *(lines per minute)*	HR-RBGS/P*PL
LPN *(licensed practical nurse)*	HR-RBGS/P*PB
LSAT *(Law School Admission Test)*	HR-RBGS/S*RBGS/A*T
LSAT	HR-RBGS/SA*T
LSD *(lysergic acid diethylamide)*	HR-RBGS/S*D
Ltd. *(limited)*	HR-TD
lubricant	HRAOUB/KAPBT
lubricate	HRAOUB/KAEUT
lubrication	HRAOUB/KAEUGS
lubricator	HRAOUB/KAEU/TOR
lumpiness	HRUFRP/P*EUPBS
lumpiness	HRUPL/P*EUPBS
luncheonette	HRUFRPBLG/TPHET
lurid	HRAOURD
luxuriance	HRUBG/SHURPBS
luxuriant	HRUBG/SHURPBT
luxuriate	HRUBGS/RAEUT
luxurious	HRUBGS/ROUS
luxury	HRUBGS/REU
lyric	HRAOERBG
lyric	HREURBG

Macintosh *(computer)*	PHABG/TORB
MADD *(Mothers Against Drunk Driving)*	PHAD/-D
MADD	PH-RBGS/A*RBGS/TK*D
magisterial	PHAPBLG/STAOERL
magnanimity	PHAG/TPHEUPL/TEU
maharaja	PHA/RA/SKWRA
Maine	PH*E/PH*E
Maine	PHEFPLT
mala in se	PHAL/TPH-/SE
mala praxis	PHAL/PRABG/SEUS
mala prohibita	PHAL/PROEUBT/TA
maladminister	PHAL/PH*R
maladminister	PHAL/AD/PH*R
maladministrate	PHAL/PH*RT
maladministrate	PHAL/AD/PH*RT
maladministration	PHAL/PH*RGS
maladministration	PHAL/AD/PH*RGS
malconduct	PHAL/KUBGT
malice *(as wd)*	PHA/HREUS,
	PHAL/EUS
malice aforethought	PHAFRT
maltreatment	PHAL/TRAOEPLT
manage	PHAPBG
manageability	PHAPBG/-BLT
manageable	PHAPBG/-BL
management(s)	PH-GT(S)
management(s)	PHAPBG/-PLT(S)
manager(s)	PH-G(S)
manager(s)	PHAPBG/ER(S)
managerial	PH-G/KWRAL
managerial	PHAPBG/ER/KWRAL
managerial	PHAPB/SKWRAOERL
mange	PHAEUPBG
manger(s)	PHAEUPBG/ER(S)
mangier	PHAEUPBG/KWRER
mangiest	PHAEUPBG/KWR*ES
mangily	PHAEUPBG/HREU
manginess	PHAEUPB/SKWR*EUPBS
manginess	PHAEUPBG/*PBS
manliness	PHAPB/HR*EUPBS
manpower	PHAPB/PO*UR
manslaughter	*PLS
manslaughter	PHAPB/SHRAUR
manufacture(s)	PH-FR(S)
manufactured	PH-FRD
manufacturer(s)	PH-FR/ER(S)
manufacturing	PH-FRG
many	PH-
March	PHA*R
Mardi Gras	PHARD/TKPWRA
Mardi Gras	PHARD/TKPWRAU
marijuana	PHAEURPB
marine *(as wd)*	PHRAOEPB
Marine *(as wd)*	PHRAO*EPB
marine base	PHRAOEPBS

Marine Base	PHRAO*EPBS	may find	PHAEUFPBD
Marine Corps	PHRAOEPB/KOERP	may have	PHAEUF
Marine Corps	PHRAOEPB/KOERPZ	may have been	PHAEUFB
Marine Corps	PHRAO*EPB/KOERP	may have been the	PHAEUFBT
Marine Corps	PHRAO*EPB/KOERPZ	may have had	PHAEUFD
marine	PHRAOEPB	may have the	PHAEUFT
Marine	PHRAO*EPB	may I approach	PHAEUFP
mark(ed) *(as wd)*	PHARBG(/-D)	may I approach the bench	PHAEUFPT
mark for identification	PHOEUF	may it please the Court	PHAEURPLTS
marked for identification	PHOEUD, PHOEUFD	may not	PHAEUPBT
market	PHARBGT	may recall	PHAEURL
marketability	PHARBGT/-BLT	may recollect	PHAEURBG
marketable	PHARBGT/-BL	may remember	PHAEURPL
marketeer	PHARBGT/TAOER	may understand	PHAEUPBDZ
marketeer	PHARBG/TAOER	may want	PHAEUPT
marketer(s)	PHARBGT/ER(S)	MBA *(Master of Business Administration)*	
marketplace	PHARBGT/PHRAEUS		PH-RBGS/PWA*
marriage	PHAEURPBLG	MCI *(Microwave Communications Incorporated)*	
marriageable	PHAEURPBLG/-BL		PH-RBGS/KR*EU
marshal *(as wd)*	PHAR/-RBL	McIntosh *(the apple)*	PH*BG/TORB
THE MARSHAL: *(colloquy)*		MCP *(male chauvinist pig)*	PH-RBGS/KR*P
	PHARL/PHARL	MCRI *(Master Certified Reporting Instructor)*	
Martindale-Hubbell	PHART/TKAEUL/HUBL		PH-RBGS/KR*RBGS/R*EU
marvel	PHAFRBL	M.D. *(medical doctor)*	PH*D
Maryland	PH*D/PH*D, PH-D	MDMA *(methylene dioxymethamphetamine [Ecstasy])*	
Massachusetts	PHA*/PHA*		PH-RBGS/TK*RBGS/PHA*
Massachusetts	PHAFPLT	MDMA	PH-RBGS/TKPHA*
master *(as wd)*	PHA*S/ER	me	PHE
master bedroom	PHA*RPL	mealiness	PHAOE/HR*EUPBS
Master's degree	PH-RD	mealiness	PHAOEL/HR*EUPBS
material	TERL	measurable	PH-RB/-BL
materialism	TERL/EUFPL	measurably	PH-RB/PWHREU
materialist	TERL/*EUS	measure(s)	PH-RB(S)
materialistic	TERL/*EUS/EUBG	measured	PH-RBD
materialistically	TERL/*EUS/KHREU	measurement(s)	PH-RB/-PLT(S)
materiality	TERL/TEU	measuring	PH-RBG
materialize	TERL/AOEUZ	mechanic(s)	PH-BG(S)
materially	TERL/HREU	mechanical	PH-BG/KAL
matriarch	PHAEU/TRARBG	mechanically	PH-BG/HREU
matriarch	PHAEUT/RARBG	mechanization	PHEBG/SA*EUGS
matriarchal	PHAEU/TRAR/KAL	medical *(as wd)*	PHED/KAL
matriarchal	PHAEUT/RAR/KAL	medical examiner	PHEBGS
matriarchy	PHAEU/TRAR/KEU	medical record	PHORD
matriarchy	PHAEUT/RAR/KEU	medical report	PHORT
matrimonial	PHA/TREU/PHOEPBL	medical school	PHAOL
matrimonial	PHAT/REU/PHOEPBL	Medical School	PHAO*L
matrimony	PHAT/PHOE/TPH*EU	medicolegal	PHED/KO/HRAOEL
matter(s) *(as wd)*	PHAT/ER(S)	melange	PHAEU/HRAPBG
matter of fact	PHAFT	melange	PHE/HRAPBG
matters of fact	PHAFTS	member(s) *(as wd)*	PHEB(/-S)
matter of facts	PHAFT/-S	members of the jury	PHEPBLG
matter of law	PHAFL	Members of the Jury	PH*EPBLG
matters of law	PHAFLS	membership	PHEB/SHEUP
matter of laws	PHAFL/-S	memento	PHEPLT/TOE
matter of minutes	PHAFPLTS	memorabilia	PHEPL/PWAOEL/KWRA
matter of record	PHAFRD	memorabilia	PHEPL/PWEUL/KWRA
mausoleum	PHAUS/HRAOEPL	menace	PHEPBS
mausoleum	PHAUZ/HRAOEPL	meningitis	PHEPB/SKWRAOEUTS
may *(as wd)*	PHAEU	mental *(as wd)*	PHEPB/TAL
maybe	PHAEUB	mental anguish	PHEURB
may be	PHAEU/PW-	mental cruelty	PHAOULT
may believe	PHAEUBL	mentally	PHEPBT/HREU
may feel	PHAEUFL		

© 2004 *StenEd®* Briefs & Phrases (Excerpted from StenEd's Realtime Professional Dictionary)

merchandise	PH-DZ	midst	PH*EUDZ
merchandiser(s)	PH-DZ/ER(S)	Midwestern	PHEUD/W*ERPB
merit	PHERT	Midwesterner(s)	PHEUD/W*ERPB/ER(S)
merriment	PHER/-PLT	might *(as wd)*	PHAOEUGT
merriness	PHER/R*EUPBS	might be	PHAOEUB
messenger	PHESZ/SKWRER	might have	PHAOEUF
messiness	PHES/S*EUPBS	might have been	PHAOEUFB
Messrs.	PHR-FPLTS	might have had	PHAOEUFD
metaphysical	PHET/TP-L	mightiness	PHAOEU/T*EUPBS
meteorologist	PHAOET/RO*LGS	mightiness	PHAOEUT/T*EUPBS
meteorology	PHAOET/ROLG	mighty	PHAOEU/TEU
method(s)	PH*ETD(Z)	mighty	PHAOEUT/TEU
methodical	PH*ETD/KAL	mile(s) *(as wd)*	PHAOEUL(/-S)
methodically	PH*ETD/KHREU	miles an hour	PHARP
methodism	PH*ETD/EUFPL	miles per hour	PHEURP
Methodist	K-P/PH*ETD/*EUS	militariness	PHEUL/TA*EURPBS
methodist	PH*ETD/*EUS	militariness	PHEUL/TR*EUPBS
methodology	PH*ETD/OLG	milkiness	PHEUL/K*EUPBS
metropolitan	PHET/POL/TAPB	million(s) *(as wd)*	PH-L(S)
mg *(milligram)*	PH*G	million dollar(s)	PH-LD(Z)
MGM *(Metro-Goldwyn-Mayer)*		millionaire	PH-L/TPHAEUR
	PH-RBGS/TKPW*PL	millionairess	PH-L/TPHAEUR/ESZ
MIA *(missing in action)*	PH-RBGS/A*EU	millionth	PH*LT
Miami	PHAOEUPL/PHAOE	millisecond(s)	PHEUL/SEBGD(Z)
Michigan	PH*EU/PH*EU	minicomputer	PHEUPB/KPAOURT
Michigan	PHEUFPLT	minicomputer	PHEUPB/KPAOUT/ER
microcomputer	PHAOEU/KRO/KPAOURT	miniseries	PHEUPB/SAOERZ
microcomputer	PHAOEU/KRO/KPAOUT/ER	minisystem	PHEUPB/S-PL
microcomputer	PHAOEUBG/RO/KPAOURT	minitower	PHEUPB/TO*UR
microcomputer	PHAOEUBG/RO/	mink	PH*EUPBG
	KPAOUT/ER	Minnesota	PH*PB/PH*PB
micrographic(s)	PHAOEU/KRO/	Minnesota	PH-PB
	TKPWRAFBG/-S	minute(s)	PH*EUPB(S)
micrographic(s)	PHAOEUBG/RO/	minuteman	PH*EUPB/PHAPB
	TKPWRAFBG/-S	minutemen	PH*EUPB/PHEPB
micromanage	PHAOEU/KRO/PHAPBG	Miranda	PH-RPBD
micromanage	PHAOEUBG/RO/PHAPBG	Miranda rights	PH-RTS
micromanagement	PHAOEU/KRO/PH-GT	Miranda rule	PH-RL
micromanagement	PHAOEUBG/RO/PH-GT	Miranda warning(s)	PH-RPBG(S)
micromanagement	PHAOEU/KRO/	Mirandize	PH-RPBD/AOEUZ
	PHAPBG/-PLT	misadventure(s)	PHEUS/SR*EFP(-/S)
micromanagement	PHAOEUBG/RO/	misapplication	PHEUS/PHR*EUBGS
	PHAPBG/-PLT	misappropriate	PHEUS/PROEPT
micromanager(s)	PHAOEU/KRO/PH-G(S)	misappropriation	PHEUS/PROEPGS
micromanager(s)	PHAOEUBG/RO/PH-G(S)	misbehave	PHEUS/PWHA*EUF
micromanager(s)	PHAOEU/KRO/	misbehavior	PHEUS/PWHA*EUF/
	PHAPBG/ER(S)		KWROR
micromanager(s)	PHAOEUBG/RO/	miscalculate	PHEUS/KAL/KHRAEUT
	PHAPBG/ER(S)	miscalculation	PHEUS/KAL/KHRAEUGS
microsecond(s)	PHAOEU/KRO/SEBGD(Z)	miscarriage	PHEUS/KAEURPBLG
microsecond(s)	PHAOEUBG/RO/SEBGD(Z)	mischaracterization	PHEUS/KARBGT/
middle *(as wd)*	PHEUD/-L		SA*EUGS
middle age	PHAEUPBLG	mischaracterize	PHEUS/KARBGT/AOEUZ
middle-aged	PHAEUPBLG/-D	misconduct	PHEUS/KUBGT
Middle East	PHAO*ELS	misdemeanant	PHEUS/TKPHAOEPBT
middle school	PHRAOL	misdemeanor	STKPHAOERPB
Middle School	PHRA*OL	misdemeanor	PHEUS/TKPHAOE/TPHOR
Mideast	PHAO*ES	misdirect	PHEUS/TKREBGT
Mideastern	PHEUD/AO*ERPB	miserably	PHEUZ/PWHREU
Mideasterner(s)	PHEUD/AO*ERPB/ER(S)	misfortune	PHEUS/TP-RPB
midget	PHEUPBLGT	misinform	PHEUS/TPH-F
mid-morning	PHEUD/PHORPBG	misinterpret	PHEUS/SPWERPT
midnight	PHAOEUPBT	misinterpretation	PHEUS/SPWERPGS

misinterpretation	PHEUS/SPWERP/TAEUGS	mortgagee	PHORPBLG/SKWRAOE
misjudgment	PHEUS/SKWRUPLT	mortgagor	PHORG/SKWROR
mismanage	PHEUS/PHAPBG	mortgagor	PHORPBLG/SKWROR
mismanagement	PHEUS/PH-GT	mosaic	PHO/SA*EUBG
mismanagement	PHEUS/PHAPBG/-PLT	mosaic	PHOE/SA*EUBG
misprison	PHEUS/PREUZ	mother(s) *(as wd)*	PHOER(/-S)
misrepresent	PHEUS/REPT	mother and father	PHAFR
misrepresentation	PHEUS/REPGS	mothers and fathers	PHAFRS, PHAFR/-S
Miss	PH-S	mother lode(s)	PHOER/HRO*ED(Z)
Mississippi	PH*S/PH*S	mother or father	PHOFR
Missouri	PHO*/PHO*	mothers or fathers	PHOFRS, PHOFR/-S
Missouri	PHOFPLT	motherboard(s)	PHOER/PWAORD(Z)
misspoken	PHEUS/SPOEPB	motherfucker(s)	PH-FRBG(S)
misstatement	PHEUS/STAEUPLT	mother-in-law	PHOERPBL
mistreatment	PHEUS/TRAOEPLT	mothers-in-law	PHOERPBLS
misunderstand	PHEUS/UPBS	mother-in-laws	PHOERPBL/-S
misunderstanding(s)	PHEUS/UPBS/-G(S)	motherless	PHOER/HRES
misunderstood	PHEUS/UPBD	motherly	PHOER/HREU
MIT *(Massachusetts Institute of Technology)*		motion	PHOEGS
	PH-RBGS/*EUT	motor *(as wd)*	PHOE/TOR
mitigate *(as wd)*	PHEUT/TKPWAEUT	motor vehicle	PHO*EFBG
mitigating circumstance	PHEURBG	motorbike	PHOEUB
mitigating circumstances	PHEURBGZ, PHEURBG/-S	motorboat	PHOET/PWOET
		motorcade(s)	PHOET/KAEUD(Z)
mm *(millimeter)*	PH*PL	motorcycle	PHOEUBG
mobile	PHOEBL	motorcyclist	PHOEUBG/*EUS
mobility	PHOEBLT	mountainside	PHOUPB/TAEUPBDZ
Mohammed *(var of Muhammad)*		movability	PHO*FBLT
	PHO/HAPLD	movable	PHO*FBL
Mohammed	PHOE/HAPLD	movably	PHO*F/PWHREU
moldiness	PHOEL/TK*EUPBS	movant	PHO*FPBT
moldiness	PHOL/TK*EUPBS	move	PHO*F
molestation	PHOLS/TAEUGS	movement	PHO*FPLT
Monday(s)	PHOPBD(Z)	mover	PHO*FR
money *(as wd)*	PHUPB	movie	PHO*F/SRAOE
moneybag	PHUPB/PWAG	mower	PHO*UR
moneymaker(s)	PHUPB/PHAEUBG/ER(S)	mpg *(miles per gallon)*	PH*/P*G
money order(s)	PHUPB/ORD/ER(S)	mph *(miles per hour)*	PH*P/H*BGZ
moneywise	PHUPB/WAO*EUZ	Mr.	PHR-, PHR-FPLT
monk	PHO*PBG	Mr. and Mrs.	PHRARPLS
monosyllabic	PHOPB/SHRAB/EUBG	Mr. Chairman	PHR-F
Montana	PH*T/PH*T	Mr. Chairperson	PHR*FP
Monte Carlo	PHOPBT/KAR/HROE	Mr. Foreman	PHR-FPL
moodiness	PHAO/TK*EUPBS	Mr. Foreperson	PHR*FPL
moodiness	PHAOD/TK*EUPBS	Mr. or Mrs.	PHRORPLS
moonlight	PHAOLGT	Mr. President	PHR-PT
mopiness	PHOE/P*EUPBS	Mr. Speaker	PHR-BG
mopiness	PHOEP/P*EUPBS	Mr. Vice President	PHR*FPT
moratorium	PHOR/TOEURPL	MRI *(magnetic resonance imaging)*	
morbid	PHORBD		PH-RBGS/R*EU
morbidity	PHORBD/TEU	Mrs.	PHR-S
more *(as wd)*	PH-R	Ms.	PH-Z
more or less	PHORLS	Ms. Chairperson	PH*FP
moreover	PHRO*FR, PHROFR	Ms. Foreperson	PH*FPL
more over	PH-R/O*EFR, PH-R/OEFR	Ms. President	PH*PT
		Ms. Speaker	PH*BGS
more than	PH-RPB	Ms. Vice President	PH*FPT
morning	PHORPBG	MS-DOS *(Microsoft Disk Operating System)*	
mortgage	PHORPBLG		PH-S/TKO*S
mortgageability	PHORPBLG/-BLT	MSG *(monosodium glutamate)*	
mortgageable	PHORPBLG/-BL		PH-RBGS/S*G
mortgagee	PHORG/SKWRAOE	MSN *(Microsoft Network)*	PH-RBGS/S*PB

© 2004 *StenEd*® Briefs & Phrases (Excerpted from StenEd's Realtime Professional Dictionary)

MSNBC *(Microsoft & National Broadcasting Company)*	
	PH-RBGS/S*PB/PW*BG
Mt.	PH-T
MTV *(Music Television)*	PH-RBGS/T*F
muddiness	PHUD/TK*EUPBS
muffin	PHUFPB
mugginess	PHUG/TKPW*EUPBS
Muhammad *(var of Mohammad)*	
	PHU/HAPLD
mulct	PHUBGT
multimillion	PHULT/PH-L
multinational	PHULT/TPHARBL
multipurpose	PHULT/PURP
multisyllabic	PHULT/SHRAB/EUBG
mumps	PHUFRPS
municipal *(as wd)*	PHAOU/TPHEUS/PAL
municipal *(as wd)*	PHAOUPB/EUS/PAL
municipal court	PHOURT
Municipal Court	PHO*URT
murder(s) *(as wd)*	PHURD(Z)
murder in the first	PH*UFRS
murder in the first degree	PH*UFRD
murder in the second	PH*UBG
murder in the second degree	PH*UBGD
murder in the third	PH*UR
murder in the third degree	PH*URD
murderer	PHURD/RER
murderous	PHURD/OUS
murderous	PHURD/ROUS
murkiness	PHUR/K*EUPBS
mushiness	PHURB/SH*EUPBS
muskiness	PHUS/K*EUPBS
must *(as wd)*	PH*US
mustn't	PHUPBT
must've	PH*UF
must be	PHUB
must believe	PHUBL
must find	PHUFPBD
must have been	PHUFB
must have believed	PHUFBLD
must have had	PHUFD
must have recalled	PHUFRLD
must have recollected	PHUFRBGD
must have remembered	PHUFRPLD
must recall	PHURL
must remember	PHURPL
must understand	PHUPBDZ
must want	PHUPT
mutual *(as wd)*	PHAOU/KHAL
mutual *(as wd)*	PHAOU/KHUL
mutual fund(s)	PHAOUFD(Z)
mutually	PHAOUFP/HREU
MVP *(most valuable player)*	PH-RBGS/SR*P
MX missile	PH*BGS/PHEUS/SEUL
MX missile	PH-BGS/PHEUS/SEUL
my	PHEU
myself	PHAO*EUS
mysterious	PHEUS/TAOERS

NAACP *(National Association for the Advancement of Colored People)*	TPHA*EUPBG
NAACP	TPH-RBGS/TKOUBL/A*RBGS/KR*P
NAACP	TPH-RBGS/TKUBL/A*RBGS/KR*P
NAFTA *(North American Free Trade Agreement)*	TPHAF/TA
naked	TPHAEUBGD
nakedness	TPHAEUBGD/*PBS
nanosecond(s)	TPHA/TPHO/SEBGD(Z)
NAR *(National Association of Realtors)*	TPH-RBGS/A*R
NARAL *(National Abortion [and Reproductive] Rights Action League)*	TPHA*EU/RAL
narcissism	TPHARS/SEUFPL
narcissist	TPHARS/S*EUS
narcissistic	TPHARS/S*EUS/EUBG
narcissus	TPHARS/SUS
narcotic(s) *(as wd)*	TPHARBGT(S)
narcotics officer	TPHAFR
narcotics officers	TPHAFRS
NASA *(National Aeronautics and Space Administration)*	TPHA/SA
NASA	TPH-RBGS/A*RBGS/SA*
NASA	TPHA/SA*
NASCAR *(National Association for Stock Car Auto Racing)*	TPHAS/KAR
NASD *(National Association of Securities Dealers)*	TPH-RBGS/A*RBGS/S*D
Nasdaq *(National Association of Securities Dealers Automated Quotations)*	TPHAS/TKABG
NASDAQ	TPHA*S/TKABG
nastiness	TPHAS/T*EUPBS
national	TPHARBL
National	TPHA*RBL
National Guard	TPHARBL/TKPWARD
nationalism	TPHARBL/EUFPL
nationalist	TPHARBL/*EUS
nationalistic	TPHARBL/*EUS/EUBG
nationality	TPHARBL/TEU
nationalization	TPHARBL/SA*EUGS
nationalize	TPHARBL/AOEUZ
nationally	TPHARBL/HREU
Native American	TPHAEUT/PHERPB
nativity	TPHAEU/T*EUFT
nativity	TPHAEUT/*EUFT
NATO *(North Atlantic Treaty Organization)*	TPHAEU/TOE
NATO	TPH-RBGS/A*RBGS/TO*
naturally	TPHAFP/HREU
nature	TPHAEUFP
naught	TPHAUT
naughtier	TPHAUT/KWRER
naughtiest	TPHAUT/KWR*ES
naughtily	TPHAUT/HREU

naughtiness	TPHAU/T*EUPBS	nervousness	TPH*EFRBS/*PBS
naughtiness	TPHAUT/T*EUPBS	nervousness	TPHEFRBS/*PBS
naughty	TPHAU/TEU	.net *(suf)*	TPHEFPLT
naughty	TPHAUT/TEU	network	TPHERBG
navy *(as wd)*	TPHAEU/SREU	neuron	TPHAOURPB
Navy *(as wd)*	TPHA*EU/SREU	neuropsychiatry	TPHAOUR/SKRAOE
navy base	TPHAEUBS	neuropsychiatry	TPHAOU/RO/SKRAOE
Navy Base	TPHA*EUBS	neurosurgeon	TPHAOUR/S-RPB

NBA *(National Basketball Association)*
       TPH-RBGS/PWA*   neurosurgeon   TPHAOU/RO/S-RPB
NBC *(National Broadcasting Company)*   neurosurgery   TPHAOUR/S-RPBLG
       TPH-RBGS/PW*BG   neurosurgery   TPHAOU/RO/S-RPBLG

		Nevada	TPH*F/TPH*F
NCAA *(National Collegiate Athletic Association)*		Nevada	TPH*EF
	TPH*BG/TKOUBL/A*RBGS	never	TPH*EFR, TPHEFR
NCAA	TPH*BG/TKUBL/A*RBGS	nevertheless	TPH*EFRLS
NCO *(noncommissioned officer)*		nevertheless	TPHEFRLS
	TPH-RBGS/KRO*	new *(as wd)*	TPHU
NCRA *(National Court Reporters Association)*		Newark	TPHAOURBG
	TPH-RBGS/KRA*	New Hampshire	H*PB/H*PB
NCRA	TPH-RBGS/KR*RBGS/RA*	New Jersey	TPH*PBLG/TPH*PBLG
NCRF *(National Court Reporters Foundation)*		New Jersey	TPHAOUPBLG
	TPH-RBGS/KR*RBGS/R*F	New Mexico	TPH*PL/TPH*PL
nearby	TPHAOERB	New Mexico	TPH-PL
nearsighted	TPHAOER/SAOEUGTD	New Orleans	TPHORLS
nearsightedness	TPHAOER/	New Year's Eve	TPHU/KWRAO*EFRS
	SAOEUGTD/*PBS	New York	TPHAO*EU/TPHAO*EU
Nebraska	TPH*E/TPH*E	New York	TPHORBG
Nebraska	TPHEB	New York City	TPHORBGS
necessarily	TPHES/HREU	New York City	TPHORBG/STEU
necessariness	TPHES/*PBS	New York City	TPHORBG/ST*EU
necessary	TPHES	news *(as wd)*	TPHAOUZ
necessitas	TPHES/TAS	news, weather,	
necessitate	TPHES/TAEUT	and sports	TPHO*RTS
necessitous	TPHES/TOUS	newspaper	TPHAOUP
necessity	TPHES/TEU	newsworthiness	TPHAOUS/
needn't	TPHAOEPBT		WOR/TH*EUPBS
negligence	TPHEPBLGS	newsworthiness	TPHAOUZ/
negligent	TPHEPBLGT		WOR/TH*EUPBS
negligently	TPHEPBLGT/HREU	NFC *(National Football Conference)*	
negotiability	TKPWOERBLT		TPH-RBGS/TP*BG
negotiable	TKPWOERBL	NFL *(National Football League)*	
negotiant	TKPWOERB/KWRAPBT		TPH-RBGS/TP*L
negotiate	TKPWOERBT	NGRI *(not guilty by reason of insanity)*	
negotiation	TKPWOERBGS		TPH-RBGS/
negotiator	TKPWOERBT/TOR		TKPW*RBGS/R*EU
neighbor	TPHAEUB	NGRI	TPH-RBGS/TKPWR*EU
neighborhood(s)	TPHAEUBD(Z)	NHL *(National Hockey League)*	
neighborhood(s)	TPHAEUB/HAOD(Z)		TPH-RBGS/H*L
neighborliness	TPHAEUB/HR*EUPBS	nighttime	TPHAOEUPLT
neighborliness	TPHAEU/PWOR/	NIMBY *(not in my back yard)*	
	HR*EUPBS		TPH*EUPL/PWEU
neighborly	TPHAEUB/HREU	9/11	9/HR*FPB
neither	TPHAOERT	9/11	TPHAO*EUFPB
nerviness	TPH*EFRB/SR*EUPBS	ninety	TPHAOEUPBT
nerviness	TPHEFRB/*PBS	NIOSH *(National Institute for Occupational Safety*	
nerviness	TPHEFRB/SR*EUPBS	*and Health)*	TPHAOEU/ORB
nerviness	TPHER/SR*EUPBS	NIRA *(National Industrial Recovery Act)*	
nervous	TPH*EFRBS		TPH-RBGS/*EURBGS/RA*
nervous	TPHEFRBS	NLRA *(National Labor Relations Act)*	
nervously	TPH*EFRB/SHREU		TPH-RBGS/HR*RBGS/RA*
nervously	TPH*EFRBS/HREU	NLRA	TPH-RBGS/HRA*R
nervously	TPHEFRB/SHREU	NLRB *(National Labor Relations Board)*	
nervously	TPHEFRBS/HREU		TPH-RBGS/HR*RB

NLRB	TPH-RBGS/HR*RBGS/R*B	nonviolent	TPHOPB/SRAOEUPBLT
no *(as wd)*	TPHO	nor	TPH-R
No,	TPHO*RBGS	normalization	TPHORPL/SA*EUGS
No.	TPHO*FPLT	north *(as wd)*	TPHO*RT
No.	TPHOFPLT	North America	TPHA*/TPHA*
nobody	TPHOEB	North America	TPHO*RT/PHERBG
nobody else	TPHOEBLS	North American	TPHO*RT/PHERPB
no-fault	TPHAULT	northbound	TPH*B
no-fault divorce	TPHAULT/TKWORS	northbound lane	TPH*BL
no-fault insurance	TPHAULT/STPHURPBS	northbound traffic	TPH*BT
no further questions	TPHUFRGS	North Carolina	TPH*BG/TPH*BG
no more questions	TPHORGS	North Dakota	TPH*D/TPH*D
no objection	TPHO*BGS	northeast	TPHO*ES
no such	TPHOUFP	Northeast	K-P/TPHO*ES
no, ma'am	TPHOPL	northeaster	TPHO*ES/ER
No, ma'am	TPHO*PL	northeasterly	TPHAO*ERL
no, sir	TPHORS	northeastern	TPHAO*ERPB
No, sir	TPHO*RS	northeasterner(s)	TPHAO*ERPB/ER(S)
nowhere	TPHO/WR*, TPHO/WR-	Northeasterner(s)	K-P/TPHAO*ERPB/ER(S)
no, your Honor	TPHURPB	northerly	TPHO*RL
No, your Honor	TPH*URPB	northern	TPHO*RPB
noise pollution	TPHOEUPLGS	northern	TPHORPB
noise pollution	TPHOEUZ/PHRAOUGS	Northern	K-P/TPHO*RPB
noisiness	TPHOEU/S*EUPBS	Northern	K-P/TPHORPB
noisiness	TPHOEUZ/S*EUPBS	northerner(s)	TPHO*RPB/ER(S)
nomad(s)	TPHOEPLD(Z)	northerner(s)	TPHORPB/ER(S)
nomadic	TPHOEPLD/EUBG	Northerner(s)	K-P/TPHO*RPB/ER(S)
nomographic	TPHOPL/TKPWRAFBG	Northerner(s)	K-P/TPHORPB/ER(S)
nomographic	TPHOEPL/TKPWRAFBG	Northern Ireland	TPHO*RPB/ AOEUR/HRAPBD
nonalcoholic	TPHOPB/KHROEUBG		
nonalcoholic	TPHOPB/KHOL/EUBG	Northern Ireland	TPHORPB/ AOEUR/HRAPBD
noncompliance	TPHOPB/KPHRAOEUPBS		
noncontroversial	TPHOPB/TRO*EFRL	Northern Territory	TPHO*RPB/TER/TOEUR
nondescript	TPHOPB/TKREUPT	Northern Territory	TPHORPB/TER/TOEUR
nondestructive	TPHOPB/TKRUBGT/*EUF	North Korea	TPHOERBG
nondestructive	TPHOPB/TKRUBG/T*EUF	North Korean	TPHOERBG/KWRAPB
nonessential	TPHOPB/SERBL	north side	TPH*DZ
nonetheless	TPHUPBLS	Northwest	K-P/TPWHO*ES
nonetheless	TPHUPB/THELS	northwest	TPWHO*ES
nonidentifying	TPHOPB/AOEUF/-G	northwester	TPWHO*ES/ER
nonidentifying	TPHOPB/ AOEUD/TPEU/-G	northwesterly	TPWH*ERL
		northwestern	TPWH*ERPB
nonjudgmental	TPHOPB/SKWRUPLT/TAL	Northwesterner(s)	K-P/TPWH*ERPB/ER(S)
nonjuror	TPHOPB/SKWRAOR	northwesterner(s)	TPWH*ERPB/ER(S)
nonlegal	TPHOPB/HRAOEL	Nos.	TPHOFPLTS
nonnegotiable	TPHOPB/TKPWOERBL	Nos.	TPHOFPLT/-S
nonobjective	TPHOPB/OBT/*EUF	nosiness	TPHOE/S*EUPBS
nonperformance	TPHOPB/P-FRPBS	nosiness	TPHOEZ/S*EUPBS
nonperformance	TPHOPB/P-FRPL/PHAPBS	not *(as wd)*	TPHOT
nonperson	TPHOPB/PERPB	not guilty	TPHOLT
nonproductive	TPHOPB/PRUBGT/*EUF	not to answer	TPHAOPBS
nonproductive	TPHOPB/PRUBG/T*EUF	not to answer the question	TPHAOPBGS
nonprofit	TPHOPB/PROFT	not to my knowledge	TPHAOEUPBLG
nonrenewable	TPHOPB/RE/TPHUBL	notwithstanding	TPHAPBG
(No response.)	TPHO*RPS	notary(ies) *(as wd)*	TPHOET/REU(/-S)
nonresponsive	TPHOPB/SPOPBS/*EUF	notaries public	TPHOPS
nonreturnable	TPHOPB/RURPB/-BL	notary public	TPHOP
non sequitur	TPHOPB/SEBG/TUR	noteworthiness	TPHOET/ WOR/TH*EUPBS
nonspecific	TPHOPB/SPEFBG		
nonstandard	TPHOPB/STARD	nothing *(as wd)*	TPHOG
nonsupport	TPHOPB/SPO*RT	nothing further	TPHURT
nonverbal	TPHOPB/SRERBL	notice	TPHOETS
nonviolence	TPHOPB/SRAOEUPBLS	noticeable	TPHOETS/-BL

noticeably	TPHOETS/PWHREU
November	TPHO*F, TPHOF
novice	TPHO*FS
now *(as wd)*	TPHOU
Now,	TPHOURBGS
NOW *(National Organization for Women)*	TPH-RBGS/O*U
nowadays	TPHOU/AEU/TKAEUS
now have	TPHOUF
NPR *(National Public Radio)*	TPH-RBGS/P*R
NRA *(National Rifle Association)*	TPH-RBGS/RA*
NRC *(Nuclear Regulatory Commission)*	TPH-RBGS/R*BG
NSA *(National Security Agency)*	TPH-RBGS/SA*
NSAID *(nonsteroidal anti-inflammatory drug)*	TPH-RBGS/SAEUD
NSPCA *(National Society for the Prevention of Cruelty to Animals)*	TPH-RBGS/S*RBGS/P*RBGS/KRA*
NSPCA	TPH-RBGS/SP*RBGS/KRA*
N.S.P.C.A.	TPH-FPLT/S*FPLT/P*FPLT/KRA*
N.S.P.C.A.	TPH-FPLT/SP*FPLT/KRA*
nuance	TPHAOUPBS
nugget	TPHUGT
number *(as wd)*	TPHURPL
Number	TPH*URPL
number of	TPHUFRPL
number of days	TPHUFDZ
number of days	TPHUFRPL/TKAEU/-S
number of times	TPHUFTS
number of times	TPHUFRPL/TAOEUPL/-S
number of witnesses	TPHUFPBS
number of witnesses	TPHUFRPL/W-PBS/-S
numeric	TPHAOUPL/ERBG
nu-uh *(negative)*	TPH*U/U
NYC *(New York City)*	TKPWHR*BG
NYC	TPH-RBGS/KWR*BG
N.Y.C.	TPH-FPLT/KWR*BG
NYPD *(New York Police Department)*	TKPWHR-RBGS/P*D
NYPD	TKPWHR*PD
NYPD	TPH-RBGS/KWR*RBGS/P*D
NYSE *(New York Stock Exchange)*	TKPWHR-RBGS/S*E
NYSE	TPH-RBGS/KWR*RBGS/S*E

O+	O/P*LS, ORBGS/P*LS
OAS *(Organization of American States)*	ORBGS/A*S
object *(as wd)*	OBT
object to the form	OFRPL
object to the form of the question	OFRPLGS
objected	OBTD
objectify	OBT/TPEU
objection	O*BGS
objectionable	O*BGS/-BL
objectionably	O*BGS/PWHREU
objectional	O*BGS/TPHAL
objective(s)	OBT/*EUF(S)
objectively	OBT/*EUF/HREU
objectivism	OBT/SREUFPL
objectivism	OBT/*EUF/EUFPL
objectivity	OBT/*EUFT
objectivity	OBT/*EUF/TEU
objector	OBT/TOR
objects	OBTS
obligate	OBL/TKPWAEUT
obligation	OBL/TKPWAEUGS
obligative	OBL/TKPWAEUT/*EUF
observation	OBS/SRAEUGS
obstetrician	O*BS/TREUGS
obstetrician	OBS/TREUGS
obvious	OFB
obviously	OFB/HREU
obviously	OFBL
occupancy	OUPS
occupancy	OUPT/SEU
occupant	OUPT
occupation	OUPGS
occupational	OUPGS/TPHAL
occupier(s)	OUP/ER(S)
occupy	OUP
ocean	OEGS
Ocean	O*EGS
o'clock	KHR*OBG
OCR *(optical character recognition)*	ORBGS/KR*R
OCS *(officer candidate school)*	ORBGS/KR*S
October	OBGT
OD *(overdose, olive drab)*	*OD
OD'd *(overdosed)*	O*D/-D, O*D/AOED
OEM *(outside equipment manufacturer)*	ORBGS/*EPL
of *(as wd)*	OF
of course	OFBG
of the	OFT
off *(as wd)*	AUF
off the	AUFT
off the record	AUFRBGD

offend(s)	OFPBD(Z)	one-zillion	WUPB/H-F/S*L
offender(s)	OFPBD/ER(S)	one-zillionth	WUPB/S*LT
offense	OFPBS	ongoing	OPB/TKPWOEUPBG
offensive(s)	OFPBS/*EUF(S)	only	OPBL
offensively	OFPBS/*EUF/HREU	ooziness	AO/S*EUPBS
office	AUFS	ooziness	AOZ/S*EUPBS
officer	AUFRS	OPEC *(Organization of Petroleum Exporting Countries)*	
officer	AUFS/ER		O/PEBG
Officer	A*UFRS	open	OEP
Officer	A*UFS/ER	opener(s)	OEP/ER(S)
official	TPEURBL	opening *(as wd)*	OEP/-G
officialese	TPEURBL/AOEZ	opening statement(s)	OEPGT(S)
officially	TPEURBL/HREU	openings	OEP/-GS
officiate	TPEURB/KWRAEUT	openly	OEP/HREU
officiate	TPEURB/SHAEUT	operate	OERPT
often	AUFPB	operatic	OERPT/EUBG
oftener	AUFPB/ER	operating *(as wd)*	OERPT/-G
oftentimes	AUFPB/TAOEUPLS	operating room	O*RPL
oh *(as wd)*	O*E	operation	OERPGS
oh,	OERBGS	operational	OERPGS/TPHAL
Oh,	O*ERBGS	operative(s)	OERPT/*EUF(S)
Ohio	HO*/HO*	operator	OERPT/TOR
Ohio	HAOEU/KWROE	opinion(s)	P-PB(S)
o.k.	O*BG	opinionated	P-PB/TPHAEUT/-D
okay	O*EBG	OPM *(Office of Personnel Management)*	
Oklahoma	O*BG/O*BG		ORBGS/P*PL
Oklahoma City	O*BG/O*BG/ST*EU	opponent	O/POEPBT
Oklahoma City	O*BG/O*BG/STEU	opportune	OP/TAOUPB
Oldsmobile	OELDZ/PHOEBL	opportunism	OP/TAOUPB/EUFPL
Oldsmobile	OLDZ/PHOEBL	opportunist	OP/TAOUPB/*EUS
OMB *(Office of Management and Budget)*		opportunistic	OP/TAOUPB/*EUS/EUBG
	ORBGS/PH*B	opportunity	TUPBT
omit	OEPLT	opportunity	OP/TAOUPB/TEU
on *(as wd)*	OPB	opposite	OP/SEUT
on or about	TPHORBT	opposition	OP/POGS
on the	OPBT	opposition	OP/SEUGS
on the ground(s)	OEGD(Z)	or *(as wd)*	OR
on the other hand	OERPBD	or not	ORPBT
on the part	OEPT	orange	ORPBG
on the record	OERBGD	orbit	ORBT
one *(as wd)*	WUPB	orbiter(s)	ORBT/ER(S)
one billion	WUPB/PW-L	orderliness	ORD/HR*EUPBS
one-billion	WUPB/H-F/PW-L	orderliness	ORD/HREU/*PBS
one-billionth	WUPB/PW*LT	ordinariness	ORD/TPHA*EURPBS
one-fourth	WUPB/TPO*URT	ordinary *(as wd)*	ORD/TPHAEUR
one-half	WUPB/HAF	ordinary care	OERBG
1/2 *(one half symbol)(suf)*	HAFS	ordinary care	
one hundred	WUPB/HUPB	and diligence	OERPBLG
one-hundred	WUPB/H-F/HUPB	ordinary person	OERP
one-hundredth	WUPB/H*UPBT	ordinary reason	OERPB
one million	WUPB/PH-L	ordinary reason	
one-million	WUPB/H-F/PH-L	and prudence	OERPBS
one-millionth	WUPB/PH*LT	ordinary, reasonable,	
1/4 *(one quarter symbol)(suf)*	KWARS	and prudent	OERPBT
oneself	W*UPBS	Oregon	O*R/O*R
one-third	WUPB/THEURD	.org *(suf)*	OFRPLT
one thousand	WUPB/THOU	organization	ORGS
one-thousand	WUPB/H-F/THOU	organization	ORG/SA*EUGS
one-thousandth	WUPB/THO*UT	organizational	ORGS/TPHAL
one trillion	WUPB/TR-L	organizational	ORG/SA*EUGS/TPHAL
one-trillion	WUPB/H-F/TR-L	organize	ORG
one-trillionth	WUPB/TR*LT	organizer(s)	ORG/ER(S)
one zillion	WUPB/S*L	orient	OEURPBT

Orient	O*EURPBT
oriental	OEURPBL
Oriental	O*EURPBL
orientation	OEURPB/TAEUGS
origin	ORPBLG
original	ORPBLG/TPHAL
originality	ORPBLG/TPHAL/TEU
originally	ORPBLG/HREU
originate	ORPBLG/TPHAEUT
origination	ORPBLG/TPHAEUGS
originator	ORPBLG/TPHAEU/TOR
Orlando	ORLD
orphan	OFRPB
orphanage	OFRPB/APBLG
OSHA *(Occupational Safety and Health Administration)*	O/SHA
OTC *(over-the-counter)*	ORBGS/T*BG
other *(as wd)*	O*ER
other side	O*ERDZ
other than the	O*ERPBT
other than	O*ERPB
otherwise	O*ERZ
otherwise	O*ER/WAO*EUZ
ourself	O*URS
ourselves	O*URS/-S
out *(as wd)*	OUT
out of	OUF
out of the	OUFT
outgoing	O*UT/TKPWOEUPBG
outnumber	O*UT/TPHURPL
outpatient	O*UT/PAEURBT
outside	OUDZ
outsider(s)	OUDZ/ER(S)
outspoken	O*UT/SPOEPB
outthink	O*UT/THEU
over *(as wd)*	O*EFR, OEFR
over the	OEFRT
overage *(n)*	O*EFRPBLG
overburden(s)	O*FR/PWURD(Z)
overcapitalization	O*FR/KAPT/SA*EUGS
overdevelop	O*FR/TKWOP
overindulge	O*FR/EUPB/TKULG
overpopulate	O*FR/PO*P/HRAEUT
overpopulation	O*FR/POP/HRAEUGS
overpower	O*FR/PO*UR
overqualify(ied)	O*FR/KW-F(D)
overrule	O*FRL
overruled	O*FRLD
oversimplify	O*FR/SEUFRP/TPEU
overt	O*EFRT
overtly	O*EFRT/HREU
overwork	O*FRBG
ovum	O*EFPL
oz *(ounce)*	OZ
oz.	O*Z

PABA *(para-aminobenzoic acid)*	P-RBGS/A*RBGS/PWA*
PAC *(political action committee)*	PA*BG
PAC	P-RBGS/A*BG
Pacific	PA/SEUFBG
Pacific Ocean	PA/SEUFBG/O*EGS
pain *(as wd)*	PAEUPB
pain and suffering	PUFRG
palatial	PHRAEURBL
palladium	PHRAEUD/KWRUPL
palooka	PHRAO/KA
paltriness	PAUL/TR*EUPBS
paltriness	PAULT/R*EUPBS
panegyric	PAPB/SKWREURBG
pants	PAPBTS
par delictum	PAR/TKHREUBG/TUPL
par delictum	PAR/TKHREUBGT/UPL
par excellence	PAR/KPHREPBS
parade(s)	PRAEUD(Z)
paragraph	PRAF
paralegal	PHRAOEL
paralegal	PAR/HRAOEL
paralyses	PRAL/SAOEZ
paralysis	PRAL/SEUS
paramedic(s)	PARPLD(Z)
parameter	PRAPL/TER
parameter(s)	PRAPLT/ER(S)
paraphernalia	PAEURPB
paraphernalia	PRAF/TPHAEUL/KWRA
paraprofessional	PAR/PROFL
paraprofessional	PAR/PROFGS/TPHAL
parapsychology	PAR/SKOLG
pardon *(as wd)*	PAR/TKOPB
pardon me	PARPL
paregoric	PAR/TKPWOERBG
paregoric	PAR/TKPWORBG
paren	PREPB
parentheses	PA*RPBT/SAOEZ
parentheses	PR*EPBT/SAOEZ
parenthesis	PA*RPBT/SEUS
parenthesis	PR*EPBT/SEUS
parietal	PRAOEU/TAL
parishioner	PREURB/TPHER
Park Avenue	PARBG/A*F
park(ing) *(as wd)*	PARBG(/-G)
parking light(s)	P-LT(S)
parking lot	PARLT
parkway	PRAE
Parkway	PRA*E
parochial	PROEBG/KWRAL
parol *(as wd)*	PARL, PA/ROL
parol evidence	PRO*EFD, PROEFD
parole *(as wd)*	PAERL, PA/ROEL
parole office	PROEFS
parole officer	PROEFR

parole officers	PROEFRS	people('s) *(as wd)*	PAOEPL(/AOES)
parolee	PROEL/HRAOE	People's Exhibit	P-BGS
paroxysm	PROBGS/EUFPL	People's Exhibit No.	P*BGS
participant	PARPT	per curiam	PER/KAOURPL
participate	PARP	per diem	PER/TKAOEPL
participation	PARPGS	peremptorily	PREFRP/TOEUR/HREU
participatory	PARP/TOEUR	peremptorily	PREFRP/TREU/HREU
particular	PHRAR	peremptorily	PREFRPT/REU/HREU
particularity	PHRAR/TEU	peremptoriness	PREFRP/TO*EURPBS
particularly	PHRAR/HREU	peremptoriness	PREFRP/TR*EUPBS
part-time	PAOEUPL	peremptoriness	PREFRPT/R*EUPBS
par value	PAR/SRAL	peremptoriness	PREFRPT/REU/*PBS
passenger('s) *(as wd)*	PASZ/SKWRER(/AOES)	peremptory	PREFRP/TOEUR
passenger side	P-DZ	peremptory	PREFRP/TREU
passenger's side	P-DZ/AOE	peremptory	PREFRPT/REU
passivity	PASZ/*EUFT	perennial	PREPB/KWRAL
passivity	PAS/S*EUFT	perfect	PEFRT
patchiness	PAFP/KH*EUPBS	perfectibility	PEFRT/-BLT
patience	PAEURBS	perfectible	PEFRT/-BL
patient	PAEURBT	perfection	P*EFRGS
patiently	PAEURBT/HREU	perfectionism	P*EFRGS/EUFPL
patriarch	PAEU/TRARBG	perfectionist	P*EFRGS/*EUS
patriarch	PAEUT/RARBG	perfectly	PEFRT/HREU
patriarchal	PAEU/TRAR/KAL	perform(s)	P-FRPL(S)
patriarchal	PAEUT/RAR/KAL	performance	P-FRPBS
patriarchy	PAEU/TRAR/KEU	performance	P-FRPL/PHAPBS
patriarchy	PAEUT/RAR/KEU	performed	P-FRPLD
patrimonial	PA/TREU/PHOEPBL	performer(s)	P-FRPL/ER(S)
patrimonial	PAT/REU/PHOEPBL	performing	P-FRPLG
patriot	PAEU/TROT	perhaps	PRAPS
patriot	PAEUT/ROT	peril	P*ERL
patriotism	PAEU/TREUFPL	perilous	P*ERL/OUS
patriotism	PAEUT/REUFPL	perilous	PERL/OUS
patrol	PROL	perimeter	PREUPL/TER
patrolman	PROL/PHAPB	perimeter(s)	PREUPLT/ER(S)
patrolmen	PROL/PHEPB	period(s) *(as wd)*	PAOERD(Z)
patrolwoman	PROL/WOPL	period of time	PR-FT
patrolwomen	PROL/WEUPL	periodic	PAOERD/EUBG
paunchiness	PAUFRPBLG/KH*EUPBS	periodical	PAOERD/KAL
paunchiness	PAUPB/KH*EUPBS	periodically	PAOERD/KHREU
payoff	PAUF	peripheral	PREUF/RAL
payroll	PAEURL	periphery	PREUF/REU
PBS *(Public Broadcasting Service)*		periwinkle	PER/W*EUPBG/-L
	P-RBGS/PW*S	perjury	P-RPBLG
PBX *(private branch exchange)*		perkiness	PER/K*EUPBS
	P-RBGS/PW*BGS	permission	PERPLGS
PCB *(polychlorinated biphenyl)*		permit	PERPLT
	P-RBGS/KR*B	peroxide(s)	PROBG/SAOEUD(Z)
PCP *(phencyclidine pill)*	P-RBGS/KR*P	peroxide(s)	PROBGS/AOEUD(Z)
PDA *(personal digital assistant)*		perpetrator	PERP/TRAEURT
	P-RBGS/TKA*	person	PERPB
PDR *(Physicians' Desk Reference)*		persona	PERPB/TPHA
	P-RBGS/TK*R	personable	PERPB/-BL
peace *(as wd)*	PAES	personal *(as wd)*	PERPBL
peace officer	PAUFR	personal injury	PEUPBLG
peace officers	PAUFRS	personality	PERPBLT
pearliness	PER/HR*EUPBS	personality	PERPBL/TEU
pearliness	PERL/HR*EUPBS	personalization	PERPBL/SA*EUGS
pedestrian	P*ED	personalize	PERPBL/AOEUZ
penalty	PEPBLT	personally	PERPB/HREU
penicillin	PEPB/SHREUPB	personally	PERPBL/HREU
penitentiary	PEPBT/REU	personalty	P*ERPBLT
Pennsylvania	PA*/PA*, PAFPLT	personalty	P*ERPBL/TEU

personification	PERPB/TPEU/KAEUGS	picturesque	PEUBG/KHUR/*ES
personify	PERPB/TPEU	pigeon-toed	PEUPBLG/
personnel	PERPB/EL		SKWROPB/TOED
Peruvian	PRAO*UF/KWRAPB	pimple	PEUFRPL
peskiness	PES/K*EUPBS	PIN *(personal identification number)*	
PETA *(People for the Ethical Treatment of Animals)*			P-RBGS/*EUPB
	PAO*E/TA	PIN	P*EUPB
PETA	P-RBGS/*ERBGS/TA*	pink	P*EUPBG
petit *(as wd)*	PE/TAOE, PET/TAOE	pinkie	P*EUPBG/KAOE
petit jury	PET/TAOE/SKWRUR	pinkish	P*EUPBG/EURB
petit larceny	PHRARS	pinko	P*EUPBG/KOE
pettiness	PET/T*EUPBS	pinky	P*EUPBG/KEU
petty jury	PET/TEU/SKWRUR	pirate	PAOEURT
PGA *(Professional Golfers Association)*		pistol	P*EULS
	P-RBGS/TKPWA*	pithiness	P*EUT/TH*EUPBS
pH	PAEUFP	PITI *(principal, interest, taxes, and insurance)*	
Ph.D. *(Philosophiae Doctor)*	PAEUFPD		P-RBGS/*EURBGS/T*EU
Ph.D.	P-RBGS/H*D	pivot	P*EUFT
Philadelphia	TP-FLD	place *(as wd)*	PHRAEUS
Philadelphia	TPEUL/TKEL/TPA	place of business	PHRAEUBS
philander(s)	TPHRAPBD/ER(S)	place of employment	PHRAEUPLT
philandered	TPHRAPBD/ERD	plaintiff(s) *(as wd)*	PHR-F(S)
philandering	TPHRAPBD/ERG	THE PLAINTIFF: *(colloquy)*	
philanthropic	TPHRAPB/THROP/EUBG		PHR-F/PHR-F
philanthropist	TPHRAPB/THRO/P*EUS	plaintiff's attorney	PHROERPB
philanthropist	TPHRAPB/THROP/*EUS	Plaintiff's Attorney	PHRO*ERPB
philanthropy	TPHRAPB/THRO/PEU	Plaintiff's Exhibit	PHR-BGS
philosopher	TPHROS/TPER	Plaintiff's Exhibit No.	PHR*BGS
philosophic	TPEUL/SOFBG	planetarium	PHRAPB/TAEURPL
philosophize	TPHROS/TPAOEUZ	plank	PHRA*PBG
philosophy	TPHROS/TPEU	plankton	PHRA*PBG/TOPB
phone *(as wd)*	TPOEPB	plastic *(as wd)*	PHRA*S/EUBG
phone conference	TP-FRPBS	plastic surgery	PHR-RPBLG
phone line	TPHRAOEUPB	plea *(as wd)*	PHRAOE
phoniness	TPOE/TPH*EUPBS	plea agreement	PHRAOEPLT
phoniness	TPOEPB/TPH*EUPBS	plea bargain	PHRARG
photocomposition	TPOET/KOPL/POGS	plea of guilty	PHROFGT
photocomposition	TPOET/KOFRP/SEUGS	plea of no contest	PHROFPBG
photograph	TPRAF	plea of nolo contendere	PHROFPBLT
photographer	TPRAFR	plea of not guilty	PHROFPBGT
photographer(s)	TPRAF/ER(S)	plead *(as wd)*	PHRAOED
photographic	TPRAFBG	plead guilty	PHRAOEGT
photographic	TPRAF/EUBG	please *(as wd)*	PHRAOEZ
photography	TPRAF/TPEU	please raise	
photovoltaic	TPOET/SROEL/TAEUBG	your right hand	PHRAEURPBDZ
photovoltaic	TPOET/SROL/TAEUBG	please, ma'am	PHRAOEPL
physical(ly) *(as wd)*	TP-L/(HREU)	please, ma'am,	PHRAOEPLZ
physical abuse	TPABS	please, sir	PHRAOERS
physical examination	TP-BGS	please, sir,	PHRAOERSZ
physical injury	TPEUPBLG	pleasurable	PHR-RB/-BL
physical therapist	TPA*EURPS	pleasurably	PHR-RB/PWHREU
physical therapy	TPAEURP	pleasure(s)	PHR-RB(S)
physicality	TP-L/TEU	pliers	PHRAOEURS
physically abuse	TPAEBS	PLO *(Palestine Liberation Organization)*	
physically abused	TPAEBS/-D		P-RBGS/HRO*
physician	TP-GS	plunge	PHRUPBG
physiotherapy	TPEUZ/KWRO/THAEURP	plunger(s)	PHRUPBG/ER(S)
picket	PEUBGT	plunk	PHR*UPBG
pick-me-up *(n)*	PEUBG/PH*UP	plushiness	PHRURB/SH*EUPBS
pickpocket	PEUBG/POBGT	p.m.	P*PL
pickup *(as wd)*	P*UP	PMS *(premenstrual syndrome)*	
pickup truck	P*UPT		P*PLS
picosecond(s)	PAOEUBG/SEBGD(Z)	PMS	P-RBGS/PH*S

© 2004 *StenEd®* Briefs & Phrases (Excerpted from StenEd's Realtime Professional Dictionary)

POB *(post office box)*	PO*B	polluter(s)	PHRAOUT/ER(S)
POB	P-RBGS/O*B	pollution	PHRAOUGS
PO Box *(post office box)*	PO/PWOBGS	polygamist	PHREUG/PH*EUS
P.O. Box	PO*/PWOBGS	polygamous	PHREUG/PHOUS
pocket	POBGT	polygamy	PHREUG/PH*EU
pocketbook	POBGT/PWAOBG	polygynist	PHREUPBLG/TPH*EUS
pocketknife	POBGT/TPHAOEUF	polygynous	PHREUPBLG/TPHOUS
point(s) *(as wd)*	POEUPBT(/-S)	polygyny	PHREUPBLG/TPH*EU
point-blank	POEUPBT/PWHRA*PBG	pompously	POFRP/SHREU
point of fact	POEUFT	populace	POP/HRAS
points of fact	POEUFTS	popular	PO*P/HRAR
point of facts	POEUFT/-S	popularity	PO*P/HRAEUR/TEU
point of impact	POEUBGT	popularity	PO*P/HRAR/TEU
points of impact	POEUBGTS	popularity	POP/HRAEUR/TEU
point of impacts	POEUBGT/-S	popularity	POP/HRAR/TEU
point of law	POEUFL	popularize	PO*P/HRAR/AOEUZ
points of law	POEUFLS	popularly	PO*P/HRAR/HREU
point of laws	POEUFL/-S	populate	PO*P/HRAEUT
point of origin	POEURPB	population	PO*P/HRAEUGS
point of origins	POEURPB/-S	populism	POP/HREUFPL
points of origin	POEURPBS	populist	PO*P/HR*EUS
point of view	PO*EUF	populous	POP/HROUS
point of views	PO*EUF/-S	porkiness	POR/K*EUPBS
points of view	PO*EUFS	position	POGS
point of view	POEUF	positional	POGS/TPHAL
point of views	POEUF/-S	positivity	POS/T*EUFT
points of view	POEUFS	positivity	POZ/T*EUFT
polarization	POEL/SA*EUGS	possess	PESZ
polarize	POEL/RAOEUZ	possession *(as wd)*	PEGS
police *(as wd)*	PHREUS	possession	PO/SEGS
police action	PHRA*BGS	possession of a	
police chief	PHRAOEF	controlled substance	POFBGS
police department	PHR-D	possession of a weapon	POFP
police departments	PHR-DZ	possession of cocaine	POFBG
police force	PHRORS	possession of crack cocaine	POFRBG
police officer	PHRAUFR	possession of marijuana	POFRPL
police officer	PHREUFR	possessive	PESZ/*EUF
police officers	PHRAUFRS	possessively	PESZ/*EUF/HREU
police officers	PHREUFRS	possessiveness	PESZ/*EUFPBS
police report	PHRORT	possessiveness	PESZ/*EUF/*PBS
police reports	PHRORTS	possessives	PESZ/*EUFS
police station	PHRAEUGS	possessor	PESZ/SOR
police vehicle	PHRAOEBG	possessory	PESZ/REU
policeman	PHRAPL	possessory	PESZ/SOEUR
policeman	PHREUS/PHAPB	possibilities	POBLTS, POBLT/-S
policemen	PHREPL	possibility	POBLT
policemen	PHREUS/PHEPB	possible	POBL
policewoman	PWHRAPL	possibly	POEBL
policewoman	PHREUS/WOPL	POSSLQ *(person of the opposite sex sharing living*	
policewomen	PWHREPL	*quarters)*	POSZ/-L/KAOU
policewomen	PHREUS/WEUPL	POSSLQ	POSZ/-L/KWAOU
polite	PHRAOEUT	post diem	PO*ES/TKAOEPL
politely	PHRAOEUT/HREU	post office	PO*ES/AUFS
politeness	PHRAOEUT/*PBS	postconviction	PO*S/KW*EUBGS
political	PHREUT/KAL	postoperative	PO*S/OERPT/*EUF
politically	PHREUT/KHREU	potpourri	POE/PRAOE
politically correct	PHREUT/KREBGT	POW *(prisoner of war)*	P-RBGS/O*U
politicization	PHREUT/SAOEU/ SA*EUGS	POW	PO*U
politicize	PHREUT/SAOEUZ	power	PO*UR
politics	POL/TEUBGS	powerful	PO*UR/-FL
pollutant	PHRAOU/TAPBT	powerfully	PO*UR/TPHREU
pollute	PHRAOUT	powerfulness	PO*UR/TPHR*PBS
		powerhouse	PO*UR/HOUS

powerless	PO*UR/HRES
powerlessly	PO*UR/HRES/HREU
powerlessness	PO*UR/HRES/*PBS
PPO *(preferred-provider organization)*	P-RBGS/PO*
PPS *(post postscript)*	P-RBGS/P*S
practicable	PRABGT/KABL
practical	PRABGT/KAL
practically	PRABGT/KHREU
practicum	PRABGT/KUPL
praiseworthiness	PRAEUZ/WOR/TH*EUPBS
prank	PRA*PBG
prayer	PRAEUR
prearrange	PRE/ARPBG
prearrangement(s)	PRE/ARPBG/-PLT(S)
precinct	PREUPBGT
precipitate	PR*EUPT
precipitation	PR*EUPGS
precipitator	PR*EUPT/TOR
pre-Columbian	PRE/KHRUPL/KWRAPB
precomputer	PRE/KPAOURT
precomputer	PRE/KPAOUT/ER
precondition(s)	PRE/K-PB(S)
preconditioned	PRE/K-PBD
preconditioning	PRE/K-PBG
precontract	PRE/KR-T
predatoriness	PRED/TO*EURPBS
predetermination	PRE/TKERPLGS
predetermination	PRE/TKERPL/TPHAEUGS
predetermine	PRE/TKERPL
predisposition	PRE/TKEUS/POGS
prefabricate	PRE/TPAB/KAEUT
prefabrication	PRE/TPAB/KAEUGS
prefer	PREFR
preferable	PREFRBL
preferably	PREFR/PWHREU
preference	PREFRPBS
preferential	PREFRPB/-RBL
pregnancy	PREGT/SEU
pregnant	PREGT
prehearing	PRE/HAERG
prehistoric	PRE/HEUS/TORBG
prehistoric	PRE/HEUS/TOERBG
prehuman	PRE/HAOUPL
prejudgment	PRE/SKWRUPLT
prelim	PHREUPL
preliminarily	PHREUPL/TPHAEUR/HREU
preliminary *(as wd)*	PHREUPL/TPHAEUR
preliminary examination	PRAOEBGS
preliminary hearing	PRAOERG
preliminary injunction	PRAOEPBGS
premature	PRAOEPL/KHUR
prematurely	PRAOEPL/KHUR/HREU
premise	PREPLS
premises	PREPLSZ, PREPLS/-S
preoccupation	PRE/OUPGS
preoccupied	PRE/OUP/-D
preoperative	PRE/OERPT/*EUF
preparatorily	PREP/TOEUR/HREU
preparatory	PREP/TOEUR
preponderance *(as wd)*	P-P
preponderance	
of the evidence	P-PD
preponderate(s)	P-PT(S)
preposition	PREP/POGS, PREP/SEUGS
preproduction	PRE/PR*UBGS
prerecord(ed)	PRE/RORD(/-D)
preregistration	PRE/REGS
prerequisite	PRE/REBG/SEUT
prerequisite	PRE/REBG/S*EUT
prerogative	PROG/T*EUF
preschool	PRAOL
Preschool	PRA*OL
preschooler(s)	PRAOL/ER(S)
prescribe	PRAOEUB
prescription	PREUPGS
prescriptive	PREUPT/*EUF
preselect	PRE/SHREBGT
presence	PREPBS
present	PREPBT
presentable	PREPBT/-BL
presentably	PREPBT/PWHREU
presentation	PREGS
presentation	PREPBT/TAEUGS
presentence	PRE/STPH-PBS
presenter(s)	PREPBT/ER(S)
presently	PREPBT/HREU
presentment	PREPBT/-PLT
presidency	P-T/SEU
president(s)	P-T(S)
President(s)	P*T(S)
President Bush	P*T/PW*URB
President Carter	P*T/KA*RT/ER
President Clinton	P*T/KHR*PBT
President Clinton	P*T/KHREUPB/TOPB
President Clinton	PHR*EUBG
President Ford	P*T/TPO*RD
President Johnson	P*T/SKWROPB/SOPB
President Kennedy	P*T/KEPB/TKEU
President Nixon	P*T/TPHEUBG/SOPB
president pro tem	P-T/PROE/TEPL
President Reagan	P*T/RAEU/TKPWAPB
President Reagan	P*T/RAOE/TKPWAPB
presidential	P-T/-RBL
pressure(s)	PR-RB(S)
pressured	PR-RBD
pressuring	PR-RBG
pressurize	PR-RB/AOEUZ
pressurizer	PR-RB/AOEUZ/ER
presumable	PRAOUPL/-BL
presumably	PRAOUPL/PWHREU
presume	PRAOUPL
presumedly	PRAOUPL/TKHREU
presumption *(as wd)*	PRUFRPGS, PRUPLGS
presumption of guilt	PRULT
presumption of innocence	PRUPBS
presumptive	PRUFRPT, PRUPLT
presumptuous	PRURBS
presumptuously	PRURBS/HREU
presuppose	PRE/SPOEZ
presupposition	PRE/SUP/POGS
preteenager	PRE/TAEURPBLG
pretrial *(as wd)*	PRE/TRAOEUL
pretrial conference	PR-FRPBS

prettiness	PRET/T*EUPBS	producer(s)	PRAOUS/ER(S)
prettiness	PREUT/*PBS	producible	PRAOUS/-BL
pretty	PREUT	product	PRUBGT
prevent	PR*EFPBT	production	PR*UBGS
preventability	PR*EFPBT/-BLT	productive	PRUBGT/*EUF
preventable	PR*EFPBT/-BL	productive	PRUBG/T*EUF
preventative	PR*EFPBT/T*EUF	productivity	PRUBG/T*EUFT
prevention	PR*EFPBGS	productivity	PRUBGT/*EUFT
preventive(s)	PR*EFPBT/*EUF(S)	productivity	PRUBGT/*EUF/TEU
previous (as wd)	PRAO*EFS	profert	PROEFRT
previous to	PR*EFT, PREFT	profess	PROFS
previously	PRAO*EF/SHREU	profession	PROFGS
previously	PRAO*EFS/HREU	professional	PROFL
preyer	PRA*EUR	professional	PROFGS/TPHAL
priciness	PRAOEU/S*EUPBS	professionalism	PROFL/EUFPL
priciness	PRAOEUS/S*EUPBS	professionalism	PROFGS/TPHAL/EUFPL
prima facie	PRAOEUPL/TPAEURB	professionally	PROFL/HREU
princeliness	PREUPBS/HR*EUPBS	professionally	PROFGS/HREU
principally	PREUPBS/PHREU	professor	PROFS/SOR
prior (as wd)	PRAOEUR	proffer	PROFR
prior to	PRAOEURT	profit (as wd)	PROFT
prison	PREUZ	profit and loss	PR-FLS
prisoner	PREURZ	profitability	PROFT/-BLT
prisoner	PREUZ/TPHER	profitable	PROFT/-BL
private (as wd)	PRAO*EUFT	profitably	PROFT/PWHREU
private school	PRAOEUL	profiteer	PROF/TAOER
privately	PRAO*EUFT/HREU	profiteer	PROFT/TAOER
privet	PR*EUFT	program	PRAPL
privilege (as wd)	PR*EUF/HREPBLG	programmable	PRAPL/-BL
privileged information	PREUFGS	programmer(s)	PRAPL/ER(S)
prn (med)	P*/R*PB	progress	PROG
p.r.n. (med)	P*RPB, PR*PB	progression	PROGS
p.r.n.	P*PD/R*PB	progressive	PROG/*EUF
pro-America	PRO/PHERBG	progressively	PROG/*EUF/HREU
pro-American	PRO/PHERPB	prohibit	PROEUBT
probabilities	PROBLTS, PROBLT/-S	prohibit	PRO/HEUBT
probability	PROBLT	prohibition	PROEUBGS
probable (as wd)	PROBL	prohibition	PRO/PWEUGS
probable cause	PROBLZ	prohibitive	PROEUBT/*EUF
probably	PROEBL	prohibitively	PROEUBT/*EUF/HREU
probation (as wd)	PRO/PWAEUGS	project	PROPBLGT
probation office	PRAUFS	projective	PROPBLGT/*EUF
probation officer	PRAUFR	projector	PROPBLGT/TOR
probation officers	PRAUFRS	projector	PROPBLG/TOR
probation report	PRORT	prolific	PRO/HREUFBG
problem	PROB	promise	PROPLS
problematic	PROB/PHAT/EUBG	promisee	PROPLS/SAOE
problems	PROBS, PROB/-S	promiser(s)	PROPLS/ER(S)
procedural	PRAOERL	promisor	PROPLS/SOR
procedural	PRAOED/KWRURL	promissorily	PROPLS/SOEUR/HREU
procedurally	PRAOERL/HREU	promissorily	PROPL/SOEUR/HREU
procedurally	PRAOED/KWRUR/HREU	promissory	PROPLS/SOEUR
procedurally	PRAOED/KWRURL/HREU	promissory	PROPL/SOEUR
procedure	PRAOER	pronouncement (as wd)	PRO/TPHOUPBS/-PLT
procedure	PRAOED/KWRUR	pronouncement of judgment	PROUPBLG
proceed(s)	PRAOED(Z)	pronouncements of judgment	PROUPBLGS
proceeding(s)	PRAOED/-G(S)		
proclamation	PROBG/PHAEUGS		
proclivity	PRO/KHR*EUFT	pronouncement of judgments	PROUPBLG/-S
procreate	PRO/KRAET	property	PROT
procreation	PRO/KRAEGS	proponent	PRO/POEPBT
procreative	PRO/KRAET/*EUF	proposition	PROP/POGS
produce	PRAOUS		

proposition	PROP/SEUGS	public *(as wd)*	PUB/HREUBG
prosaic	PRO/SAEUBG	public school	PHRAOUL
prosaic	PRO/SA*EUBG	publication	PUBL/KAEUGS
prosecutable	PR-T/-BL	publicize	PUBL/SAOEUZ
prosecute(s)	PR-T(S)	PUC *(Public Utilities Commission)*	
prosecuted	PR-TD		P-RBGS/*UBG
prosecuting	PR-GT, PR-T/-G	PUD *(planned unit development)*	
prosecution	PR-GS		P-RBGS/*UD
prosecutor	PR-RT, PR-T/TOR	PUD	P*UD
prosecutorial	PR-T/TOEURL	pudginess	PUD/SKWR*EUPBS
prosecutrix	PR-T/REUBGS	pudginess	PUPBLG/SKWR*EUPBS
protect	PREBGT	puerile	PAOURL
protectee	PREBG/TAOE	Puerto Rico	PR*/PR*
protection	PR*EBGS	puffiness	PUF/TP*EUPBS
protectionism	PR*EBGS/EUFPL	pulmonary	PUPL/TPHAEUR
protective	PREBGT/*EUF	pumpkin	PUPL/KEUPB
protector	PREBGT/TOR	punchdrunk	PUFRPBLG/TKR*UPBG
protector	PREBG/TOR	punishment	PUPLT
protectorate	PREBGT/TRAT	punk	P*UPBG
protectorate	PREBG/TRAT	pupil	PAOUPL
protectory	PREBGT/TOEUR	puppeteer	PUP/TAOER
protectory	PREBGT/REU	puppetry	PUP/TREU
protectory	PREBG/TOEUR	purpose	PURP
provability	PRO*FBLT	purposeful	PURP/-FL
provable	PRO*FBL	purposefully	PURP/TPHREU
provably	PRO*F/PWHREU	purposeless	PURP/HRES
prove	PRO*F	purposely	PURP/HREU
proven	PRO*FPB	pushiness	PURB/SH*EUPBS
prover	PRO*FR	putrefaction	PAOUT/TPA*BGS
province	PRO*FPBS, PROFPBS	putrefactive	PAOUT/TPABGT/*EUF
provocativeness	PRO/SROBG/T*EUFPBS	putrefy	PAOUT/TPEU
provocativeness	PRO/SROBGT/*EUFPBS	puzzlement	PUZ/HR-PLT
proximate *(as wd)*	PR-BGS		
proximate cause	PRAUZ		
proximate result	PR-RLT		
proximately	PR-BGS/HREU		
proximation	PR-BGS/PHAEUGS		
prudence	PRAOUPBS		
prudent *(as wd)*	PRAOUPBT		
prudent person	PRAOUP		
prudential	PRAOUPBT/-RBL		
prudently	PRAOUPBT/HREU		
pseudosophistication	SAOUD/ STP*EUS/KAEUGS		
psychiatric	SKREUBG		
psychiatrist	SKR*EUS		
psychiatry	SKRAOE		
psychoanalysis	SAOEUBG/APBL/SEUS		
psychological	SKOL		
psychologically	SKOL/HREU		
psychologist	SKO*LGS		
psychology	SKOLG		
psychosomatic	SAOEUBG/SPHAT/EUBG		
psychotherapist	SAOEUBG/THA*EURPS		
psychotherapy	SAOEUBG/THAEURP		
PTA *(Parent-Teacher Association)*	P-RBGS/TA*		
PTI *(pretrial intervention)*	P-RBGS/T*EU		
PTL *(Praise the Lord)*	P-RBGS/T*L		
PTO *(Parent-Teacher Organization)*	P-RBGS/TO*		
puberty	PAOUB/TEU		
pubes	PAOUBS		

Q. *(question bank)*	STKPWHR-
Q. Are	STKPWHR*R
Q. Is	STKPWHR*S
Q. Ma'am,	STKPWHR*PL
Q. Now,	STKPWHRO*U
Q. Oh	STKPWHROE
Q. Oh,	STKPWHRO*E
Q. Sir,	STKPWHR*RS
Q. So	STKPWHRO
Q. So,	STKPWHRO*
Q. Was	STKPWHR*FS
Q. Well,	STKPWHR*EL
Q. Were	STKPWHR*RP
Q. Will	STKPWHR*L
Q&A *(question & answer)*	KW-RBGS/SKPA*
Q&A	KW-RBGS/TPHA*
quadriplegic(s)	KWAD/PHRAOEPBLG/EUBG(S)
quadriplegic(s)	KWAUD/PHRAOEPBLG/EUBG(S)
quadruplicate *(j)*	KWAD/RAOUP/KAT
quadruplicate *(j)*	KWAD/RUP/KAT
quadruplicate *(j)*	KWAUD/RAOUP/KAT
quadruplicate *(j)*	KWAUD/RUP/KAT
quadruplicate *(v)*	KWAD/RAOUP/KAEUT
quadruplicate *(v)*	KWAD/RUP/KAEUT
quadruplicate *(v)*	KWAUD/RAOUP/KAEUT
quadruplicate *(v)*	KWAUD/RUP/KAEUT
qualifiable	KW-FBL
qualification	KW-FGS
qualified	KW-FD
qualifiedly	KW-F/TKHREU
qualifier(s)	KW-FR(S)
qualifies	KW-FS
qualify	KW-F
qualifying	KW-FG
quality	KWALT, KWAULT
quantity	KWAPBT, KWAUPBT
1/4 *(quarter symbol)(suf)*	KWARS
queasiness	KWAOE/S*EUPBS
queasiness	KWAOEZ/S*EUPBS
question bank *(Q.)*	STKPWHR-
question *(as wd)*	KWE
questions	KWES, KWE/-S
question of fact	KWEFT
question of facts	KWEFT/-S
questions of fact	KWEFTS
question of law	KWEFL
questions of law	KWEFLS
question of laws	KWEFL/-S
question read	KWAED
(Question read.)	KWA*ED
questionable	KWEBL
questionably	KWE/PWHREU
questionably	KWEBL/HREU
questioned	KWED, KWE/-D
questioner(s)	KWE/ER(S)
questioning	KWEG, KWE/-G
questionnaire	KWE/TPHAEUR
quiet	KWAO*EUT
quieter	KWAO*EUT/ER
quietest	KWAO*EUT/*ES
quietly	KWAO*EUT/HREU
quorum	KWOERPL
quorum	KWORPL
quotient	KWOERBT
QWERTY	KWER/TEU

rabbit	RABT
rabid	RABD
raciness	RAEU/S*EUPBS
raciness	RAEUS/S*EUPBS
racket	RABGT
racquetball	RABGT/PWAL
radioactivity	RAEUD/KWRO/ABGT/*EUFT
radioactivity	RAEUD/KWRO/ABG/T*EUFT
ragamuffin	RAG/PHUFPB
railroad(s)	R-RD(Z)
rainfall	RAEUFL
raininess	RAEU/TPH*EUPBS
raininess	RAEUPB/TPH*EUPBS
RAM (random-access memory)	R-RBGS/A*PL
RAM	RA*PL
R&B (rhythm & blues)	R-RBGS/SKP*B
R&D (research & development)	R-RBGS/SKP*D
R&R (rock & roll, rest & recreation)	R-RBGS/SKP*R
range	RAEUPBG
ranger(s)	RAEUPBG/ER(S)
rank	RA*PBG
rankle(s)	RA*PBG/-L(S)
rankled	RA*PBG/-LD
rankling	RA*PBG/-LG
rankly	RA*PBG/HREU
rapid	RAPD
rapidity	RAPD/TEU
rapidly	RAPD/HREU
RapidText	RAPD/T*EBGS
RapidWrite	RAPD/WRAO*EUT
ratchet	RAFPT
rather (as wd)	RA*T/ER
rather than	RARPB
rather than the	RARPBT
ration (as wd)	RAEUGS, RAGS
rational	RARBL
rationalism	RARBL/EUFPL
rationalism	RAGS/HREUFPL
rationalist	RARBL/*EUS
rationalist	RAGS/HR*EUS
rationality	RARBL/TEU
rationalization	RARBL/SA*EUGS
rationalization	RAGS/SA*EUGS
rationalize	RARBL/AOEUZ
rationalize	RAGS/HRAOEUZ
rationally	RARBL/HREU
rationally	RAGS/HREU
raunchiness	RAUFRPBLG/KH*EUPBS
raunchiness	RAUPB/KH*EUPBS
ravage	RA*FPBLG
RBI (runs batted in)	R-RBGS/PW*EU
RCA (Radio Corporation of America)	R-RBGS/KRA*
RDR (Registered Diplomate Reporter)	R-RBGS/TK*R
re (as wd)	R*E
re:	REFRPLT
readiness	RED/TK*EUPBS
Reagan (as wd)	RAEU/TKPWAPB, RE/TKPWAPB
Reagan Administration	R*ERGS
reagent	RE/AGT
real (as wd)	RAEL
real estate	RA*ELS
real estate agent	RA*ELGT
reality	RAELT
realization	RAELGS
realize	RAELZ
really	RA*EL
realtime	RA*ELT
rear (as wd)	RAOER
rear end	RAOERPBD
rear-end	RAO*ERPBD
rearraignment(s)	RE/AEURPBG/-PLT(S)
rearrange	RE/ARPBG
rearrangement(s)	RE/ARPBG/-PLT(S)
re-ask	RE/SK-
re-asked	RE/SK-D
re-asking	RE/SK-G
re-asks	RE/SK-S
reason(s)	R-PB(S)
reasonable (as wd)	R-PBL, R-PB/-BL
reasonable care	R-BG
reasonable certainty	RERPBT
reasonable doubt	R-PBLD
reasonableness	R-PBL/*PBS
reasonableness	R-PB/-BL/*PBS
reasonably	R-PBL/HREU
reasonably	R-PB/PWHREU
reasoned	R-PBD
reasoning	R-PBG
reauthorize	RE/THORZ
rebel	REBL
rebellion	REBL/KWROPB
rebellious	REBL/KWROUS
recall	RAUL
recapitalization	RE/KAPT/SA*EUGS
recapitulate	RE/KPEUFP/HRAEUT
recapitulation	RE/KPEUFP/HRAEUGS
receivable	SEFBL
receive	RE/SAO*EF
receive(d) (as wd)	SEF(/-D)
received in evidence	STPH*EFD, STPHEFD
received in evidence	S*EFD/TPH*EFD
received in evidence	SEFD/TPHEFD
receiver	SEFR
receivership	SEFR/SHEUP
recess (as wd)	RE/SESZ
(Recess.)	R*ESZ
reclaimant	RE/KHRAEUPLT
recognition	REBG/TPHEUGS
recognizable	REBG/TPHAOEUZ/-BL
recognizably	REBG/TPHAOEUZ/PWHREU

recognizance	RE/KOG/SA*PBS	redistribute	RE/TKREUBT
recognize	REBG/TPHAOEUZ	redistribution	RE/TKREUBGS
recognizee	REBG/TPHAOEU/SAO*E	redo	RE/TKO
recognizor	REBG/TPHAOEU/SO*R	reduction	R*UBGS
re-collect	RE/H-F/KHREBGT	redundancy	RE/TKUPBD/SEU
recollect	REBGT	reeducate	RE/EGT
recollection	R*EBGS	reeducation	RE/EGS
recommend(s)	REPLD(Z)	reelect	RE/HREBGT
recommendation	REPLGS	reelection	RE/HR*EBGS
recommendation	REPLD/TKAEUGS	reemployment	RE/PHROEUPLT
reconcilable	REBG/SAOEUBL	reenter(s)	RE/SPWR-(S)
reconcilable	REBG/SAOEUL/-BL	reentered	RE/SPWR-D
reconcilably	REBG/SAOEUL/PWHREU	reentering	RE/SPWR-G
reconcile	REBG/SAOEUL	reentry	RE/SPWREU
reconcilement	REBG/SAOEUL/-PLT	reestablish	RE/PWHREURB
reconciliate	REBG/SEULT	reevaluate	RE/*EFLT
reconciliate	REBG/SEUL/KWRAEUT	reevaluation	RE/*EFLGS
reconciliation	REBG/SEULGS	re-examination	RE/KP-GS
reconciliation	REBG/SEUL/KWRAEUGS	re-examination	RE/KP-PLGS
reconciliatory	REBG/SEUL/TOEUR	re-examine(s)	RE/KP-PL(S)
recondition(s)	RE/K-PB(S)	re-examined	RE/KP-PLD
reconditioned	RE/K-PBD	re-examining	RE/KP-PLG
reconditioning	RE/K-PBG	reference	REFRPBS
reconnect	RE/KEBGT	referendum	REFRPB/TKUPL
reconsider(s)	RE/K-R(S)	referendum	REFRPBD/UPL
reconsideration	RE/K-RGS	referent	REFRPBT
reconsidered	RE/K-RD	referral	REFRL
reconsidering	RE/K-RG	referred *(as wd)*	REFR/-D
reconstitute	RE/TAOUT	referred to	REFRTD
reconstruct	RE/KRUBGT	referring *(as wd)*	REFR/-G
reconstruction	RE/KR*UBGS	referring to	REFRGT
reconstructive	RE/KRUBGT/*EUF	refinance	RE/TP-PBS
record(s)	RORD(Z)	reforest	RE/TPO*RS
recordation	RORD/TKAEUGS	reform(s)	R-FRPL(S)
recorder(s)	RORD/ER(S)	reformation	R-FRPLGS
recordkeeping	RORD/KAOEP/-G	reformation	REFR/PHAEUGS
recoupable	RE/KAOUPBL	reformation	R-FRPL/PHAEUGS
recoupable	RE/KOUPBL	reformatory	R-FRPL/TOEUR
recreate	RE/KRAET	reformed	R-FRPLD
re-create	RE/H-F/KRAET	reformer(s)	R-FRPL/ER(S)
recreation	RE/KRAEGS	reforming	R-FRPLG
re-creation	RE/H-F/KRAEGS	refractoriness	RE/TPRABG/TO*EURPBS
recreation	REBG/RAEUGS	refractoriness	RE/TPRABG/TR*EUPBS
recreational	RE/KRAEGS/TPHAL	refractoriness	RE/TPRABGT/R*EUPBS
recreational	REBG/RAEUGS/TPHAL	refresh *(as wd)*	RE/TPRERB
recriminate	RE/KREUPLT	refresh her memory	TPRERPL
recrimination	RE/KREUPLGS	refresh her recollection	TPRERBGS
recross *(as wd)*	RE/KROSZ	refresh his memory	TPREURPL
recross examination	R-BGS	refresh his recollection	TPREURBGS
RECROSS EXAMINATION *(cap & center)*		refresh my memory	TPRAOEURPL
	R-BGS/R-BGS	refresh my recollection	TPRAOEURBGS
red *(as wd)*	RED	refresh our memory	TPROURPL
red light(s)	R-LT(S)	refresh our recollection	TPROURBGS
redelivery	RE/TKHR*EUF/REU	refresh your memory	TPRURPL
redelivery	RE/TKHR*EUFR/REU	refresh your recollection	TPRURBGS
redemise	RE/TKPHAOEUZ	regard(s)	RARD(Z)
redevelop	RE/TKWOP	regardless	RARD/HRES
redevelopment	RE/TKWOPLT	registration	REGS
redevelopment	RE/TKWOP/-PLT	regular	REG
redirect *(as wd)*	RE/TKREBGT	regularity	REG/TEU
redirect examination	R-D	regularly	REG/HREU
REDIRECT EXAMINATION *(cap & center)*		regulatory	REG/TOEUR
	R-D/R-D	rehabilitant	RE/HABL/TAPBT

rehabilitate	RE/HABLT	renewal	RE/TPHUL
rehabilitation	RE/HABLGS	reopen	RE/OEP
rehabilitative	RE/HABLT/*EUF	reorganization	RE/ORGS
rehabilitator	RE/HABLT/TOR	reorganize	RE/ORG
rehearing	RE/HAERG	rephrase *(as wd)*	RE/TPRAEUZ
reindict	RE/TKAO*EUT	rephrase the question	R-FRGS
reindictment	RE/EUPB/ TKAOEUT/-PLT(S)	report	RORT
		reportable	RORT/-BL
reindictment	RE/TKAO*EUPLT	reportedly	RORT/TKHREU
reindictment	RE/TKAOEUPLT	reporter(s)	RORT/ER(S)
reindictment	RE/TKAO*EUT/-PLT	reposition	RE/POGS
reinjure	RE/SKWREUR	repossess	RE/PESZ
reinoculation	RE/TPHOBG/HRAEUGS	repossession	RE/PEGS
reinstatement	RE/EUPB/STAEUPLT	re-present	RE/H-F/PREPBT
reinstitute	RE/EUPB/STAOUT	represent	REPT
reinstitute	RE/EUPBS/TAOUT	representation	REPGS
reinstitute	RE/STAOUT	representation	REPT/TAEUGS
reinsurance	RE/STPHURPBS	representative	REPT/T*EUF
reinsure	RE/STPHUR	reprimand(s)	REP/PHAPBD(Z)
reinvest	RE/TPH*FS	reproduce	RE/PRAOUS
REIT *(real estate investment trust)*		reproduction	RE/PR*UBGS
	R-RBGS/*ERBGS/*EUT	reproductive	RE/PRUBGT/*EUF
reiterate	RE/EUT/RAEUT	reprogram	RE/PRAPL
reiteration	RE/EUT/RAEUGS	reprove	RE/PRO*F
relate	RELT	republican	RE/PUBL/KAPB
relatedly	RELT/TKHREU	Republican	R*E/PUBL/KAPB
relation	RELGS	republication	RE/PUBL/KAEUGS
relational	RELGS/TPHAL	request(s)	KW-(S)
relationship	RELGS/SHEUP	requested	KW-D
relativity	REL/T*EUFT	requester(s)	KW-R(S)
religion	HREUPBLG	requesting	KW-G
religions	HREUPBLG/-S	requestor	KW-/TOR
religious	HREUPBLGS	require	RAOEUR
religiously	HREUPBLGS/HREU	requirement	RAOEURPLT
REM *(rapid eye movement)* R*EPL		resin	REZ/-PB
remark	RARBG	resolve	RE/SO*F
remarkable	RARBG/-BL	respect(s)	R-PT(S)
remarkably	RARBG/PWHREU	respectabilities	R-PT/-BLTS
remarriage	RE/PHAEURPBLG	respectability	R-PT/-BLT
remember	REB	respectable	R-PT/-BL
remember	RE/PHEB	respectably	R-PT/PWHREU
remembrance	REB/RAPBS	respected	R-PTD
remembrance	REB/PWRAPBS	respecter(s)	R-PT/ER(S)
remit	REPLT	respectful	R-PT/-FL
remittal	REPLT/TAL	respectfully	R-PT/TPHREU
remittance	REPLT/TAPBS	respecting	R-PT/-G
remittee	REPLT/TAOE	respective	R-PT/*EUF
remittence	REPLT/EPBS	respectively	R-PT/*EUF/HREU
remittence	REPLT/TEPBS	respond(s)	SPOPBD(Z)
remittent	REPLT/EPBT	respondeat	SPOPBD/KWRAT
remittent	REPLT/TEPBT	respondent *(as wd)*	SPOPBT
remitter(s)	REPLT/ER(S)	respondent *(as wd)*	SPOPBD/EPBT
removable	RE/PHO*FBL	Respondent's Exhibit	R-PBGS
removal	RE/PHO*FL	Respondent's Exhibit No.	R*PBGS
remove	RE/PHO*F	respondentia	SPOPB/TKEPB/SHA
remover	RE/PHO*FR	responder(s)	SPOPBD/ER(S)
rendezvous	RAUPBD/SRAOU	response	SPOPBS
rendezvous	ROPBD/SRAOU	responsibilities	SPOPBLT/-S
rendezvous	RAUPB/SRAOU	responsibilities	SPOPBS/-BLTS
renegotiate	RE/TKPWOERBT	responsibility	SPOPBLT
renegotiation	RE/TKPWOERBGS	responsibility	SPOPBS/-BLT
renew	RE/TPHU	responsible	SPOPBL
renewable	RE/TPHUBL	responsible	SPOPBS/-BL

responsibly	SPOEPBL	rink	R*EUPBG
responsibly	SPOPBS/PWHREU	RIP *(rest in peace)*	R-RBGS/*EUP
responsive	SPOPBS/*EUF	riskiness	REUS/K*EUPBS
responsively	SPOPBS/*EUF/HREU	rivet	R*EUFT
responsiveness	SPOPBS/*EUFPBS	riveter	R*EUFT/ER
responsiveness	SPOPBS/*EUF/*PBS	RMR *(Registered Merit Reporter)*	
restatement	RE/STAEUPLT		R-RBGS/PH*R
restroom	R*ERPL	R.N. *(registered nurse)*	R*PB
resubmit	RE/SPHEUT	RNA *(ribonucleic acid)*	R-RBGS/TPHA*
result	RULT	Robert	RO*BT, ROBT
resultant	RULT/TAPBT	Roberts	RO*BTS, ROBTS
rethink	RE/THEU	rock 'n' roll	ROBG/-PB/ROL
retribution	RET/PWAOUGS	rock 'n' roll	ROBG/TPH-/ROL
retrovert	RET/RO*EFRT	rocket	ROBGT
return	RURPB	rocketry	ROBGT/REU
returnable	RURPB/-BL	ROM *(read-only memory)*	RO*PL
revaluate	R*EFLT	Ronald	RO*PBLD
revaluation	R*EFLGS	roominess	RAO/PH*EUPBS
revalue	RE/SRAL	roominess	RAOPL/PH*EUPBS
revenge	RE/SREPBG	rosin	ROZ/-PB
reverence	R*EFRPBS	rosiness	ROE/S*EUPBS
reverend(s)	R*EFRPBD(Z)	rosiness	ROEZ/S*EUPBS
reverent	R*EFRPBT	ROTC *(Reserve Officers Training Corps)*	
revolver	RO*FRL		ROT/KR*RBGS
rewrite	RE/WREU	ROTC	ROT/SEU
rewritten	RE/WREUPB	rowdiness	ROU/TK*EUPBS
rewritten	RE/WREU/-PB	rowdiness	ROUD/TK*EUPBS
rewrote	RE/WRO	royal	ROEUL
RFD *(rural free delivery)*	R-RBGS/TP*D	royalty	ROEUL/TEU
RFP *(request for proposal)*	R-RBGS/TP*P	RPR *(Registered Professional Reporter)*	
Rh *(Rhesus [factor])*	RAEUFP		R-RBGS/P*R
Rh factor	RAEUFP/TPABG/TOR	RSVP *(repondez s'il vous plait)*	
Rh-negative	RAEUFP/TPHEG/T*EUF		R-RBGS/S*RBGS/SR*P
Rh-positive	RAEUFP/POS/T*EUF	RTF *(rich text format)*	R-RBGS/T*F
Rh-positive	RAEUFP/POZ/T*EUF	RTF/CRE *(rich text format/court reporter extensions)*	
Rhode Island	R*EU/R*EU, REUFPLT		R-RBGS/T*F/SHR-RB/
Rhode Island	ROED/AO*EULD		KR*RBGS/R*E
Rhode Island	ROED/AOEULD	RTF/CRE	R-RBGS/T*F/SHR-RB/
Richard(s)	REUFPD(Z)		KR-RBGS/R*E
rickets	REUBGTS, REUBGT/-S	ruddiness	RUD/TK*EUPBS
		rudimentariness	RAOUD/-PLT/R*EUPBS
rickety	REUBGT/TEU	rudimentariness	RAOUD/-PLT/
right *(as wd)*	RAOEUGT		TA*EURPBS
right arm	R*RPL	rule(s) *(as wd)*	RAOUL(/-S)
right fender(s)	R*FPBD(Z)	rules and regulations	R*EGZ
right foot	R*FT	rumple	RUFRPL
right hand *(j+n)*	RAOEUGT/HAPBD	Russian	RUGS
right-hand *(j)*	R*PBD	RV *(recreational vehicle)*	R*F
right-handed *(j)*	R*PBD/-D	Rwanda	WRAPB/TKA
right-hand lane	R*PBLD	Rwandan	WRAPB/TKAPB
right-hand side	R*PBDZ	Rx *(recipe x/prescription)*	R*BGS
right-hand turn	R*PBTD		
right lane	R*L		
right leg	R*LG		
right of way	RAEGT		
right side	R*DZ		
right to remain silent	R*RS		
right turn	R*T		
rigid	REUPBLGD		
rigidity	REUPBLGD/TEU		
rigidly	REUPBLGD/HREU		
rigidness	REUPBLGD/*PBS		
rigor mortis	REUG/PHORTS		

sabbatical	SPWAT/KAL
sacrilege	SABG/HREPBLG
sacrilege	SABG/HREUPBLG
sacrilegious	SABG/HREPBLG/OUS
sacrilegious	SABG/HREUPBLG/OUS
safari	STPA/RAOE
safari	STPAR/RAOE
safflower	SA/TPHRO*UR
safflower	SA/TPHROUR
Saint Louis	SAEUPBT/HRAOUS
saintliness	SAEUPBT/HR*EUPBS
salacious	SHRAEURBS
salaciously	SHRAEURBS/HREU
salaciousness	SHRAEURBS/*PBS
salami	SHRA/PHAOE
sale *(as wd)*	SAEL
sale of a controlled substance	SAEFBGS
sale of a weapon	SAEFP
sale of cocaine	SAEFBG
sale of crack cocaine	SAEFRBG
sale of marijuana	SAEFRPL
salesclerk	SKHRERBG
salesgirl	STKPWEURL
saleslady	SHRAEU/TKEU
saleslady	SHRAEUD/TKEU
salesman	SPHAPB
salesmanship	SPHAPB/SHEUP
salesmen	SPHEPB
salespeople	SPAOEPL, SAELS/PAOEPL
salesperson	SPERPB, SAELS/PERPB
saleswoman	SWOPL, SAELS/WOPL
saleswomen	SW*EUPL, SAELS/WEUPL
saliva	SHRAOEU/SRA
salon	SHROPB
saloon	SHRAOPB
salute	SHRAOUT
salvation *(as wd)*	SAL/SRAEUGS
Salvation Army	SA*ERPL
SAM *(surface-to-air missile)*	S-RBGS/A*PL
Samantha	SPHA*PBT/THA
Samaria *(Palestine)*	SPHAEUR/KWRA
Samarian	SPHAEUR/KWRAPB
Samarian	SPHAEURPB
samaritan	SPHAEUR/TAPB
samaritan	SPHAR/TAPB
Samaritan	SPHA*EUR/TAPB
Samaritan	SPHA*R/TAPB
same *(as wd)*	SAEUPL
same objection	SAO*BGS
same or similar circumstance	SAEURBG
same or similar circumstances	SAEURBGZ, SAEURBG/-S
Samoa	SPHOE/WA
Samoan	SPHOE/WAPB
sample	SAFRPL
San Diego	SAPB/TKAEU/TKPWOE
San Francisco	STPO
San Salvador	SAPB/SAL/TKOR
sanatorium	SAPB/TOEURPL
sandiness	SAPB/TK*EUPBS
S&L *(savings & loan)*	S-RBGS/SKP*L
S&L	STPH*L
S&P *(Standard and Poor's)*	S-RBGS/SKP*P
S&P	STPH*P
sanitariness	SAPB/TA*EURPBS
sanitarium	SAPB/TAEURPL
sanitization	SAPBT/SA*EUGS
sank	SA*PBG
Santa Claus	SKHRAUZ
Santa Claus	SAPBT/KHRAUZ
Santa Cruz	SAPBT/KRAOUZ
Santa Fe	SAPBT/TPAEU
Santo Domingo	SAPBT/TKPHEUPB/TKPWOE
SAR *(search and rescue)*	S-RBGS/A*R
SARS *(severe acute respiratory syndrome)*	S-RBGS/A*RS
SARS	S-RBGS/A*RBGS/R*S
SARS	SA*RS
SASE *(self-addressed stamped envelope)*	S-RBGS/A*RBGS/S*E
SAT *(Scholastic Aptitude Test)*	S-RBGS/A*T
SAT	SA*T
satellite	SAT/HRAOEUT
satiric	SA/TAOERBG
satiric	SA/TEURBG
satisfaction	STPA*BGS
satisfactorily	STPOEUR/HREU
satisfactoriness	STPO*EURPBS
satisfactoriness	STPOEUR/*PBS
satisfactory	STPOEUR
satisfy	STPAOEU
Saturday(s) *(as wd)*	SATD(Z), SARD(Z)
Saturday night	SAOEUPBT
Saturday night	STPHAOEUGT
sauciness	SAU/S*EUPBS
sauciness	SAUS/S*EUPBS
Saudi Arabia	SAUD/RAEUB/KWRA
Saudi Arabian	SAUD/RAEUB/KWRAPB
savage	SA*FPBLG
savagely	SA*FPBLG/HREU
savagery	SA*FPBLG/REU
savings *(as wd)*	SA*EUF/-GS
savings account	SAEUBGT
savings and loan	SHROEPB
savings and loan association	SHROEPBGS
savoriness	SA*EUF/R*EUPBS
savoriness	SAEU/SRO*EURPBS
says	SEZ, SAEUS

SBA *(Small Business Administration)*		season(s)	S-PB(S)
	S-RBGS/PWA*	seasonable	S-PB/-BL
scaliness	SKAEU/HR*EUPBS	seasonably	S-PB/PWHREU
scaliness	SKAEUL/HR*EUPBS	seasonal	S-PBL
scantiness	SKAPB/T*EUPBS	seasoned	S-PBD
scarlet	SKARLT	seasoning	S-PBG
Scarlet	SKA*RLT	seat *(as wd)*	SAOET
scatterbrained	SKAT/ER/PWRAEUPBD	seat belt	SPWELT
scavenge	SKA*FPBG	seaworthiness	SAE/WOR/TH*EUPBS
scavenge	SKA*F/EPBG	SEC *(Securities and Exchange Commission)*	
scavenger(s)	SKA*FPBG/ER(S)		S-RBGS/*EBG
scavenger(s)	SKA*F/EPBG/ER(S)	second(s) *(as wd)*	SEBGD(Z)
scenario	STPHAEUR/KWROE	Second	S*EBGD
scenario	STPHAR/KWROE	second degree	S*D
scene *(as wd)*	SAEPB	second-degree	S-D
scene of that accident	STPHABGS	second-degree murder	S-PLD
scene of the accident	STPHEBGS	Second World War	SEBGD/WORLD/WAR
scene of this accident	STPHEUBGS	secondarily	SEBG/TKAEUR/HREU
schilling	SH*EULG	secondary	SEBG/TKAEUR
schlemiel	SHRE/PHAOEL	secondary	SEBGD/TKAEUR
schmaltz	SPHAULTS, SPHALTS	secondhand	SEBGD/HAPBD
schmaltzy	SPHALT/S*EU, SPHALT/SEU	secondly	SEBGD/HREU
		secrecy	SKRET/SEU
schmaltzy	SPHAULT/S*EU, SPHAULT/SEU	secret	SKRET
		secretarial	SEBG/TAEURL
scholastic	SKHRA*S/EUBG	secretary	SEBG/TAEUR
scholastically	SKHRA*S/KHREU	Secretary	S*EBG/TAEUR
school *(as wd)*	SKAOL	secretive	SKRET/*EUF
school board(s)	SKAORD(Z)	secretively	SKRET/*EUF/HREU
school district	SKEUBGT	secretly	SKRET/HREU
schoolboy	SKOEU	secure	SKUR
schoolgirl	SKEURL	securely	SKUR/HREU
schoolhouse	SKOUS	securement	SKURPLT
schoolteacher	SKAOERFP	securities	SKURTS, SKURT/-S
schoolwork	SKAORBG	security	SKUR/TEU
schoolyard(s)	SKARD(Z)	sedentariness	SED/SPWA*EURPBS
scientific	SAOEUPB/TEUFBG	segregate	SEG/TKPWAEUT
scientifically	SAOEUPB/TEUFBG/HREU	segregation	SEG/TKPWAEUGS
scissors	SEUZ/SO*RS	segregationist	SEG/TKPWAEUGS/*EUS
scissors	SEUZ/SORS	seismographic(s)	SAOEUS/PHO/ TKPWRAFBG(/-S)
S corporation	S-RBGS/KORPGS		
scratchiness	SKRAFP/KH*EUPBS	seismographic(s)	SAOEUZ/PHO/ TKPWRAFBG(/-S)
scrawniness	SKRAU/TPH*EUPBS		
scrawniness	SKRAUPB/TPH*EUPBS	select	SHREBGT
screw *(as wd)*	SKRAOU	selection	SHR*EBGS
screwup	SKR*UP	selective	SHREBGT/*EUF
screw up	SKRUP	selectively	SHREBGT/*EUF/HREU
scrounge	SKROUPBG	selectivity	SHREBGT/*EUFT
SCSI *(small computer system interface)*		selectivity	SHREBG/T*EUFT
	SKUZ/SAOE	selector	SHREBG/TOR
SCSI	SKUZ/SAO*E	selector	SHREBGT/TOR
sculpt	SKUPT	self *(as wd)*	SEL/-F
sculptor	SKUP/TOR	self- *(pre w/hyphen)*	SEFL
sculptural	SKUP/KHURL	self-advancement	SEFL/SRAPBS/-PLT
sculpture(s)	SKUP/KHUR(S)	self-analysis	SEFL/APBL/SEUS
sculptured	SKUP/KHURD	self-confidence	SEFL/K-FD
sculpturing	SKUP/KHURG	self-confident	SEFL/K-FT
SDS *(Students for a Democratic Society)*		self-conscious	SEFL/KORBS
	S-RBGS/TK*S	self-consciously	SEFL/KORBS/HREU
seance	SAEUPBS	self-consciousness	SEFL/KORBS/*PBS
search *(as wd)*	S*ERPBLG, SER/-FP	self-contradiction	SEFL/KR*GS
search and seizure	S-FPZ	self-control	SEFL/KROL
search warrant	SWARPBT	self-defense	STKEFS

self-defense	SEFL/TKEFPBS
self-defense	SEFL/TKEFS
self-delusion	SEFL/TKHRAOUGS
self-destruct	SEFL/TKRUBGT
self-destruction	SEFL/TKR*UBGS
self-destructive	SEFL/TKRUBGT/*EUF
self-determination	SEFL/TKERPLGS
self-determination	SEFL/TKERPL/TPHAEUGS
self-diagnosis	SEFL/TKAOEUGS
self-educated	SEFL/EGT/-D
self-employment	SEFL/PHROEUPLT
self-evident	SEFL/*EFT
self-examination	SEFL/KP-GS
self-examination	SEFL/KP-PLGS
self-government	SEFL/TKPWO*FT
self-government	SEFL/TKPWOFT
self-help	SEFL/H*EP
self-important	SEFL/PORPBT
self-improvement	SEFL/EUPL/PRO*FPLT
self-incriminate	SKREUPLT
self-incriminate	SEFL/EUPB/KREUPLT
self-incriminating	SKREUPLT/-G
self-incriminating	SEFL/EUPB/KREUPLT/-G
self-incrimination	SKREUPLGS
self-incrimination	SEFL/EUPB/KREUPLGS
self-indulgence	SEFL/EUPB/TKULG/EPBS
self-indulgent	SEFL/EUPB/TKULG/EPBT
self-insurance	SEFL/STPHURPBS
self-insure	SEFL/STPHUR
self-interest	SEFL/SPWR*ES
self-limiting	SEFL/HREUPLT/-G
self-possessed	SEFL/PESZ/-D
self-realization	SEFL/RAELGS
self-respect	SEFL/R-PT
self-satisfaction	SEFL/STPA*BGS
self-satisfied	SEFL/STPAOEU/-D
self-service	SEFL/S-FS
self-slaughter	SEFL/SHRAUR
self-sufficient	SEFL/SUF
self-supporting	SEFL/SPO*RT/-G
self-sustaining	SEFL/STAEPBG
self-sustaining	SEFL/STAEPB/-G
semantic	SPHAPBT/EUBG
semester(s)	SPH*ES/ER(S)
semiconductor	SEPL/KUBG/TOR
semiconductor	SEPL/KUBGT/TOR
semiconscious	SEPL/KORBS
semiconsciousness	SEPL/KORBS/*PBS
semiprivate	SEPL/PRAO*EUFT
semiserious	SEPL/SAOERS
Semitic	SPHEUT/EUBG
senate	STPHAT
Senate	STPHA*T
senator	STPHART
senator	STPHAT/TOR
Senator	STPHA*RT
Senator	STPHA*T/TOR
senatorial	STPHAT/TOEURL
senile	STPHAOEUL
senility	STPHEUL/TEU
senior (as wd)	SAOEPB/KWROR
senior high school	SRAOL
Senior High School	SRAO*L
sensitivity	SEPBS/T*EUFT
sentence	STPH-PBS
sentenced	STPH-PBD
sentences	STPH-PBSZ, STPH-PBS(/-S)
sentencing	STPH-PBG
separate (n&j)	SPRAT
separate (v)	SPRAEUT
separately	SPRAT/HREU
separation (as wd)	SPRAEUGS
separation agreement	SPRAEUPLT
separatist	SPRAT/*EUS
separator	SPRAEUT/TOR
September	SEPT
sequel	SKWEL
sequelize	SKWEL/AOEUZ
sequence	SKWEPBS
sequential	SKWEPB/-RBL
sequentially	SKWEPB/-RBL/HREU
sequester(s)	SKW*ES/ER(S)
sequestered	SKW*ES/ERD
sequestering	SKW*ES/ERG
sequestrate	SKWES/TRAEUT
sequestrate	SKW*ES/RAEUT
sequestration	SKWES/TRAEUGS
sequestration	SKW*ES/RAEUGS
sergeant(s)	S-GT(S)
sergeant(s)	SARGT(/-S)
Sergeant	K-P/S-GT
Sergeant	SA*RGT
sergeant-at-arms	SARGT/AT/ARPL/-S
sergeant-at-arms	S-GT/AT/ARPL/-S
series	SAOERZ
serious (as wd)	SAOERS
serious bodily harm	SPWORPL
serious bodily injury	SPWOPBLG
seriously	SAOERS/HREU
seriousness	SAOERS/*PBS
serum	SAOERPL
service	S-FS
serviceability	S-FS/-BLT
serviceable	S-FS/-BL
serviceman	S-FS/PHAPB
servicemen	S-FS/PHEPB
servicewoman	S-FS/WOPL
servicewomen	S-FS/WEUPL
settlement (as wd)	SET/HR-PLT
settlement conference	ST-FRPBS
seventh	S*EFPBT
seventy	S*EFT
several	S*EFRL
severance	S*EFRPBS
sewage	SAOUPBLG
sewer	SAOUR
sewerage	SAOURPBLG
sex (as wd)	SEBGS
sex abuse	SWABS
sex abuse syndrome	SWABSZ
sex discrimination	SWAPLGS
sexiness	SEBG/S*EUPBS
sexiness	SEBGS/S*EUPBS
sexual (as wd)	SWAUL
sexual abuse	SWAUBS

© 2004 StenEd® Briefs & Phrases (Excerpted from StenEd's Realtime Professional Dictionary)

sexual abuse syndrome	SWAUBSZ	she just want	SHEFPT
sexual and physical abuse	SWAUFBS	she just wanted	SHEFPTD
sexual assault	SWAULT	she just wants	SHEFPTS
sexual conduct	SWAUBGT	she knows	SH*EPBS
sexual discrimination	SWAUPLGS	she recalled	SHERLD
sexual harassment	SWAURPLT	she recalls	SHERLS
sexual intercourse	SWAOURS	she recollected	SHERBGD
sexual misconduct	SWAUPBLGT	she recollects	SHERBGS
sexuality	SWAUL/TEU	she remembered	SHERPLD
sexually *(as wd)*	SWAEUL	she remembers	SHERPLS
sexually abuse	SWAEUBS	she said	SHEBS
sexually abused	SWAEUBS/-D	she say	SHEBZ
sexually and physical abuse	SWAEUFBS	she says	SHEBSZ
		she shall	SHERB
sexually and physically abused	SWAEUFBS/-D	she should	SHERBD
		she think	SHEPBG
sexually assault	SWAEULT	she thinks	SHEPBGS
sexually discriminate	SWAEUPLGT	she understand	SHEPBDZ
sexually harass	SWAEURSZ	she understands	SHEPBDZ/-S
sexually transmitted disease	SWAEUTD, SWAEUTDZ	she understood	SH*EPBDZ
		she want	SHEPT
Sgt.	S*GT	she wanted	SHEPTD
shabbiness	SHAB/PW*EUPBS	she wants	SHEPTS
shadiness	SHAEU/TK*EUPBS	she was	SHEFS
shadiness	SHAEUD/TK*EUPBS	she were	SHERP
shagginess	SHAG/TKPW*EUPBS	she were the	SHERPT
shakiness	SHAEU/K*EUPBS	she will	SHE/HR-
shakiness	SHAEUBG/K*EUPBS	she would	SHELD
shall *(as wd)*	SHAL	sheriff(s) *(as wd)*	SHR-F(S)
shall be	SH-B	sheriff's department	SHR-FD
shall be the	SH-BT	sheriff's office	SHRAUFS
shall believe	SH-BL	Shiite	SHAOEUT
shall feel	SH-FL	shilling	SHEULG
shall have	SH-F	shininess	SHAOEU/TPH*EUPBS
shall have been	SH-FB	shininess	SHAOEUPB/TPH*EUPBS
shall have had	SH-FD	shipment	SHEUPLT
shall recall	SH-RL	shittiness	SHEUT/T*EUPBS
shall recollect	SH-RBG	shoes	SHAOUZ
shall remember	SH-RPL	shop(ping) *(as wd)*	SHOP(/-G)
shall understand	SH-PBDZ	shoplift	SHREUFT
shall want	SH-PT	shoplifter(s)	SHREUFRT(/-S)
shank	SHA*PBG	shoplifter(s)	SHREUFT/ER(S)
shapeliness	SHAEU/PHR*EUPBS	shopping center	SHOPGS
shapeliness	SHAEUP/HR*EUPBS	shortchange	SHORT/KHAEUPBG
shareholder(s)	SHAEURLD(Z)	shorthand	SHAPBD
she *(as wd)*	SHE	shortsighted	SHORT/SAOEUGTD
she'd	SHAO*ED	short-term	SHERPL
she'll	SHAO*EL	shotgun	SH-G
she's	SHAO*ES	should *(as wd)*	SHOULD
she been	SHEB	should've	SHO*UF
she believe	SHEBL	should be	SHOUB
she believed	SHEBLD	should be the	SHOUBT
she believes	SHEBLS	should believe	SHOUBL
she can	SHEBG	should feel	SHOUFL
she cannot	SHEBG/TPHOT	should find	SHOUFPBD
she can't	SHE/K-PBT	should go	SHOUG
she can't	SHEBG/-PBT	should have	SHOUF
she could	SHEBGD	should have been	SHOUFB
she ever	SHEFR	should have been the	SHOUFBT
she feels	SHEFLS	should have believed	SHOUFBLD
she felt	SHEFLT	should have had	SHOUFD
she has	SHEZ	should have recalled	SHOUFRLD
she is	SHES	should have recollected	SHOUFRBGD

should have remembered	SHOUFRPLD
should have the	SHOUFT
should have wanted	SHOUFPTD
shouldn't	SHO*PBT
should recall	SHOURL
should recollect	SHOURBG
should remember	SHOURPL
should understand	SHOUPBDZ
should want	SHOUPT
shower	SHO*UR
showiness	SHOE/W*EUPBS
shrank	SHRA*PBG
shrewd	SHRAOUD
shrewder	SHRAOUD/ER
shrewdest	SHRAOUD/*ES
shriller	SHREUL/ER
shrillest	SHREUL/*ES
shrimp	SHREUFRP
shrimp	SHREUPL/-P
shrimper(s)	SHREUFRP/ER(S)
shrimper(s)	SHREUPL/PER(/-S)
shrine	SHRAOEUPB
shrink	SHR*EUPBG
shrinkage	SHR*EUPBG/APBLG
shrinkage	SHR*EUPB/KAPBLG
shroud(s)	SHROUD(Z)
shrub	SHRUB
shrubbery	SHRUB/REU
shrubby	SHRUB/PWEU
shut *(as wd)*	SHUT
shut up	SHUP
sidewalk	SWAUBG
SIDS *(sudden infant death syndrome)*	S-RBGS/*EUDZ
SIDS	SEUDZ
signature	SEUGT
significance	SEUG/KAPBS
significant	SEUG/KAPBT
significantly	SEUG/KAPBT/HREU
signify	SEUG/TPEU
silkiness	SEUL/K*EUPBS
silliness	SEUL/HR*EUPBS
similar	SHRAR
similarity	SHRART
similarity	SHRAR/TEU
similarly	SHRAR/HREU
similitude	SPHEUL/TAOUD
simple	SEUFRPL
simpleminded	SEUFRPL/ PHAOEUPBD/-D
simpler	SEUFRPL/ER
simplest	SEUFRPL/*ES
simpleton	SEUFRPL/TOPB
simplification	SEUFRP/TPEU/KAEUGS
simplify	SEUFRP/TPEU
simultaneous	SPHULT
simultaneously	SPHULT/HREU
sincerely *(as wd)*	SEUPB/SAOER/HREU
Sincerely yours,	SKWROURS
sine die	SAO*EUPB/TKAOEU
sister(s) *(as wd)*	ST-R(S)
sister and brother	STABT
sisters and brothers	STABTS, STABT/-S
sister or brother	STOBT
sisters or brothers	STOBTS, STOBT/-S
sisterhood	ST-R/HAOD
sister-in-law	ST-RPBL
sisters-in-law	ST-RPBLS
sister-in-laws	ST-RPBL/-S
sisterly	ST-R/HREU
situate	SEUFPT
situation	SEUFPGS
six-pack	SPABG
sixty	SEUBGT
sketchiness	SKEFP/KH*EUPBS
skid *(as wd)*	SKEUD
skid mark	SKPHARBG
skimpiness	SKEUFRP/P*EUPBS
skimpiness	SKEUPL/P*EUPBS
skinniness	SKEUPB/TPH*EUPBS
skunk	SK*UPBG
skylight	SKAOEULGT
skyrocket	SKAOEU/ROBGT
slaughter	SHRAUR
sleaziness	SHRAOE/S*EUPBS
sleaziness	SHRAOEZ/*PBS
sleaziness	SHRAOEZ/S*EUPBS
sleepiness	SHRAOE/P*EUPBS
sleepiness	SHRAOEP/P*EUPBS
sliminess	SHRAOEU/PH*EUPBS
sliminess	SHRAOEUPL/PH*EUPBS
slipperiness	SHREUP/R*EUPBS
sloppiness	SHROP/P*EUPBS
slovenliness	SHRO*FPB/HR*EUPBS
slumminess	SHRUPL/PH*EUPBS
slunk	SHR*UPBG
slushiness	SHRURB/SH*EUPBS
s-mail	SPHA*EUL
smeariness	SPHAOE/R*EUPBS
smeariness	SPHAOER/R*EUPBS
smelliness	SPHEL/HR*EUPBS
smoke *(as wd)*	SPHOEBG
smoke detector	SPHEBGT
smokiness	SPHOE/K*EUPBS
smokiness	SPHOEBG/K*EUPBS
smudginess	SPHUPBLG/ SKWR*EUPBS
snail mail	SPHAEUL
snappiness	STPHAP/P*EUPBS
sneakiness	STPHAOE/K*EUPBS
sneakiness	STPHAOEBG/K*EUPBS
snippet	STPHEUPT
snippety	STPHEUPT/TEU
snippiness	STPHEUP/P*EUPBS
snobbiness	STPHOB/PW*EUPBS
snow *(as wd)*	STPHOE
snow and ice	STPHAOEUS
snowball	STPHOEBL
snowfall	STPHOEFL
snowmobile	STPHOE/PHOEBL
so *(as wd)*	SO
so far	SOFR
so far as	SOFRS
so fast	SOFZ
so find	SOFPBD
so forth	SO*FRT

so he believed	SOEBLD	so she say	SHOEBZ
so he believes	SOEBLS	so she says	SHOEBSZ
so he could	SOEBGD	so she should	SHOERBD
so he feels	SOEFLS	so she thinks	SHOEPBGS
so he felt	SOEFLT	so she understand	SHOEPBDZ
so he recalled	SOERLD	so she understands	SHOEPBDZ/-S
so he recalls	SOERLS	so she understood	SHO*EPBDZ
so he recollected	SOERBGD	so she wanted	SHOEPTD
so he remembered	SOERPLD	so she wants	SHOEPTS
so he remembers	SOERPLS	so she was	SHOEFS
so he said	SOEBS	so you believe	SOUBL
so he say	SOEBZ	so you believed	SOUBLD
so he says	SOEBSZ	so you can	SOUBG
so he should	SOERBD	so you could	SOUBGD
so he thinks	SOEPBGS	so you feel	SOUFL
so he understand	SOEPBDZ	so you felt	SOUFLT
so he understands	SOEPBDZ/-S	so you have	SOUF
so he understood	SO*EPBDZ	so you have been	SOUFB
so he wanted	SOEPTD	so you have had	SOUFD
so he wants	SOEPTS	so you have the	SOUFT
so he was	SOEFS	so you recall	SOURL
so I believe	SOEUBL	so you recalled	SOURLD
so I believed	SOEUBLD	so you recollect	SOURBG
so I can	SOEUBG	so you recollected	SOURBGD
so I could	SOEUBGD	so you remember	SOURPL
so I feel	SOEUFL	so you remembered	SOURPLD
so I felt	SOEUFLT	so you said	SOUBS
so I have	SOEUF	so you say	SOUBZ
so I have been	SOEUFB	so you says	SOUBSZ
so I have had	SOEUFD	so you shall	SOURB
so I recall	SOEURL	so you should	SOURBD
so I recalled	SOEURLD	so you think	SOUPBG
so I recollect	SOEURBG	so you think the	SOUPBGT
so I recollected	SOEURBGD	so you want	SOUPT
so I remember	SOEURPL	so you wanted	SOUPTD
so I remembered	SOEURPLD	so you were	SOURP
so I said	SOEUBS	so you were the	SOURPT
so I say	SOEUBZ	soapiness	SOE/P*EUPBS
so I says	SOEUBSZ	soapiness	SOEP/P*EUPBS
so I shall	SOEURB	SOB *(son of a bitch)*	S-RBGS/O*B
so I should	SOEURBD	SOB	SO*B
so I think	SOEUPBG	sobriety	SPWRAOEU/TEU
so I think the	SOEUPBGT	social *(as wd)*	SOERBL
so I understand	SOEUPBDZ	Social Security	S*S
so I understood	SO*EUPBDZ	social work	SOERBG
so I want	SOEUPT	social worker(s)	SOERBG/ER(S)
so I wanted	SOEUPTD	socially	SOERB/HREU
so I was	SOEUFS	societal	SOET/TAL
so long as	SO/HROPBGS	society	SOET
so marked	SPHARBGD	socioeconomic	SOERB/KPHEUBG
so much	SOFP	socioeconomic	SOERB/KWRO/KPHEUBG
so on and so forth	SOPB/SO*FRT	socket	SOBGT
so she believed	SHOEBLD	soft	SOF
so she believes	SHOEBLS	softball	SOFBL
so she could	SHOEBGD	sogginess	SOG/TKPW*EUPBS
so she feels	SHOEFLS	solarium	SHRAEURPL
so she felt	SHOEFLT	sole *(as wd)*	SOEL
so she recalled	SHOERLD	sole and exclusive	SOEBGS
so she recalls	SHOERLS	sole and exclusive judge	SOEPBLG
so she recollected	SHOERBGD	sole and exclusive judges	SOEPBLGS, SOEPBLG/-S
so she remembered	SHOERPLD		
so she remembers	SHOERPLS	sole judge	SOPBLG
so she said	SHOEBS		

sole judges	SOPBLGS, SOPBLG/-S	sonorous	STPHOER/OUS
solemnify	SHREPL/TPHEU/TPEU	sonorously	STPHOR/SHREU
solemnity	SHREPL/TPHEU/TEU	sonorously	STPHOR/OUS/HREU
solemnize	SHREPL/TPHAOEUZ	sonorously	STPHOER/SHREU
solicit	SHREUS/SEUT	sonorously	STPHOER/OUS/HREU
solicitation	SHREUS/TAEUGS	SOP *(standard operating procedure)*	
solicitor	SHREUS/TOR		S-RBGS/O*P
solicitor general	SHREUS/TOR/ SKWREPB	SOP	SO*P
		sophisticate	STP*EUS/KAEUT
Solicitor General	SHR*EUS/TOR/ SKWREPB	sophisticate	STP*EUS/KAT
		sophistication	STP*EUS/KAEUGS
solicitous	SHREUS/TOUS	sophomoric	SOF/PHOERBG
solicitude	SHREUS/TAOUD	sophomoric	SOF/PHORBG
solidify	SHREUD/TPEU	soprano	SPRA/TPHOE
solidity	SHREUD/TEU	SOS *(save our ship)*	S-RBGS/O*S
soliloquist	SHREUL/KW*EUS	SOS	SO*S
soliloquize	SHREUL/KWAOEUZ	sought	SAUT
soliloquy	SHREUL/KWAOE	sourness	SO*URPBS
solitariness	SOL/TA*EURPBS	south *(as wd)*	SO*UT
solution	SHRAOUGS	South Africa	SO*UT/AFR/KA
solvable	SO*FBL	South African	SO*UT/AFR/KAPB
solve	SO*F	South America	SA*/SA*
Somali	SPHA/HRAOE	South America	SO*UT/PHERBG
Somalia	SPHAL/KWRA	South American	SO*UT/PHERPB
Somalian	SPHAL/KWRAPB	southbound	S*B
somatic	SPHAT/EUBG	southbound lane	S*BL
some *(as wd)*	SOPL	southbound traffic	S*BT
somebodies	SPH-BS	South Carolina	S*BG/S*BG
somebody	SPH-B	South Dakota	S*D/S*D
somebody else	SPH-BLS	southeast	SO*ES
somebody else	SPH-B/ELS	Southeast	K-P/SO*ES
someday	STKAEU	southeaster	SO*ES/ER
somehow	SPHOU	southeasterly	SAO*ERL
some of	SPHOF	southeastern	SAO*ERPB
some of the	SPHOFT	southeasterner(s)	SAO*ERPB/ER(S)
someone	SWUPB	Southeasterner(s)	K-P/SAO*ERPB/ER(S)
someone	SPH-PB	southerly	SO*RL, SORL
someone else	SWUPBLS	southern	SO*RPB, SORPB
someone else	SWUPB/ELS	Southern	K-P/SO*RPB, K-P/SORPB
someone else	SPH-PBLS	southerner(s)	SO*RPB/ER(S)
someone else	SPH-PB/ELS	southerner(s)	SORPB/ER(S)
someplace	SPHRAEUS	Southerner(s)	K-P/SO*RPB/ER(S)
something	STHEUPBG	Southerner(s)	K-P/SORPB/ER(S)
something	SPH-G	south side	S*DZ
sometime	STAOEUPL	southernmost	SO*RPB/PHO*ES
sometimes	STAOEUPLS, STAOEUPL/-S	southernmost	SORPB/PHO*ES
		southwest	SWO*ES
somewhat	SWHA	Southwest	K-P/SWO*ES
some what	SOPL/WHA	southwester	SWO*ES/ER
somewhere(s)	SWR-(S)	southwesterly	SW*ERL
some where	SOPL/WR-	southwestern	SW*ERPB
son(s) *(as wd)*	SOPB(/-S)	southwesterner(s)	SW*ERPB/ER(S)
son and daughter	STPHAD	Southwesterner(s)	K-P/SW*ERPB/ER(S)
sons and daughters	STPHADZ	sovereign	SO*FRPB
son or daughter	STPHOD	sovereignty	SO*FRPB/TEU
sons or daughters	STPHODZ	soviet	SO*EFT
son-in-law	SOPBL	Soviet	K-P/SO*EFT
sons-in-law	SOPBLS	space *(as wd)*	SPAEUS
son-in-laws	SOPBL/-S	space shuttle	SPULT
sonata	STPHAT/TA	spank	SPA*PBG
sonority	STPHOR/TEU	SPCA *(Society for the Prevention of Cruelty to Animals)*	
sonority	STPHOER/TEU		S-RBGS/P*RBGS/KRA*
sonorous	STPHOR/OUS	speaker *(as wd)*	SPAOEBG/ER

Speaker of the House	SPHO*US
special *(as wd)*	SPERBL
special circumstance	SPERBG
special circumstances	SPERBGZ, SPERBG/-S
specific	SPEFBG
specifically	SPEFBG/HREU
specification	SPEFBGS
specification	SPEF/KAEUGS
specify	SPEF
speedometer	SPOPLT
speedwriter	SPAOED/WREUR
speedwriter	SPAOED/WREU/ER
speedwriting	SPAOED/WREUG
speedwriting	SPAOED/WREU/-G
spell *(as wd)*	SPEL
spell your first name	SP*UFRPB
spell your first name, please	SP*UFRPBLS
spell your full name	SPUFRPB
spell your full name, please	SPUFRPBLS
spell your last name	SP*URPBL
spell your last name, please	SP*URPBLS
spell your name	SPURPBL
spell your name, please	SPURPBLS
spelunker(s)	SPHR*UPBG/ER(S)
spelunking	SPHR*UPBG/-G
spiciness	SPAOEU/S*EUPBS
spiciness	SPAOEUS/S*EUPBS
spirit	SPAOERT, SPEURT
spite *(as wd)*	SPAOEUT
spite of	SPAOEUF
spite of the	SPAOEUFT
spoken	SPOEPB
spokespeople	SPOEBGS/PAOEPL
spokesperson	SPOEBGS/PERPB
spokeswoman	SPOEBGS/WOPL
spokeswomen	SPOEBGS/WEUPL
sponge	SPOPBG
spongier	SPOPBG/KWRER
spongiest	SPOPBG/KWR*ES
sponginess	SPOPBG/*PBS
spookiness	SPAO/K*EUPBS
spookiness	SPAOBG/K*EUPBS
sporadic	SPRAD/EUBG
sporadically	SPRAD/KHREU
sportswoman	SPORTS/WOPL
spotlight(s)	SP-LT(S)
sprinkle(s)	SPR*EUPBG/-L(S)
sprinkled	SPR*EUPBG/-LD
sprinkler	SPR*EUPBG/HRER
sprinkling	SPR*EUPBG/-LG
sprocket	SPROBGT
spunk	SP*UPBG
spunkier	SP*UPBG/KWRER
spunkiest	SP*UPBG/KWR*ES
spunkiness	SP*UPBG/K*EUPBS
spunkiness	SPUPB/K*EUPBS
spunky	SP*UPBG/KEU
square *(as wd)*	SKWAEUR
square feet	SKWAEUFT
square feet	SKWAOEFT
square foot	SKWAOFT
Sr.	S-R
SRAM *(static random-access memory)*	S-RBGS/R*RBGS/A*PL
SRAM	S-RBGS/RA*PL
S. Rept. *(Senate report)*	S-FPLT/R*EPT
S. Res. *(Senate resolution)*	S-FPLT/REZ
S. Res.	S-FPLT/RES
SRO *(standing room only)*	S-RBGS/R*O
SSA *(Social Security Administration)*	S-RBGS/SA*
SSI *(supplemental security income)*	S-RBGS/S*EU
SSM *(surface-to-surface missile)*	S-RBGS/S*PL
SSN *(Social Security number)*	S-RBGS/S*PB
SSS *(Selective Service System)*	S-RBGS/S*S
SST *(supersonic transport)*	S-RBGS/S*T
St.	ST-FPLT
St. Bernard	ST-FPLT/PWERPBD
St. Louis	ST-FPLT/HRAOUS
St. Valentine	ST-FPLT/SRAL/TAOEUPB
standard *(as wd)*	STARD, STAPB/TKARD
Standard & Poor's	STARD/PH-PBD/PAOR/AOES
standard of care	ST-FBG
standard of living	ST-FLG
standardization	STARD/SA*EUGS
standardize	STARD/AOEUZ
standpoint	STAPT
stank	STA*PBG
starchiness	STA*RPBLG/KH*EUPBS
starchiness	STAR/KH*EUPBS
starlet	STARLT
starlight	STARLGT
starling	STARLG
state *(as wd)*	STAEUT
State *(as wd)*	STA*EUT
state court	STOURT
State Court	STO*URT
state government	STKPWOFT, STKPWO*FT
state of	STAOF
State of	STAO*F
state of mind	STAOFPLD
state of mind	STAEUPLD
state of the	STAOFT
state of the	STAEUFT
state-of-the-art *(j)*	STAO*FRT
state-of-the-art *(j)*	STA*EUFRT
state of the art	STAOFRT
state of the art	STAEUFRT
state of the union	STAOUPB
State of the Union	STAO*UPB
state of war	STAOFR
State Police	STPHREUS
state police officer(s)	STPHREUFR(S)
state police officer(s)	STPHRAUFR(S)
state prison	STPREUZ

state's attorney	STOERPB	stickiness	STEUBG/K*EUPBS
State's Attorney	STO*ERPB	sticky wicket	STEUBG/KEU/WEUBGT
State's Exhibit	ST-BGS	stinginess	STEUPB/SKWR*EUPBS
State's Exhibit No.	ST*BGS	stink	ST*EUPBG
state your full name	STUFRPB, STUFPB	stinker(s)	ST*EUPBG/ER(S)
state your full name and address	STUFRPBDZ	stinkier	ST*EUPBG/KWRER
		stinkiest	ST*EUPBG/KWR*ES
state your full name for the record	STUFRPBD	stock *(as wd)*	STOBG
		stockbroker	STPWROERBG
state your full legal name	STUFRPBL	stock exchange	STEBGS
		stockholder(s)	STHORLD(Z)
state your full legal name for the record	STUFRPBLD	stockholder(s)	STHOERLD(Z)
		stock market	STPHAORBGT
state your legal name	STURPBL	stocks and bonds	STPWOPBDZ
state your legal name for the record	STURPBLD	stoic	STOEUBG
		stoical	STOEUBG/KAL
state your name	STURPB	stoically	STOEUBG/HREU
state your name and address	STURPBDZ	STOL *(short takeoff and landing)*	
			S-RBGS/T*RBGS/O*L
state your name for the record	STURPBD	STOL	S-RBGS/TO*L
		stomach	STUPL
statement(s) *(as wd)*	STAEUPLT(S)	stomachache	STUPL/A*EUBG
statement of fact	STOFT	stomach ache	STUPL/AEUBG
statements of fact	STOFTS	Stonehenge	STOEPB/HEPBG
statement of facts	STOFT/-S	stop *(as wd)*	STOP
Staten Island	STAT/-PB/AO*EULD	stop sign(s)	ST-PB(S)
Staten Island	STAT/-PB/AOEULD	stoplight(s)	ST-LT(S)
statistician	STAT/STEUGS	stoppable	STOPBL
statistician	STATS/TEUGS	storage	STORPBLG, STOERPBLG
statue *(as wd)*	STAFP/KWRAOU, STAT/KHAOU		
		storm *(as wd)*	STORPL
Statue of Liberty	STAFPL	storm warning	STORPBG
statute *(as wd)*	STAFP/KWRAOUT	storm watch	STWAFP
statute *(as wd)*	STAT/KHAOUT	storminess	STOR/PH*EUPBS
statute of limitations	STHREUPLTS	storminess	STORPL/PH*EUPBS
stay *(as wd)*	STAEU	story	STOEUR
stay tuned	STAOUPBD	storybook	STOEUR/PWAOBG
STD *(sexually transmitted disease)*		stouthearted	STOUT/HARTD
	S-RBGS/T*D	stowage	STOEPBLG
steadiness	STED/TK*EUPBS	STP *(dimethoxy-methamphetamine)*	
stealthiness	STEL/TH*EUPBS		S-RBGS/T*P
steer(ing) *(as wd)*	STAOER(/-G)	straightforward	STRAEUGT/TPWARD
steering wheel	STWAOEL	straitjacket	STRAEUT/SKWRABGT
StenEducator	STEPB/ERGT	strange	STRAEUPBG
stenographic	STEPB/TKPWRAFBG	strangely	STRAEUPBG/HREU
stenographically	STEPB/TKPWRAFBG/HREU	strangeness	STRAEUPBG/*PBS
stenoscription	STREUPGS	stranger(s)	STRAEUPBG/ER(S)
stenoscriptioner(s)	STREUPGS/ER(S)	strangest	STRAEUPBG/*ES
stenowriter	STEPB/WREUR	stratospheric	STRAT/STPAOERBG
stenowriter	STEPB/WREU/ER	stratospheric	STRATS/TPAOERBG
stepbrother	STEP/PWROER	street *(as wd)*	STRAOET
stepchildren	STEP/KHEURPB	street light(s)	STR-LT(S)
stepdaughter	STEP/TKAUR	street sign(s)	STR-PB(S)
stepfather	STEP/TPAUR	strength	STR*EPBT
stepmother	STEP/PHOER	strengthen(s)	STR*EPBT/-PB(S)
stepparent	STEP/PAEURPBT	strengthened	STR*EPBT/-PBD
stepparent	STEP/PARPBT	strengthening	STR*EPBT/-PBG
stepping-stone	STEPG/STOEPB	strike *(as wd)*	STRAOEUBG
stepsister(s)	STEP/ST-R(S)	strike that	STRAT
sterling	STERLG	stringiness	STREUPB/TKPW*EUPBS
steward(s)	STAOURD(Z)	stubbiness	STUB/PW*EUPBS
stewardess	STAOURD/ESZ	student	STAOUPBT
stewardship	STAOURD/SHEUP	stuffiness	STUF/TP*EUPBS

stunk	ST*UPBG
stupid	STAOUPD
stupider	STAOUPD/ER
stupidest	STAOUPD/*ES
stupidity	STAOUPD/TEU
sturdiness	STUR/TK*EUPBS
subagent	SUB/AGT
subaverage	SUB/A*FRPBLG
subcentral	SUB/STRAL
subconscious	SUB/KORBS
subconsciously	SUB/KORBS/HREU
subconsciousness	SUB/KORBS/*PBS
subcontract(s)	SKR-T(S)
subcontract(s)	SUB/KR-T(S)
subcontracted	SKR-TD
subcontracted	SUB/KR-TD
subcontractor(s)	SKR-RT(S)
subcontractor(s)	SKR-T/TOR(/-S)
subcontractor(s)	SUB/KR-T/TOR(/-S)
subdivide	SUB/TKWAOEUD
subdivision	SUB/TKWEUGS
subhuman	SUB/HAOUPL
subject	SUPBLGT
subjection	S*UPBLGTS
subjective	SUPBLGT/*EUF
subjectively	SUPBLGT/*EUF/HREU
subjectivism	SUPBLGT/SREUFPL
subjectivity	SUPBLGT/*EUF/TEU
subjectivity	SUPBLGT/*EUFT
sublicense	SUB/HRAOEUPBS
sublimate	SUBL/PHAEUT
sublimation	SUBL/PHAEUGS
submarine	SUB/PHRAOEPB
submission	SPHEUGS
submit	SPHEUT
submortgage	SUB/PHORPBLG
subordinate (j)	SPWORD/TPHAT
subordinate (v)	SPWORD/TPHAEUT
subordination	SPWORD/TPHAEUGS
subparagraph	SUB/PRAF
subpoena(s) (as wd)	S-P(S)
subpoena ad testificandum	S-P/T-FPL
subpoena duces tecum	S-P/TK-T
subpoenaed	S-PD
subpoenaing	S-PG
subsequent	SKWEPBT
subsequently	SKWEPBT/HREU
subside	SUBDZ
subsidence	SUB/STKEPBS
subsidize	SUB/STKAOEUZ
subsidize	SUBS/TKAOEUZ
substance (as wd)	SUB/STAPBS
substance abuse	SPWAOUS
substance abuser(s)	SPWAOUS/ER(S)
substandard	SUB/STARD
substantial (as wd)	STAPBL
substantial doubt	STAPBLD
substantiality	STAPBL/TEU
substantially	STAPBL/HREU
substantiate	STAPBT
substantiation	STAPBGS
substitutability	STUT/-BLT
substitutable	STUT/-BL
substitute	STUT
substitution	STUGS
substitutive	STUT/*EUF
subsystem(s)	SUB/S-PL(S)
subterranean	SUB/TRAEUPB/KWRAPB
subway	SPWAE
succotash	SUBG/TARB
such (as wd)	SUFP
such as	SUFPS
sufficiency	SUF/SEU
sufficient	SUF
sufficiently	SUF/HREU
suffrage	SUFRPBLG
suffragette	SUFRPBLG/ET
sugariness	SHUG/R*EUPBS
suggest	SUGT
suggestibility	SUGT/-BLT
suggestible	SUGT/-BL
suggestibly	SUGT/PWHREU
suggestion	S*UGS, SUGS
suggestive	SUGT/*EUF
suggestively	SUGT/*EUF/HREU
suicidal	S-DZ/TKAL
suicide (as wd)	S-DZ
suicide bomber(s)	SPWOPL/ER(S)
sulfuric	SUL/TPAOURBG
sultriness	SUL/TR*EUPBS
sultriness	SULT/R*EUPBS
summa cum laude	SAOUPL/KAOUPL/HRAUD
summa cum laude	SAOUPL/KUPL/HRAUD
summit	SUPLT
summon	SPHUPB
summons (n, sing)	SPHUPBS
summonses (n, pl)	SPHUPBS/-S
Sunday(s)	SUPBD(Z)
sundriness	SUPB/TKR*EUPBS
sundriness	SUPBD/R*EUPBS
sunflower	SUPB/TPHRO*UR
sunk	S*UPBG
sunlight	SULGT
sunniness	SUPB/TPH*EUPBS
superconductivity	SAO*UP/KUBG/T*EUFT
superconductivity	SAO*UP/KUBGT/*EUFT
superconductivity	SAO*UP/KUBGT/*EUF/TEU
supergovernment	SAO*UP/TKPWOFT
supergovernment	SAO*UP/TKPWO*FT
superhighway	SAO*UP/HAE
superhuman	SAO*UP/HAOUPL
superintelligent	SAO*UP/SPWEPBLGT
superintendent	SUPT
superior (as wd)	SPAOER/KWROR
superior court	SPROURT
Superior Court	SPRO*URT
superiority	SPAOER/KWROR/TEU
supermarket	SAO*UP/PHARBGT
superpower	SAO*UP/PO*UR
supertanker	SAO*UP/TA*PBG/ER
supervise	SAO*UFPZ
supervision	SAO*UFPGS

supervisor	SAO*UFRPZ	svelte	STPELT
supervisory	SAO*EUFRPZ	SVGA *(Super VGA)*	S-RBGS/SR*RBGS/TKPWA*
supervisory	SAO*UFRPZ/REU	SWAK *(sealed with a kiss)*	S-RBGS/W*RBGS/A*BG
supplier(s)	SPHRAOEU/ER(S)	SWAK	S-RBGS/WA*BG
supply	SPHRAOEU	swampiness	SWAFRP/P*EUPBS
support	SPO*RT	swampiness	SWAPL/P*EUPBS
supporter(s)	SPO*RT/ER(S)	swank	SWA*PBG
supportive	SPO*RT/*EUF	swankier	SWA*PBG/KWRER
suppose	SPOEZ	swankiest	SWA*PBG/KWR*ES
supposedly	SPOEZ/TKHREU	swankily	SWA*PBG/HREU
supposition	SUP/POGS, SUP/SEUGS	swanky	SWA*PBG/KEU
suppository	SPOZ/TOEUR	swear(ing) *(as wd)*	SWAEUR(/-G)
suppress	SPRESZ	swearing-in	SWAEURG/TPH*
suppressant	SPRES/SAPBT	sweatiness	SWET/T*EUPBS
suppression	SPREGS	sweatpants	SWET/PAPBTS
suppressive	SPRES/S*EUF	Switzerland	SWEUTS/HRAPBD
suppressive	SPRESZ/*EUF	syllabic	SHRAB/EUBG
suppressor	SPRES/SOR	syllabus	SEUL/PWUS
supremacist	SPREPL/S*EUS	symbiosis	SEUPL/PWOE/SEUS
supremacy	SPREPL/SEU	symbiotic	SEUPL/PWOT/EUBG
supreme *(as wd)*	SPRAOEPL	symbolism	SEUPL/PWHREUFPL
supreme court	SPOURT	symbolize	SEUPL/PWHRAOEUZ
Supreme Court	SPO*URT	symmetric	SPHET/REUBG
supremely	SPRAOEPL/HREU	symmetrical	SPHET/REU/KAL
surface	STPAS	symmetrically	SPHET/REU/KHREU
surgeon(s) *(as wd)*	S-RPB(S)	symmetrically	SPHET/REUBG/HREU
surgeon general	S-RPBG	syncope	SEUPB/KPAOE
Surgeon General	S*RPBG	synonymous	STPHOPB/PHOUS
surgeons general	S-RPBGS	synonymously	STPHOPB/PHOUS/HREU
Surgeons General	S*RPBGS	synopses	STPHOP/SAOEZ
surgeries	S-RPBLGS	synopsis	STPHOP/SEUS
surgery	S-RPBLG	syringe	SEURPBG
surliness	SUR/HR*EUPBS	syringe	SEU/REUPBG
surprise	SPRAOEUZ	syrup	SEURP
surprisingly	SPRAOEUZ/TKPWHREU	system(s)	S-PL(S)
surrebuttal	SUR/PWUT/TAL	systematic	S-PL/PHAT/EUBG
surrebutter	SUR/PWUT/ER	systematically	S-PL/PHAT/KHREU
surrender(s)	SR*EPBD/ER(S)	systematize	S-PL/TAOEUZ
surrendered	SR*EPBD/ERD	systematizer	S-PL/TAOEUZ/ER
surrenderer	SR*EPBD/RER	systemic	S-PL/EUBG
surrendering	SR*EPBD/ERG	systemically	S-PL/KHREU
surreptitious	SURP/TEURBS		
surreptitiously	SURP/TEURBS/HREU		
surrogacy	SURG/SEU		
surrogate	SUR/TKPWAEUT		
surrogate	SUR/TKPWAT		
surround(s)	SROUPBD(Z)		
surrounding(s)	SROUPBD/-G(S)		
surveillance	SUR/SRAEUPBS		
surveillant	SUR/SRAEUPBT		
surveyor	SUR/SRAEUR		
suspect(s)	S-PT(S)		
suspected	S-PTD		
sustain	STAEPB		
sustainable	STAEPB/-BL		
sustained	STAEPBD, STAEPB/-D		
sustainer(s)	STAEPB/ER(S)		
sustaining	STAEPBG, STAEPB/-G		
sustains	STAEPBS, STAEPB/-S		
suture	SAOUFP		
SUV *(sport-utility vehicle)*	S-RBGS/*UF		
SUV	S*UF		

tackiness	TABG/K*EUPBS
tailgate(s)	T-GT(S)
taillight(s)	T*LT(S)
take *(as wd)*	TAEUBG
take into account	TAEUBGT
take into consideration	TAEURBGS
taleswoman	TAELZ/WOPL
taleswoman	TAEULS/WOPL
taleswomen	TAELZ/WEUPL
taleswomen	TAEULS/WEUPL
tangent	TAPBG/EPBT
tangible	TAPBG/-BL
tangibly	TAPBG/PWHREU
tanginess	TAPB/TKPW*EUPBS
tank	TA*PBG
tankard(s)	TA*PBG/ARD(Z)
tanker(s)	TA*PBG/ER(S)
tarantula	TRAFRPBLG/HRA
tardiness	TAR/TK*EUPBS
target	TARGT
tastiness	TAEUS/T*EUPBS
tawdriness	TAU/TKR*EUPBS
tawdriness	TAUD/R*EUPBS
tawniness	TAU/TPH*EUPBS
tawniness	TAUPB/TPH*EUPBS
TBS *(Turner Broadcast System)*	
	T-RBGS/PW*S
TDD *(telecommunications device for the deaf)*	
	T-RBGS/TK*D
technical	TEBG/KAL
technicality	TEBG/KAL/TEU
technically	TEBG/KHREU
technological	TEBG/HROPBLG/KAL
technologically	TEBG/HROPBLG/KHREU
teenage	TAEUPBLG
teenager(s)	TAEURPBLG(/-S)
teenager(s)	TAEUPBLG/ER(S)
teleconference	T-FRPBS
teleconference	TEL/K-FRPBS
telegraphic	TEL/TKPWRAFBG
telegraphically	TEL/TKPWRAFBG/HREU
telemarket	TEL/PHARBGT
telemarketer(s)	TEL/PHARBGT/ER(S)
telephone	T-FPB
telephonic	T-FPB/EUBG
telephotography	TEL/TPRAF/TPEU
television	T*FGS
temperature(s)	TEFRP/KHUR(S)
temple	TEFRPL
temporariness	TEFRP/RA*EURPBS
temporariness	TEPL/PRA*EURPBS
Tennessee	T*PB/T*PB
Tennessee	T-PB
tepid	TEPD
term(s) *(as wd)*	TERPL(S)
terms and conditions	TERBGS
terrarium	TRAEURPL
terrestrial	TR*ES/RAL, TRES/TRAL
terrestrial	TR*ES/REUL, TRES/TREUL
terrible	TERBL
terribly	TERBL/HREU
terrific	TREUFBG
terrifically	TREUFBG/HREU
testified	TEFD
testifies	TEFS
testify	TEF
testifying	TEFG
testimonial	T-PL/KWRAL
testimonial	T*ES/PHOEPBL
testimonies	T-PLS
testimonium	T-PL/KWRUPL
testimony	T-PL
testiness	TES/T*EUPBS
Texas	T*BGS/T*BGS
Texas	T-BGS
TGIF *(thank God it's Friday)*	T-RBGS/TKPW*EUF
thank *(as wd)*	THA*PBG
thankful	THA*PBG/-FL
thankfully	THA*PBG/TPHREU
thankfulness	THA*PBG/TPHR*PBS
thankless	THA*PBG/HRES
thanklessly	THA*PBG/HRES/HREU
thanklessness	THA*PBG/HRES/*PBS
thanks	THA*PBGS, THA*PBG/-S
Thanksgiving	THA*PBGS/TKPW*EUFG
thank you	THA*UPBG
thank you very much	THA*UFP
thank you, your Honor	THA*URPB
that *(as wd)*	THA
that'd	THA*D
that'll	THA*L
that's	THA*S
that've	THA*F
that afternoon	THAFRPB
that are	THAR
that be	THAB
that can	THABG
that cannot	THABG/TPHOT
that can't	THABG/-PBT
that could	THABGD
that fast	THAFZ
that had	THAD
that happened	THAPD
that happens	THAPS
that has	THAZ
that have	THAF
that have been	THAFB
that he	THAE
that he believed	THAEBLD
that he believes	THAEBLS
that he can	THAEBG
that he cannot	THAEBG/TPHOT
that he can't	THAEBG/-PBT
that he could	THAEBGD
that he feels	THAEFLS
that he felt	THAEFLT
that he had	THAED

that he hadn't	THAED/-PBT	that is	THAS
that he has	THAEZ	that is all	THAUL
that he is	THAES	that is correct	THABGT
that he knows	THAEPBS	that is right	THART
that he means	THAEPLS	that morning	THARPBG
that he recalled	THAERLD	that night	THAPBT
that he recalls	THAERLS	that's correct	THAEBGT
that he recollected	THAERBGD	that's correct	THABGT/AOES
that he recollects	THAERBGS	that's right	THAERT
that he remembered	THAERPLD	that's right	THART/AOES
that he remembers	THAERPLS	that shall	THARB
that he said	THAEBS	that she	STHAE
that he say	THAEBZ	that she believed	STHAEBLD
that he says	THAEBSZ	that she believes	STHAEBLS
that he shall	THAERB	that she can	STHAEBG
that he should	THAERBD	that she cannot	STHAEBG/TPHOT
that he thinks	THAEPBGS	that she can't	STHAEBG/-PBT
that he understand	THAEPBDZ	that she could	STHAEBGD
that he understands	THAEPBDZ/-S	that she feels	STHAEFLS
that he understood	THA*EPBDZ	that she felt	STHAEFLT
that he wanted	THAEPTD	that she had	STHAED
that he wants	THAEPTS	that she hadn't	STHAED/-PBT
that he was	THAEFS	that she has	STHAEZ
that he will	THAEL	that she is	STHAES
that he would	THAELD	that she knows	STHAEPBS
that he would say	THAELDZ	that she means	STHAEPLS
that I	THA*EU	that she recalled	STHAERLD
that I believe	THAEUBL	that she recalls	STHAERLS
that I believed	THAEUBLD	that she recollected	STHAERBGD
that I can	THAEUBG	that she recollects	STHAERBGS
that I cannot	THAEUBG/TPHOT	that she remembered	STHAERPLD
that I can't	THAEUBG/-PBT	that she remembers	STHAERPLS
that I could	THAEUBGD	that she said	STHAEBS
that I feel	THAEUFL	that she say	STHAEBZ
that I felt	THAEUFLT	that she says	STHAEBSZ
that I find	THAEUFPBD	that she shall	STHAERB
that I had	THAEUD	that she should	STHAERBD
that I have	THAEUF	that she thinks	STHAEPBGS
that I know	THAEUPB	that she understand	STHAEPBDZ
that I mean	THAEUPL	that she understands	STHAEPBDZ/-S
that I mean to	THAEUPLT	that she understood	STHA*EPBDZ
that I mean to say	THAEUPLTS	that she wanted	STHAEPTD
that I recall	THAEURL	that she wants	STHAEPTS
that I recalled	THAEURLD	that she was	STHAEFS
that I recollect	THAEURBG	that she will	STHAEL
that I recollected	THAEURBGD	that she would	STHAELD
that I remember	THAEURPL	that she would say	STHAELDZ
that I remembered	THAEURPLD	that should	THARBD
that I said	THAEUBS	that side	THADZ
that I say	THAEUBZ	that the	THAT
that I says	THAEUBSZ	that time	THAPLT
that I shall	THAEURB	that want	THAPT
that I should	THAEURBD	that wanted	THAPTD
that I think	THAEUPBG	that wants	THAPTS
that I think so	THAEUPBGS	that was	THAFS
that I think the	THAEUPBGT	that were	THARP
that I understand	THAEUPBDZ	that were the	THARPT
that I understood	THA*EUPBDZ	that will	THAL
that I want	THAEUPT	that would	THALD
that I wanted	THAEUPTD	that you	THA*U
that I was	THAEUFS	that you are	THAUR
that I would	THAEULD	that you are the	THAURT
that I would say	THAEULDZ	that you believe	THAUBL

that you believed	THAUBLD	THE PLAINTIFF: *(colloquy)*	PHR-F/PHR-F
that you can	THAUBG	the president	T-PT
that you cannot	THAUBG/TPHOT	the President	T*PT
that you can't	THAUBG/-PBT	the record(s)	TRORD(Z)
that you could	THAUBGD	the witness	TW-PBS
that you feel	THAUFL	THE WITNESS: *(colloquy)*	W-PBS/W-PBS, W*PBS/W*PBS
that you felt	THAUFLT		
that you find	THAUFPBD	themselves	TH*EPLS, TH*EPLS/-S
that you had	THAUD	theorem	THAOERPL
that you have	THAUF	therapist	THA*EURPS
that you have been	THAUFB	therapy	THAEURP
that you have been the	THAUFBT	there *(as wd)*	THR-
that you have the	THAUFT	there'd	THR*D
that you know	THAUPB	there'll	THR*L
that you mean	THAUPL	there's	THR*S
that you mean to	THAUPLT	there've	THR*F
that you mean to say	THAUPLTS	thereabout(s)	THR-BT(S), THRABT(S)
that you recall	THAURL		
that you recalled	THAURLD	there about	THR-/ABT
that you recollect	THAURBG	thereafter	THRAFR, THRAF
that you recollected	THAURBGD	there after	THR-/AF
that you remember	THAURPL	there are	THR-R
that you remembered	THAURPLD	thereat	THRAT
that you said	THAUBS	there at	THR-/AT
that you say	THAUBZ	thereby	THR-B
that you says	THAUBSZ	there by	THR-/PWEU
that you shall	THAURB	there can	THR-BG
that you should	THAURBD	there could	THR-BGD
that you think	THAUPBG	therefor	THR*FR
that you think so	THAUPBGS	there for	THR-/TP-R
that you think the	THAUPBGT	therefore	THR-FR
that you understand	THAUPBDZ	therefrom	THR-FRPL
that you understood	THA*UPBDZ	there from	THR-/TPR-
that you want	THAUPT	there had	THR-D
that you wanted	THAUPTD	there has	THR-Z
that you were	THAURP	there have	THR-F
that you were the	THAURPT	there have been	THR-FB
that you would	THAULD	therein	THR-PB, THREUPB
that you would say	THAULDZ	there in	THR-/TPH-
THC *(tetrahydrocannabinol)*	T-RBGS/H*BG	thereinafter	THR-PB/AFR, THREUPB/AFR
the *(as wd)*	T-		
THE BAILIFF: *(colloquy)*	PWHR-F/PWHR-F, PWAEUL/PWAEUL	there is	THR-S
		thereof	THROF
the burden of proof	TPWR-P	there of	THR-/OF
the burden of proving	TPWR-PG	thereon	THROPB
THE CHAIR: *(colloquy)*	KHAEUR/KHAEUR	there on	THR-/OPB
THE CHAIRMAN: *(colloquy)*	KHAEURPL/KHAEURPL	there shall	THR-RB
		there should	THR-RBD
THE CHAIRPERSON: *(colloquy)*	KHAEURPB/KHAEURPB	thereto	THR-T
		there to	THR-/TO
THE CHAIRWOMAN: *(colloquy)*	KWHAEURPL/KWHAEURPL	thereunder	THR-RPBD, THR-PBD
		there under	THR-/URPBD
THE CLERK: *(colloquy)*	KHRERBG/KHRERBG	thereupon	THRUP
the Court	TKOURT	there upon	THR-/POPB
THE DEFENDANT: *(colloquy)*	TK-FT/TK-FT	there was	THR-FS
		there were	THR-RP
the evidence	T*EFD	there were the	THR-RPT
THE FOREMAN: *(colloquy)*	TPORPL/TPORPL	there weren't	THR-RP/-PBT
THE FOREPERSON: *(colloquy)*	TPORPB/TPORPB	there weren't	THR-/W-RPBT
		there will	THR-L
THE FOREWOMAN: *(colloquy)*	TPWOPL/TPWOPL	therewith	THR*EUT
		therewith	THR-/W*EUT
THE MARSHAL: *(colloquy)*	PHARL/PHARL	there with	THR-/W-

there would	THR-LD	third-degree murder	TH-PLD
they (as wd)	THAEU	thirty	THEURT
they'd	THA*EUD	this (as wd)	TH-
they'll	THA*EUL	this afternoon	TH-FRPB
they're	THA*EUR	this be	TH-B
they've	THA*EUF	this can	TH-BG
they are	THER	this cannot	TH-BG/TPHOT
they believe	THEBL	this can't	TH-BG/-PBT
they believed	THEBLD	this can't	TH-/K-PBT
they can	THEBG	this could	TH-BGD
they can't	THAEU/K-PBT	this fast	TH-FZ
they can't	THEBG/-PBT	this happened	TH-PD
they cannot	THEBG/TPHOT	this happens	TH-PS
they could	THEBGD	this has	TH-Z
they ever	THEFR	this is	TH-S
they feel	THEFL	this is correct	TH-RBGT
they felt	THEFLT	this is not	TH-S/TPHOT
they had	THED	this isn't	TH-S/-PBT
they have	THEF	this isn't	TH-/S-PBT
they have been	THEFB	this is right	TH-RT
they have believed	THEFBLD	this morning	TH-RPBG
they have had	THEFD	this much	TH-FP
they have not	THEF/TPHOT	this night	TH-PBT
they haven't	THEFPBT	this shall	TH-RB
they just want	THEFPT	this should	TH-RBD
they just wanted	THEFPTD	this side	TH-DZ
they know	TH*EPB	this was	TH-FS
they recall	THERL	this were	TH-RP
they recalled	THERLD	this will	TH-L
they recollect	THERBG	this would	TH-LD
they recollected	THERBGD	Thomas	THOPLS
they said	THEBS	thoracic	THRAS/EUBG
they say	THEBZ	thorniness	THOR/TPH*EUPBS
they says	THEBSZ	thoroughfare	THOR/TPAER
they shall	THERB	those	THOZ, THOEZ
they should	THERBD	thought	THAUT
they think	THEPBG	thoughtful	THAUT/-FL
they think so	THEPBGS	thoughtfully	THAUT/TPHREU
they think the	THEPBGT	thoughtfulness	THAUT/TPHR*PBS
they understand	THEPBDZ	thoughtless	THAUT/HRES
they understood	TH*EPBDZ	thoughtlessly	THAUT/HRES/HREU
they want	THEPT	thoughtlessness	THAUT/HRES/*PBS
they wanted	THEPTD	thousand (as wd)	THOU
they was	THEFS	thousand dollar(s)	THOUD(Z)
they were	THERP	thousands	THOUS, THOU/-S
they were the	THERPT	thousandth	THO*UT
they will	THEL	thriftiness	THREUF/T*EUPBS
they would	THELD	throatiness	THROE/T*EUPBS
thicket	THEUBGT	throatiness	THROET/T*EUPBS
thigh	THAOEU	throes	THROES
think	THEU	through (as wd)	THRU
think	TH*EUPBG	through the	THRUT
thinkable	THEUBL, THEU/-BL	throughout	THROUT
thinkable	TH*EUPBG/-BL	thunderbird(s)	THUPBD/PWEURD(Z)
thinkably	THEU/PWHREU	Thunderbird(s)	K-P/THUPBD/PWEURD(Z)
thinkably	TH*EUPBG/PWHREU	thunderbolt	THUPBD/PWOELT
thinker	THEUR, THEU/ER	thunderbolt	THUPBD/PWOLT
thinker	TH*EUPBG/ER	thundercloud(s)	THUPBD/KHROUD(Z)
thinking	THEUG	thundershower	THUPBD/SHO*UR
thinks	THEUS	thunderstorm	THUPBD/STORPL
third (as wd)	THEURD	thunderstorm warning	THUPBD/STORPBG
third degree	TH*D	thunderstorm watch	THUPBD/STWAFP
third-degree	TH-D	Thursday	THURD

Thursday	THURZ	to the best of my recollection	TEURBGS
thwart	TWART	to the best of your knowledge	TURPBLG
thyself	THAO*EUS	to the best of your recollection	TURBGS
Tibet	TEUBT	to them	TO*EPLT
Tibetan	TEUBT/TAPB	to understand	TOPBDZ
ticket	TEUBGT	to us	TO*US
ticketholder(s)	TEUBGT/HOELD/ER(S)	to want	TOPT
ticketholder(s)	TEUBGT/HOLD/ER(S)	to you	TO*U
tidiness	TAOEU/TK*EUPBS	to your knowledge	TOURPBLG
tidiness	TAOEUD/TK*EUPBS	tobacco	TPWABG
time and a half	TAOEUPL/TPHAF	today	TOD
timeliness	TAOEUPL/HR*EUPBS	together	TOGT
timid	TEUPLD	toilet	TOEULT
timidity	TEUPLD/TEU	toiletry	TOEULT/REU
TIN *(taxpayer identification number)*		tomorrow	TORPL
	T-RBGS/*EUPB	tongue-tied	TUPBG/TAOEUD
TIN	T*EUPB	tonight	TOPBT
tininess	TAOEU/TPH*EUPBS	tonight	TAOEUPBT
tininess	TAOEUPB/TPH*EUPBS	too *(as wd)*	TAO
tinker(s)	T*EUPBG/ER(S)	too bad	TAOBD
tinkered	T*EUPBG/ERD	too fast	TAOFZ
tinkering	T*EUPBG/ERG	too good	TAOGD
tinkle(s)	T*EUPBG/-L(S)	too large	TAORPBLG
tinkled	T*EUPBG/-LD	too late	TAOLT
tinkling	T*EUPBG/-LG	too long	TAOPBG
tinniness	TEUPB/TPH*EUPBS	too many	TAOPL
tipsiness	TEUP/S*EUPBS	too much	TAOFP
tiredness	TAOEUR/TK*PBS	too often	TAOFPB
tireless	TAOEURLS	too old	TAOLD
tirelessly	TAOEURLS/HREU	took *(as wd)*	TAOBG
tirelessness	TAOEURLS/*PBS	took into account	TAOBGT
'tis	T*EUZ	took into consideration	TAORBGS
TKO *(technical knockout)*	T-RBGS/KO*	took place	TAOPS
TLC *(tender loving care)*	T-RBGS/HR*BG	topographic	TOP/TKPWRAFBG
TNN *(The National Network)*	T-RBGS/TPH*PB	topographic	TOEP/TKPWRAFBG
TNT *(trinitrotoluene, Turner Network Television)*		topside	TOPDZ
	T-RBGS/TPH*T	tornado *(as wd)*	TORPBD
to *(as wd)*	TO	tornado warning	TORPBG
to be	TOB	tornado watch	TWAFP
to be the	TOBT	Toronto	TROPB/TOE
to believe	TOBL	torpid	TORPD
to believe the	TOBLT	torrential	TREPB/-RBL
to do	TAOD	totalitarian	TOET/TAEURPB
to feel	TOFL	totalitarianism	TOET/TAEURPB/EUFPL
to find	TOFPBD	totally	TOET/HREU
to have	TOF	touchiness	TOUFP/KH*EUPBS
to have been	TOFB	touchiness	TUFP/KH*EUPBS
to have been the	TOFBT	toward(s)	TWARD(Z)
to have believed	TOFBLD	tower	TO*UR
to have had	TOFD	townspeople	TOUPBS/PAOEPL
to have recalled	TOFRLD	Toyota	TOEUT
to have remembered	TOFRPLD	tractor-trailer	TRARBGT/TRAEURL
to have the	TOFT	traffic *(as wd)*	TRAFBG
to have wanted	TOFPTD	traffic accident	TRAFBGS
to her	TO*ER	traffic court	TRAOURT
to him	TO*EUPL	traffic light(s)	TR-LT(S)
to it	TO*EUT	trafficability	TRAFBG/-BLT
to me	TO*EPL	trafficable	TRAFBG/-BL
to my knowledge	TOEUPBLG	trafficker(s)	TRAFBG/ER(S)
to say	TOBZ	trample	TRAFRPL
to the	TO*T		
to the best of my knowledge	TEUPBLG		

transaction	TR*BGS	TRO *(temporary restraining order)*	
transactional	TR*BGS/TPHAL		T-RBGS/RO*
transconductance	TRA*PBS/KUBGT/TAPBS	trousers	TROUZ/ERS
transcribe	TREUB	true *(as wd)*	TRAOU
transcriber(s)	TREUB/ER(S)	true and accurate	TRURBGT
transcript	TREUPT	true and accurate copy	TRURBGTS
transcription	TREUPGS	true and correct	TRORBGT
transcriptionist	TREUPGS/*EUS	true and correct copy	TRORBGTS
transcriptor	TREUPT/TOR	trunk	TR*UPBG
transfer(s)	TR-FR(S)	trunkful	TR*UPBG/-FL
transferable	TR-FRBL	trustworthiness	TR*US/WOR/TH*EUPBS
transferee	TR-FR/RAOE	T-shirt	T-RBGS/SHEURT
transference	TR-FRPBS,	TTD *(teletypewriting device for the deaf)*	
	TR-FR/EPBS		T-RBGS/T*D
transferor	TRA*PBS/TPROR	TTY *(teletypewriter)*	T-RBGS/TKWR*
transferor	TR-FR/ROR	tuberculosis	TUBLS
transferred	TR-FRD	tuberculosis	TPWERBG/HRO/SEUS
transferrer(s)	TR-FR/ER(S)	tuberculosis	TPWERBG/HROE/SEUS
transferring	TR-FRG	Tuesday	TAOUZ
transform(s)	TR-FRPL(S)	tuition	TWEUGS
transformation	TR-FRPLGS	turbid	TURBD
transformation	TR-FRPL/PHAEUGS	turgid	TURPBLGD
transformational	TR-FRPLGS/TPHAL	TV *(television)*	T*F
transformational	TR-FRPL/ PHAEUGS/TPHAL	TV	TAOE/SRAOE
		TVA *(Tennessee Valley Authority)*	
transformed	TR-FRPLD		T-RBGS/SRA*
transformer(s)	TR-FRPL/ER(S)	TWA *(Trans World Airlines)*	T-RBGS/WA*
transforming	TR-FRPLG	'twas	TWAZ, TW*UZ
transport(s)	TR-PT(S)	twelfth	TW*EFLT
transportation	TR-PGS	twelve	TW*EFL
transportation	TR-PT/TAEUGS	twenty	TWEPBT
transported	TR-PTD	24/7	24*7
transporter(s)	TR-PT/ER(S)	twilight	TWAOEULGT
transposition	TRA*PBS/POGS	twinge	TWEUPBG
transsexual	TRA*PBS/SWAUL	twinkle(s)	TW*EUPBG/-L(S)
trashiness	TRARB/SH*EUPBS	twinkled	TW*EUPBG/-LD
treasure(s)	TR-RB(S)	twinkling	TW*EUPBG/-LG
treasured	TR-RBD	'twixt	TW*EUBGS
treasurer(s)	TR-RB/ER(S)	two-thirds	TWO/THEURDZ
treasure-trove	TR-RB/TRO*EF	2000	TWOU
treasuring	TR-RBG	2001	TWUPB
treasury	TR-RB/REU	2002	TWAOU
treatment(s)	TRAOEPLT(S)	2003	TWAOE
tremendous	TRE	2004	TWOUR
tremendously	TRE/HREU	2005	TWAO*EUF
trepid	TREPD	2006	TWEUBGS
trial *(as wd)*	TRAOEUL	2007	TW*EFPB, TW*EF/-PB
trial court	TROURT	2008	TWAEUGT
trial date	TR-TD	2009	TWAO*EUPB
trial judge	TR-PBLG	2010	TWEPB
trial rights	TR-RTS	typewrite	TWREU
trial time	TR-PLT	typewrite	TAOEUP/WREU
triceps	TR*EU/SEPS	typewriter	TWREUR
trickiness	TREUBG/K*EUPBS	typewriter	TAOEUP/WREUR
tricycle	TROEUBG	typewriting	TWREUG
tried	TRAOEUD	typewriting	TAOEUP/WREUG
trillion(s) *(as wd)*	TR-L(S)	typewritten	TWREUPB
trillion dollar(s)	TR-LD(Z)	typewritten	TAOEUP/WREUPB
trillionth	TR*LT	typographic	TAOEUP/TKPWRAFBG
trinket	TR*EUPBGT	tyrant	TAOEURPBT
triplet	TREUPLT		
trivet	TR*EUFT		

© 2004 *StenEd®* Briefs & Phrases (Excerpted from StenEd's Realtime Professional Dictionary)

UAE *(United Arab Emirates)*	URBGS/A*E
U.A.E.	UFPLT/A*E
UAR *(United Arab Republic)*	URBGS/A*R
U.A.R.	UFPLT/A*R
UAW *(United Auto[mobile] Workers)*	
	URBGS/A*U
UCC *(Uniform Commercial Code)*	
	URBGS/KR*BG
UFO *(unidentified flying object)*	
	URBGS/TPO*
ugliness	UG/HR*EUPBS
UHF *(ultrahigh frequency)*	URBGS/H*F
uh-huh *(affirmative)*	U/HU
uh-oh	U/O*E
uh-uh *(negative)*	U/U
ultrahazardous	UL/TRA/HAZ/TKOUS
ultraism	UL/TRAFPL
ultraism	UL/TREUFPL
ultramarine	UL/TRA/PHRAOEPB
ultranationalism	UL/TRA/TPHARBL/EUFPL
um-hmm *(affirmative)*	UPL/H-PL
UMWA *(United Mine Workers of America)*	
	URBGS/PH*RBGS/WA*
unacceptable	UPB/SEPBL
unacceptable	UPB/SEP/-BL
unaccompanied	UPB/KPAEPB/-D
unaccomplished	UPB/PHREURB/-D
unaccountable	UPB/K-T/-BL
unaccounted	UPB/K-TD
unadulterated	UPB/TKULT/RAEUT/-D
unaffected	UPB/AFBGT/-D
unaffectionate	UPB/A*FBGS/TPHAT
unambiguous	UPB/TKPWAOUS
un-American	UPB/PHERPB
unanimous	TPHAPLS
unanimously	TPHAPLS/HREU
unanswerable	UPB/APBS/-BL
unanswered	UPB/APBS/-D
unappreciated	UPB/PRAOERBT/-D
unapproved	UPB/AEU/PRO*F/-D
unarguable	UPB/ARG/-BL
unarguably	UPB/ARG/PWHREU
unashamed	UPB/AEU/SHAEUPLD
unattached	UPB/TAFP/-D
unauthorized	UPB/THORZ/-D
unavailability	UPB/SRAEUBLT
unavailable	UPB/SRAEUBL
unbalanced	UPB/PWHRA*PBS/-D
unbecoming	UPB/PW-BG/-G
unbelievable	UPB/PWHRAO*EFBL
unbelievably	UPB/PWHRAO*EF/PWHREU
unbespoken	UPB/PWE/SPOEPB
unbiased	UPB/PWAOEUS/-D
unbroken	UPB/PWROEPB
unburden	UPB/PWURD
uncertain	UPB/SERPB
uncertainty	UPB/SERPBT
uncertainty	UPB/SERPB/TEU
unchallenged	UPB/KHAPBLG/-D
unchangeable	UPB/KHAEUPBG/-BL
unchanged	UPB/KHAEUPBG/-D
uncharacteristic	UPB/KARBGT/EUBG
uncharacteristic	UPB/KARBGT/*EUS/EUBG
uncharacteristically	UPB/KARBGT/*EUS/KHREU
uncle(s)	UPBG/-L(S)
Uncle *(as wd)*	*UPBG/-L
Uncle Sam	*UPBG/-L/SAPL
uncomfortable	UPB/K-FRBL
uncomfortable	UPB/K-FRT/-BL
uncommitted	UPB/KPHEUT/-D
uncommon	UPB/KPHOPB
uncommonly	UPB/KPHOPB/HREU
unconcerned	UPB/K-RPBD
unconditional	UPB/K-PBL
unconditional	UPB/K-PB/TPHAL
unconditionally	UPB/K-PBL/HREU
unconditionally	UPB/K-PB/HREU
unconnected	UPB/KEBGT/-D
unconscious	UPB/KORBS
unconsciously	UPB/KORBS/HREU
unconsciousness	UPB/KORBS/*PBS
unconstitutional	UPB/TAOUGS/TPHAL
uncontradicted	UPB/KR*BGT/-D
uncontrollable	UPB/KROL/-BL
uncontrolled	UPB/KROL/-D
uncontroversial	UPB/TRO*EFRL
uncontroverted	UPB/TRO*EFRT/-D
uncooperative	UPB/KAOPT/*EUF
uncorrelated	UPB/KOR/RELT/-D
uncorroborated	UPB/KROB/RAEUT/-D
unction	UPBGS
undamaged	UPB/TKAPBLG/-D
undecided	UPB/TK-DZ/-D
undefended	UPB/TKEFD/-D
undefended	UPB/TKEFPBD/-D
undependable	UPB/TKPEPBD/-BL
under *(wd)*	URPBD
under all the circumstances	ULTS
under the circumstances	UTS
under the influence	UFLS
under the same circumstances	UPLTS
underdeveloped	UPBDZ/TKWOP/-D
undereducated	UPBDZ/EGT/-D
underfinanced	UPBDZ/TP-PBS/-D
underfinanced	UPBDZ/TP-PBSD
undergoing	UPBDZ/TKPWOEUPBG
underinsurance	UPBDZ/STPHURPBS
underinsure	UPBDZ/STPHUR
underpants	UPBDZ/PAPBTS
undersecretary	UPBDZ/SEBG/TAEUR
undersheriff	UPBDZ/SHR-F
understand	UPBS
understandable	UPBS/-BL

understandably	UPBS/PWHREU	unit	KWRAOUPBT
understatement	UPBDZ/STAEUPLT	unite	KWRAOEUPBT
understood	UPBD	united *(as wd)*	KWRAOEUPBT/-D
underwrite	UPBDZ/WREU	United *(as wd)*	KWRAOEUPBTD
underwriter	UPBDZ/WREUR	United Kingdom	KWRAOEUPBTD/ KEUPBG/TKOPL
underwriter	UPBDZ/WREU/ER		
underwritten	UPBDZ/WREUPB	United Nations	KWRAOEUPBS
underwritten	UPBDZ/WREU/-PB	United Nations	KWRAOEUPBTD/ TPHAEUGS/-S
undetermined	UPB/TKERPL/-D		
undeveloped	UPB/TKWOP/-D	United States	KWRAOEUTS
undiminished	UPB/TKPHEUPB/EURB/-D	United States	KWRAOEUPBTD/STAEUTS
undistributed	UPB/TKREUBT/-D	United States Air Force	KWRAOEUTS/AEUFRS
undivided	UPB/TKWAOEUD/-D	United States Army	KWRAOEUTS/AERPL
uneasiness	UPB/AOEZ/S*EUPBS	United States Attorney	KWRAOEUTS/TOERPB
uneasiness	UPB/E/S*EUPBS	United States Coast Guard	KWRAOEUTS/ KO*ES/TKPWARD
unemployable	UPB/PHROEUBL		
unemployment	UPB/PHROEUPLT	United States District Court	KWRAOEUTS/ TKREUBGT/KOURT
UNESCO *(UN Educational, Scientific, and Cultural Organization)*	KWRAOU/TPHES/KOE		
		United States District Court	KWRAOEUTS/TKRO*URT
unessential	UPB/SERBL	United States Government	KWRAOEUTS/TKPWO*FT
uneven	UPB/*EFPB, UPB/EFPB		
uneventful	UPB/*EFPBT/-FL	United States Government	KWRAOEUTS/TKPWOFT
unexpected	UPB/KP-PTD		
unexpectedly	UPB/KP-PT/TKHREU	United States Marine Corps	KWRAOEUTS/ PHRAOEPB/KOERP
unexpectedly	UPB/KP-PTD/HREU		
unfamiliar	UPB/TPHRAR	United States Navy	KWRAOEUTS/ TPHAEU/SREU
unfamiliarity	UPB/TPHRART		
unfamiliarity	UPB/TPHRAR/TEU	United States of America	KWRAOEUPLTS
unfathomable	UPB/TPA*T/PHABL	unitization	KWRAOUPBT/SA*EUGS
unfavorable	UPB/TPA*EUFRBL	university	KWRAOUFRT
unforgettable	UPB/TPERGT/-BL	University	KWRAO*UFRT
unfortunate	UPB/TP-RPBT	unjustifiable	UPB/SKWRUFBL
unfortunate	UPB/TPORT/TPHAT	unjustifiable	UPB/SKWRUF/-BL
unfortunately	UPB/TP-RPBLT	unjustified	UPB/SKWRUF/-D
unfortunately	UPB/TP-RPBT/HREU	unless	TPH-LS
unfortunately	UPB/TPORT/ TPHAT/HREU	unlimited	UPB/HREUPLT/-D
		unmarketable	UPB/PHARBGT/-BL
ungodliness	UPB/TKPWOD/ HR*EUPBS	unnaturally	UPB/TPHAFP/HREU
		unnecessarily	UPB/TPHES/HREU
unh unh (negative)	*UPB/*UPB	unnecessary	UPB/TPHES
unhappily	UPB/HAP/HREU	unnoticeable	UPB/TPHOETS/-BL
unhappiness	UPB/HAP/*PBS	unnoticed	UPB/TPHOETS/-D
unhappiness	UPB/HAP/P*EUPBS	unnumbered	UPB/TPHURPL/-D
UNICEF *(UN [International] Children's [Emergency] Fund)*	KWRAOUPB/SEF	unoccupied	UPB/OUP/-D
		unofficial	UPB/TPEURBL
unidentified	UPB/AOEUF/-D	unofficially	UPB/TPEURBL/HREU
unidentified	UPB/AOEUD/TPEU/-D	unofficially	UPB/TPEURB/HREU
unidirection	KWRAOUPB/TKR*EBGS	unopened	UPB/OEP/-D
uniform	KWRAOUFRPL	unorganize(d)	UPB/ORG(/-D)
uniformity	KWRAOUFRPL/TEU	unpolitical	UPB/PHREUT/KAL
uniformly	KWRAOUFRPL/HREU	unpopular	UPB/PO*P/HRAR
unimaginable	UPB/PHAPBLG/-BL	unpregnant	UPB/PREGT
unimportant	UPB/PORPBT	unproductive	UPB/PRUBGT/*EUF
unincorporated	UPB/EUPB/KORPT/-D	unproductive	UPB/PRUBG/T*EUF
uninformed	UPB/TPH-FD	unprofessional	UPB/PROFL
uninhibited	UPB/EUPB/HEUBT/-D	unprofessional	UPB/PROFGS/TPHAL
uninjured	UPB/SKWREUR/-D	unprofitable	UPB/PROFT/-BL
uninsurable	UPB/STPHURBL	unpromising	UPB/PROPLS/-G
uninsured	UPB/STPHUR/-D	unprotected	UPB/PREBGT/-D
uninteresting	UPB/SPWR*ES/-G	unproven	UPB/PRO*FPB
uninterrupted	UPB/SPWRUPT/-D	unqualified	UPB/KW-FD
uninvolved	UPB/SRO*F/-D	unquestionable	UPB/KWEBL
uninvolved	UPB/SROF/-D		

© 2004 StenEd® Briefs & Phrases (Excerpted from StenEd's Realtime Professional Dictionary)

unquestionably	UPB/KWEBL/HREU	UPS *(United Parcel Service)*	URBGS/P*S
unquestionably	UPB/KWE/PWHREU	UPS	*UPS
unquestioned	UPB/KWED	upside	UPDZ
unquestioning	UPB/KWEG	upside down	UPDZ/TKOUPB
unreasonable	UPB/R-PBL	upstairs	UP/STAEURS
unreasonable	UPB/R-PB/-BL	urgency	URPBLGT/SEU
unreasonableness	UPB/R-PBL/*PBS	urgent	URPBLGT
unreasonableness	UPB/R-PB/-BL/*PBS	urgently	URPBLGT/HREU
unreasonably	UPB/R-PBL/HREU	urinal	KWRAOURPBL
unreasonably	UPB/R-PB/PWHREU	urinalyses	KWRAOURPBL/SAOEZ
unreconcilable	UPB/REBG/SAOEUBL	urinalysis	KWRAOURPBL/SEUS
unreconcilable	UPB/REBG/SAOEUL/-BL	urine	KWRAOURPB
unrecorded	UPB/RORD/-D	URL *(uniform resource locator)*	
unrelated	UPB/RELT/-D		URBGS/R*L
unremarkable	UPB/RARBG/-BL	U.S.	*US
unremitting	UPB/REPLT/-G	USA *(United States of America)*	
unreported	UPB/RORT/-D		URBGS/SA*
unresolved	UPB/RE/SO*F/-D	U.S.A.	UFPLT/SA*
unresponsive	UPB/SPOPBS/*EUF	USAF *(US Air Force)*	URBGS/S*RBGS/A*F
unruliness	UPB/RAOU/HR*EUPBS	USAF	URBGS/SA*F
unsatisfactorily	UPB/STPOEUR/HREU	USAR *(US Army Reserve)*	URBGS/S*RBGS/A*R
unsatisfactory	UPB/STPOEUR	USAR	URBGS/SA*R
unsatisfied	UPB/STPAOEU/-D	USB *(Universal Serial Bus)*	URBGS/S*B
unscientific	UPB/SAOEUPB/TEUFBG	USCG *(US Coast Guard)*	URBGS/S*RBGS/KR*G
unseasonable	UPB/S-PB/-BL	USCG	URBGS/SKR*G
unsecured	UPB/SKUR/-D	USDA *(US Dept of Agriculture)*	
unsolicited	UPB/SHREUS/SEUT/-D		URBGS/S*RBGS/TKA*
unsolved	UPB/SO*F/-D	USDA	URBGS/STKA*
unsophisticated	UPB/STP*EUS/KAEUT/-D	USDC *(US District Court)*	URBGS/S*RBGS/TK*BG
unspecific	UPB/SPEFBG	USDC	URBGS/STK*BG
unspecified	UPB/SPEF/-D	USGS *(US Geological Survey)*	
unspoken	UPB/SPOEPB		URBGS/S*RBGS/TKPW*S
unstoppable	UPB/STOPBL	USGS	URBGS/S*GS
unsubstantiated	UPB/STAPBT/-D	USI *(user system interface)*	URBGS/S*EU
unsupervised	UPB/SAO*UFPZ/-D	USMA *(US Military Academy)*	
unsuspected	UPB/S-PTD		URBGS/S*RBGS/PHA*
unsuspecting	UPB/S-PT/-G	USMA	URBGS/SPHA*
unsustainable	UPB/STAEPB/-BL	USMC *(US Marine Corps)*	URBGS/S*RBGS/PH*BG
unthinkable	UPB/THEUBL	USMC	U-RBGS/SPH*BG
unthinkable	UPB/TH*EUPBG/-BL	USN *(US Navy)*	U-RBGS/S*PB
until *(as wd)*	TPH-L	USNA *(US Naval Academy)*	URBGS/S*RBGS/TPHA*
until the	TPH-LT	USNA	URBGS/STPHA*
untoward	UPB/TWARD	USNG *(US National Guard)*	URBGS/S*RBGS/TPH*G
unusual	UPB/URBL	USNG	URBGS/STPH*G
unusually	UPB/URBL/HREU	USNR *(US Naval Reserve)*	URBGS/S*RBGS/TPH*R
unwarranted	UPB/WARPBT/-D	USNR	URBGS/STPH*R
unwelcome	UPB/W-BG	USO *(United Service Organizations)*	
unwilling	UPB/HR-G		URBGS/SO*
unwillingly	UPB/HR-G/HREU	USP *(US Pharmacopeia)*	URBGS/S*P
unwillingly	UPB/HR-G/TKPWHREU	USPO *(US Post Office)*	URBGS/S*RBGS/PO*
unwillingness	UPB/HR-G/*PBS	USPO	URBGS/SPO*
unwitnessed	UPB/W*PBS/-D	USPS *(US Postal Service)*	URBGS/S*RBGS/P*S
unwitnessed	UPB/W-PBS/-D	USPS	URBGS/SP*S
unworldliness	UPB/WORLD/HR*EUPBS	USSR *(Union of Soviet Socialist Republics, disbanded 1991)*	
unwritten	UPB/WREUPB		URBGS/S*RBGS/S*R
up *(as wd)*	UP	USSR	URBGS/S*RS
up and down	PAPBD	U.S.S.R.	UFPLT/S*FPLT/S*R
upbringing	UP/PWREU/-G	U.S.S.R.	UFPLT/S*RS
UPC *(Universal Product Code)*		usual	URBL
	URBGS/P*BG	usually	URBL/HREU
UPI *(United Press International)*		Utah	*UT/*UT
	URBGS/P*EU	UXB *(unexploded bomb)*	URBGS/KP*B
upon	POPB		

V (Roman numeral)	5R
v. (versus in legal citations)	SR-RS
VA hospital	SRA*/HOPT
VA Hospital	SRA*/HO*PT
vague (as wd)	SRAEUG
vague and ambiguous	SRAEUBS
valentine	SRAL/TAOEUPB
Valentine	SRA*L/TAOEUPB
valid	SRALD
validity	SRALD/TEU
validly	SRALD/HREU
valuable	SRAL/-BL
valuably	SRAL/PWHREU
valuate	SRAL/WAEUT
valuation	SRAL/WAEUGS
valuator	SRAL/WAEU/TOR
value	SRAL
valueless	SRAL/HRES
vapid	SRAEUPD, SRAPD
vapidity	SRAEUPD/TEU, SRAPD/TEU
vaporization	SRAEUP/SA*EUGS
variability	SRAEURBLT
variable	SRAEURBL
variance	SRAEURPBS
variant	SRAEURPBT
variation	SRAEURGS
variety	SRAEURT
various	SRAEURS
variously	SRAEURS/HREU
varmint	SRARPLT
vary	SRAEUR
VAT (value-added tax)	SR-RBGS/A*T
VCR (videocassette recorder)	SR-RBGS/KR*R
VDT (video display terminal)	SR-RBGS/TK*T
vegetable(s)	SREPBLGT/-BL(S)
vehicle (as wd)	SRAOEBG
Vehicle Code	SROED
Vehicle Code Section	SROEDZ
vehicles (as wd)	SRAOEBGS, SRAOEBG/-S
vehicular	SRAOEBG/HRAR
vehicular homicide	SRAO*EDZ
vehicular manslaughter	SRAO*EPLS
vengeance	SREPBG/EPBS
vengeful	SREPBG/-FL
veni, vidi, vici	SRAOEPB/ SRAOED/SRAOEFP
venireman	TPHAOEURPL
veniremen	TPHAO*EURPL
verdict	SRERBGT
verdicts	SRERBGTS, SRERBGT/-S
verisimilar	SRER/SHRAR
Vermont	SR*T/SR*T
Vermont	SRERPLT
very (as wd)	SR-R
very many	SR-RPL
very much	SR-FP
very much	SR-FRP
very well	SR-RL
veteran(s) (as wd)	SRET/ER/RAPB(/-S)
Veterans Administration	SR*ERGS
veterans hospital	SROPT
Veterans Hospital	SRO*PT
veterinarian	SRET/TPHAEURPB
veterinary	SRET/TPHAEUR
VFU (vertical format unit)	SR-RBGS/TP*U
VGA (video graphics array)	SR-RBGS/TKPWA*
VHF (very high frequency)	SR-RBGS/H*F
VHS (video home system)	SR-RBGS/H*S
VI (Roman numeral)	R6
vicarious	SRAOEU/KAEURS
vicariously	SRAOEU/KAEURS/HREU
vice (as wd)	SRAOEUS
vice president(s)	SR-PT(S)
Vice President	SR*PT
vichyssoise	SREURBS/SWA
vichyssoise	SREURBS/SWAZ
vichyssoise	SRAOERBS/SWA
vichyssoise	SRAOERBS/SWAZ
vicinity	SREUPBT
videocassette	SRAOBG
videodisk	SRAOD
videotape	SRAOP
viewpoint	SRAOUPT
VII (Roman numeral)	R7
VIII (Roman numeral)	R8
violate	SRAOEULT
violation	SRAOEULGS
violative	SRAOEULT/*EUF
violator	SRAOEULT/TOR
violence	SRAOEUPBLS
violent	SRAOEUPBLT
violently	SRAOEUPBLT/HREU
VIP (very important person)	SR-RBGS/*EUP
Virgin Islands	SR*EU/SR*EU
Virgin Islands	SREUFPLT
Virginia	SRA*/SRA*
Virginia	SRAFPLT
virtually	SR*EURPBLG/HREU
VISA	SRAO*E/SA, SRAO*E/SA*
vis-a-vis	SRAOEZ/SRAOE
visit	SREUT
visitation	SREUT/TAEUGS
visitor	SREUT/TOR
vitalization	SRAOEUT/SA*EUGS
vitally	SRAOEUT/HREU
vivid	SR*EUFD
vividly	SR*EUFD/HREU
voir dire	SR-RD
VOIR DIRE EXAMINATION (cap & center)	SR-RD/SR-RD
volleyball	SROBL
voluntarily	SROL/TAEUR/HREU
voluntariness	SROL/TA*EURPBS

voluntariness	SROL/TAEUR/*PBS
voluntary *(as wd)*	SROL/TAEUR
voluntary manslaughter	SRO*PLS
volunteer	SROL/TAOER
volunteerism	SROL/TAOER/EUFPL
vomit	SROPLT
voyage	SROEUPBLG
voyager(s)	SROEUPBLG/ER(S)
voyeurism	SROEUR/EUFPL
VRAM *(Video RAM)*	SR-RBGS/R-RBGS/A*PL
VRAM	SR-RBGS/RA*PL
vs.	SR*S
VSO *(very superior old)*	SR-RBGS/SO*
V.S.O.	SR-FPLT/SO*
VSOP *(very superior old pale)*	
	SR-RBGS/S*RBGS/O*P
VSOP	SR-RBGS/SO*P
V.S.O.P.	SR-FPLT/S*FPLT/O*P
V.S.O.P.	SR-FPLT/SO*P
VTR *(videotape recorder)*	SR-RBGS/T*R
vulgarism	SRUL/TKPWREUFPL

W

wait *(as wd)*	WAEUT
wait a minute	WAPLT
wait a minute	WEUPLT
wait a minute, please	WAPLTS
wait a minute, please	WEUPLTS
wait a moment	WOEPLT
wait a moment	WOPLT
wait a moment, please	WOEPLTS
wait a moment, please	WOPLTS
wait a second	WAEBGD
wait a second, please	WAEBGDZ
wallflower	WAUL/TPHRO*UR
wam *(words a minute)*	WAPL
wam	W*/A*PL
warden(s)	WARPBD(Z)
wardenry	WARPBD/REU
warehouse	WROUS
warehouseman	WROUS/PHAPB
warehousemen	WROUS/PHEPB
wariness	WAEUR/R*EUPBS
warm *(as wd)*	WARPL
warm front	WAFRT
warmhearted	WARPL/HARTD
warrant	WARPBT
warrantable	WARPBT/-BL
warrantee	WARPBT/TAOE
warrantee	WARPB/TAOE
warrantor	WARPBT/TOR
warrantor	WARPB/TOR
warranty	WARPBT/TEU
warranty	WARPB/TEU
Washington	WA*/WA*
Washington	WARBG/TOPB
Washington, D.C.	WARBDZ
wasn't	WUPBT, WAEPBT
WASP *(white Anglo-Saxon Protestant)*	
	W-RBGS/A*RBGS/S*P
watchtower	WAFP/TO*UR
wateriness	WAT/R*EUPBS
waterpower	WAT/ER/PO*UR
watery	WAT/REU
WATS line	WATS/HRAOEUPB
wavelength	WA*EF/HR*EPBT
waviness	WA*EF/SR*EUPBS
waviness	WAE/SR*EUPBS
we *(as wd)*	WE
we'd	WAO*ED
we'll	WAO*EL
we're	WAO*ER
we've	W*EF
we've	WAOEF
we are	WER
we believe	WEBL
we believe the	WEBLT
we believed	WEBLD
we can	WEBG

we cannot	WEBG/TPHOT	weighty	WAEUT/TEU
we can't	WEBG/-PBT	welcome	W-BG
we can't	WE/K-PBT	welcomed	W-BGD
we could	WEBGD	welcomes	W-BGS
we feel	WEFL	welcoming	W-BG/-G
we felt	WEFLT	well *(as wd)*	WEL
we find	WEFPBD	well- *(as pre, with hyphen)*	WHEFL, WEL/H-F
we have	WEF	Well,	WERBLGS
we have been	WEFB	well-balanced	WHEFL/PWHRA*PBS/-D
we have believed	WEFBLD		
we have had	WEFD	well-being	WHEFL/PW-G
we have the	WEF/T-, WE/SR-T	well-educated	WHEFL/EGT/-D
we haven't	WEFPBT	well-informed	WHEFL/TPH-FD
we just want	W*EFPT	Wellington	WELG/TOPB
we just wanted	W*EFPTD	well-managed	WHEFL/PHAPBG/-D
we know	W*EPB	well-spoken	WHEFL/SPOEPB
we recall	WERL	well-thought-of *(j)*	WHEFL/THAUT/OF
we recalled	WERLD	well-to-do	WHEFL/TO/TKO
we recollect	WERBG	were *(as wd)*	W-R
we recollected	WERBGD	were the	W-RT
we remember	WERPL	weren't	W-RPBT
we remembered	WERPLD	west *(as wd)*	W*ES
we said	WEBS	West *(as wd)*	K-P/W*ES
we say	WEBZ	west side	W*DZ
we says	WEBSZ	West Virginia	W*ES/SRAFPLT
we shall	WERB	West Virginia	W*F/W*F
we should	WERBD	westbound *(as wd)*	W*B
we think	WEPBG	westbound lane	W*BL
we think so	WEPBGS	westbound traffic	W*BT
we think the	WEPBGT	westerly	W*ERL
we understand	WEPBDZ	Western *(as wd)*	K-P/W*ERPB
we understood	W*EPBDZ	western *(as wd)*	W*ERPB
we want	W*EPT	Western Samoa	W*ERPB/SPHOE/WA
we wanted	W*EPTD	westerner(s)	W*ERPB/ER(S)
we was	WEFS	Westerner(s)	K-P/W*ERPB/ER(S)
we were the	WERPT	what *(as wd)*	WHA
we were	WERP	what'd	WHA*D
we will	WE/HR-	what'll	WHA*L
wealthiness	WEL/TH*EUPBS	what's *(as wd)*	WHA*S, WHA/AOES
weapon(s) *(as wd)*	WEP(S)	what've	WHA*F
weapon(s) of mass destruction	WEPLD(Z)	what about	WHABT
		what are	WHAR
weaponize	WEP/AOEUZ	what are the	WHART
weaponry	WEP/REU	what can	WHA*BG
weariness	WAOE/R*EUPBS	what can the	WHA*BGT
weariness	WAOER/R*EUPBS	what could	WHABGD
weather *(as wd)*	W*ET/ER	what could	WHA*BGD
weather conditions	WEBGS	what else	WHAELS
Wednesday	WEPBZ	what else	WHA/ELS
weediness	WAOE/TK*EUPBS	what feel	WHAFL
weediness	WAOED/TK*EUPBS	what feels	WHAFLS
weekend(s)	WAOEBGD(Z)	what felt	WHAFLT
weeknight	WAOEUPBT	what had	WHAD
weight *(as wd)*	WAEUGT	what happened	WHAPD
weight of all the evidence	WA*EUFLD	what happens	WHAPS
weight of the evidence	WA*EUFD	what has	WHAZ
weight or preponderance of all the evidence	WA*EUFPLD	what have	WHAF
		what have been the	WHAFBT
weight or preponderance of the evidence	WA*EUFPD	what have been	WHAFB
		what have the	WHAFT
weightiness	WAEU/T*EUPBS	what he	WHAE
weightiness	WAEUT/T*EUPBS	what he believed	WHAEBLD
weighty	WAEU/TEU	what he believes	WHAEBLS

what he can	WHAEBG	what I can't	WHA*EU/K-PBT
what he cannot	WHAEBG/TPHOT	what I could	WHAEUBGD
what he can't	WHAEBG/-PBT	what I could not	WHAEUBGD/TPHOT
what he can't	WHAE/K-PBT	what I couldn't	WHAEUBGD/-PBT
what he could	WHAEBGD	what I ever	WHAEUFR
what he could not	WHAEBGD/TPHOT	what I feel	WHAEUFL
what he couldn't	WHAEBGD/-PBT	what I felt	WHAEUFLT
what he feel	WHAEFL	what I find	WHAEUFPBD
what he feels	WHAEFLS	what I go	WHAEUG
what he felt	WHAEFLT	what I had	WHAEUD
what he had	WHAED	what I had not	WHAEUD/TPHOT
what he had not	WHAED/TPHOT	what I hadn't	WHAEUD/-PBT
what he hadn't	WHAED/-PBT	what I hadn't	WHA*EU/H-PBT
what he hadn't	WHAE/H-PBT	what I happen	WHAEUP
what he happened	WHAEPD	what I happened	WHAEUPD
what he happens	WHAEPS	what I have	WHAEUF
what he has	WHAEZ	what I have been	WHAEUFB
what he has not	WHAEZ/TPHOT	what I have been the	WHAEUFBT
what he hasn't	WHAEZ/-PBT	what I have believed	WHAEUFBLD
what he hasn't	WHAE/HAPBT	what I have gone	WHAEUFG
what he is	WHAES	what I have had	WHAEUFD
what he is not	WHAES/TPHOT	what I have not	WHAEUF/TPHOT
what he isn't	WHAES/-PBT	what I haven't	WHAEUFPBT
what he isn't	WHAE/S-PBT	what I haven't	WHAEUF/-PBT
what he knows	WHAEPBS	what I have the	WHAEUFT
what he recalled	WHAERLD	what I know the	WHAEUPBT
what he recalls	WHAERLS	what I know	WHAEUPB
what he recollected	WHAERBGD	what I recall the	WHAEURLT
what he recollects	WHAERBGS	what I recall	WHAEURL
what he remembered	WHAERPLD	what I recalled	WHAEURLD
what he remembers	WHAERPLS	what I recollect the	WHAEURBGT
what he said	WHAEBS	what I recollect	WHAEURBG
what he say	WHAEBZ	what I recollected	WHAEURBGD
what he says	WHAEBSZ	what I remember the	WHAEURPLT
what he shall	WHAERB	what I remember	WHAEURPL
what he should	WHAERBD	what I remembered	WHAEURPLD
what he should not	WHAERBD/TPHOT	what I said	WHAEUBS
what he shouldn't	WHAERBD/-PBT	what I say	WHAEUBZ
what he thinks	WHAEPBGS	what I says	WHAEUBSZ
what he understand	WHAEPBDZ	what I shall	WHAEURB
what he understands	WHAEPBDZ/-S	what I should	WHAEURBD
what he understood	WHA*EPBDZ	what I should not	WHAEURBD/TPHOT
what he wanted	WHAEPTD	what I shouldn't	WHAEURBD/-PBT
what he wants	WHAEPTS	what I think	WHAEUPBG
what he was	WHAEFS	what I think the	WHAEUPBGT
what he was not	WHAEFS/TPHOT	what I understand	WHAEUPBDZ
what he wasn't	WHAEFS/-PBT	what I understood	WHA*EUPBDZ
what he wasn't	WHAE/WUPBT	what I want	WHAEUPT
what he will	WHA*EL	what I wanted	WHAEUPTD
what he will go	WHA*ELG	what I was	WHAEUFS
what he will go	WHAELG	what I was not	WHAEUFS/TPHOT
what he would	WHAELD	what I wasn't	WHAEUFS/-PBT
what he would not	WHAELD/TPHOT	what I will	WHA*EUL
what he wouldn't	WHAELD/-PBT	what I will go	WHAEULG
what I	WHA*EU	what I will go	WHA*EULG
what I am	WHAEUPL	what I would	WHAEULD
what I am the	WHAEUPLT	what I would not	WHAEULD/TPHOT
what I believe	WHAEUBL	what I wouldn't	WHAEULD/-PBT
what I believe the	WHAEUBLT	what, if anything, is	WHAFPBG
what I believed	WHAEUBLD	what is	WHAS
what I can	WHAEUBG	what is your age	WHAURPBLG
what I cannot	WHAEUBG/TPHOT	what is your full name	WHAUFRPB
what I can't	WHAEUBG/-PBT	what is your name	WHAURPB

what is your occupation	WHAURBGS	what were	WHARP
what is your position	WHAURPGS	what were the	WHARPT
what part	WHAPT	what will	WHAL
what shall	WHARB	what will go	WHALG
what she	SWHAE	what will the	WHALT
what she believed	SWHAEBLD	what would	WHALD
what she believes	SWHAEBLS	what you	WHAU
what she can	SWHAEBG	what you are	WHAUR
what she cannot	SWHAEBG/TPHOT	what you are not	WHAUR/TPHOT
what she can't	SWHAEBG/-PBT	what you aren't	WHAURPBT
what she could	SWHAEBGD	what you aren't	WHAUR/-PBT
what she could not	SWHAEBGD/TPHOT	what you aren't	WHAU/R-PBT
what she couldn't	SWHAEBGD/-PBT	what you are the	WHAURT
what she feels	SWHAEFLS	what you believe	WHAUBL
what she felt	SWHAEFLT	what you believe the	WHAUBLT
what she had	SWHAED	what you believed	WHAUBLD
what she had not	SWHAED/TPHOT	what you can	WHAUBG
what she hadn't	SWHAED/-PBT	what you cannot	WHAUBG/TPHOT
what she hadn't	SWHAE/H-PBT	what you can't	WHAUBG/-PBT
what she happened	SWHAEPD	what you can't	WHAU/K-PBT
what she happens	SWHAEPS	what you could	WHAUBGD
what she has	SWHAEZ	what you could not	WHAUBGD/TPHOT
what she has not	SWHAEZ/TPHOT	what you couldn't	WHAUBGD/-PBT
what she hasn't	SWHAEZ/-PBT	what you feel	WHAUFL
what she hasn't	SWHAE/HAPBT	what you felt	WHAUFLT
what she is	SWHAES	what you find	WHAUFPBD
what she is not	SWHAES/TPHOT	what you go	WHAUG
what she isn't	SWHAE/S-PBT	what you had	WHAUD
what she isn't	SWHAES/-PBT	what you had not	WHAUD/TPHOT
what she knows	SWHAEPBS	what you hadn't	WHAUD/-PBT
what she recalled	SWHAERLD	what you hadn't	WHAU/H-PBT
what she recalls	SWHAERLS	what you happen	WHAUP
what she recollected	SWHAERBGD	what you happened	WHAUPD
what she recollects	SWHAERBGS	what you have	WHAUF
what she remembered	SWHAERPLD	what you have been	WHAUFB
what she remembers	SWHAERPLS	what you have been the	WHAUFBT
what she said	SWHAEBS	what you have believed	WHAUFBLD
what she say	SWHAEBZ	what you have gone	WHAUFG
what she says	SWHAEBSZ	what you have had	WHAUFD
what she shall	SWHAERB	what you have not	WHAUF/TPHOT
what she should	SWHAERBD	what you haven't	WHAUFPBT
what she should not	SWHAERBD/TPHOT	what you haven't	WHAUF/-PBT
what she shouldn't	SWHAERBD/-PBT	what you haven't	WHAU/SR-PBT
what she thinks	SWHAEPBGS	what you have the	WHAUFT
what she understand	SWHAEPBDZ	what you know	WHAUPB
what she understands	SWHAEPBDZ/-S	what you know the	WHAUPBT
what she understood	SWHA*EPBDZ	what you mean	WHAUPL
what she wanted	SWHAEPTD	what you recall	WHAURL
what she wants	SWHAEPTS	what you recall the	WHAURLT
what she was	SWHAEFS	what you recalled	WHAURLD
what she was not	SWHAEFS/TPHOT	what you recollect	WHAURBG
what she wasn't	SWHAEFS/-PBT	what you recollect the	WHAURBGT
what she wasn't	SWHAE/WUPBT	what you recollected	WHAURBGD
what she will	SWHAEL	what you remember	WHAURPL
what she will go	SWHAELG	what you remember the	WHAURPLT
what she would	SWHAELD	what you remembered	WHAURPLD
what she would not	SWHAELD/TPHOT	what you said	WHAUBS
what she wouldn't	SWHAELD/-PBT	what you say	WHAUBZ
what should	WHARBD	what you says	WHAUBSZ
what side	WHADZ	what you shall	WHAURB
what the	WHAT	what you should	WHAURBD
what time	WHAPLT	what you should not	WHAURBD/TPHOT
what was	WHAFS	what you shouldn't	WHAURBD/-PBT

what you think	WHAUPBG	when he is not	WHES/TPHOT
what you think the	WHAUPBGT	when he is	WHES
what you understand	WHAUPBDZ	when he isn't	WHES/-PBT
what you understood	WHA*UPBDZ	when he isn't	WHE/S-PBT
what you want	WHAUPT	when he knows	WH*EPBS
what you wanted	WHAUPTD	when he recalled	WHERLD
what you were	WHAURP	when he recalls	WHERLS
what you were not	WHAURP/TPHOT	when he recollected	WHERBGD
what you weren't	WHAURP/-PBT	when he recollects	WHERBGS
what you weren't	WHAU/W-RPBT	when he remembered	WHERPLD
what you were the	WHAURPT	when he remembers	WHERPLS
what you will	WHAUL	when he said	WHEBS
what you will go	WHAULG	when he say	WHEBZ
what you would not	WHAULD/TPHOT	when he says	WHEBSZ
what you would	WHAULD	when he shall	WHERB
what you wouldn't	WHAULD/-PBT	when he should	WHERBD
whatever	WHA*FR, WHAFR	when he should not	WHERBD/TPHOT
whatnot	WHA/TPHOT	when he shouldn't	WHERBD/-PBT
what's your age	WHA*URPBLG	when he thinks	WHEPBGS
what's your full name	WHA*UFRPB	when he understand	WHEPBDZ
what's your name	WHA*URPB	when he understands	WHEPBDZ/-S
what's your occupation	WHA*URBGS	when he understood	WH*EPBDZ
what's your position	WHA*URPGS	when he wanted	WHEPTD
whatsoever	WHA/SO*FR, WHA/SOFR	when he wants	WHEPTS
		when he was	WHEFS
wheelchair	WHAOEFP	when he was not	WHEFS/TPHOT
when (as wd)	WHEPB	when he wasn't	WHEFS/-PBT
when'd	WH*D	when he wasn't	WHE/WUPBT
when'll	WH*L	when he will	WHEL
when's	WH*S	when he will go	WHELG
when've	WH*F	when he would	WHELD
when are	WH-R	when he would not	WHELD/TPHOT
when are the	WH-RT	when he wouldn't	WHELD/-PBT
when can	WH-BG	when I	WH*EU
when can the	WH-BGT	when I am	WH*EUPL
when could	WH-BGD	when I am the	WH*EUPLT
whenever	WH*FR, WH-FR	when I believe	WHEUBL
when had	WH-D	when I believe the	WHEUBLT
when has	WH-Z	when I believed	WHEUBLD
when have	WH-F	when I can	WHEUBG
when have the	WH-FT	when I cannot	WHEUBG/TPHOT
when he	WHE	when I can't	WHEUBG/-PBT
when he believed	WHEBLD	when I can't	WH*EU/K-PBT
when he believes	WHEBLS	when I could	WHEUBGD
when he can	WHEBG	when I could not	WHEUBGD/TPHOT
when he cannot	WHEBG/TPHOT	when I couldn't	WHEUBGD/-PBT
when he can't	WHEBG/-PBT	when I feel	WHEUFL
when he can't	WHE/K-PBT	when I felt	WHEUFLT
when he could	WHEBGD	when I find	WHEUFPBD
when he could not	WHEBGD/TPHOT	when I go	WH*EUG
when he couldn't	WHEBGD/-PBT	when I had	WHEUD
when he feels	WHEFLS	when I had not	WHEUD/TPHOT
when he felt	WHEFLT	when I hadn't	WHEUD/-PBT
when he had	WHED	when I hadn't	WH*EU/H-PBT
when he had not	WHED/TPHOT	when I happen	WH*EUP
when he hadn't	WHED/-PBT	when I happened	WHEUPD
when he hadn't	WHE/H-PBT	when I happened	WH*EUPD
when he happened	WHEPD	when I have	WH*EUF
when he happens	WHEPS	when I have	WHEPB/EUF
when he has	WHEZ	when I have been	WHEUFB
when he has not	WHEZ/TPHOT	when I have been	WH*EUFB
when he hasn't	WHEZ/-PBT	when I have been the	WHEUFBT
when he hasn't	WHE/HAPBT	when I have been the	WH*EUFBT

when I have gone	WHEUFG	when she had not	SWHED/TPHOT
when I have gone	WH*EUFG	when she hadn't	SWHED/-PBT
when I have had	WHEUFD	when she hadn't	SWHE/H-PBT
when I have had	WH*EUFD	when she happened	SWHEPD
when I have not	WH*EUF/TPHOT	when she happens	SWHEPS
when I have not	WHEPB/EUF/TPHOT	when she has	SWHEZ
when I haven't	WHEUFPBT	when she has not	SWHEZ/TPHOT
when I haven't	WH*EUFPBT	when she hasn't	SWHEZ/-PBT
when I haven't	WH*EUF/-PBT	when she hasn't	SWHE/HAPBT
when I haven't	WH*EU/SR-PBT	when she is	SWHES
when I have the	WHEUFT	when she is not	SWHES/TPHOT
when I have the	WH*EUFT	when she isn't	SWHES/-PBT
when I know	WHEUPB	when she isn't	SWHE/S-PBT
when I know the	WHEUPBT	when she knows	SWHEPBS
when I recall	WH*EURL	when she recalled	SWHERLD
when I recall	WHEPB/EURL	when she recalls	SWHERLS
when I recall the	WHEURLT	when she recollected	SWHERBGD
when I recall the	WH*EURLT	when she recollects	SWHERBGS
when I recalled	WHEURLD	when she remembered	SWHERPLD
when I recalled	WH*EURLD	when she remembers	SWHERPLS
when I recollect	WHEURBG	when she said	SWHEBS
when I recollect the	WHEURBGT	when she say	SWHEBZ
when I recollected	WHEURBGD	when she says	SWHEBSZ
when I remember	WHEURPL	when she shall	SWHERB
when I remember the	WHEURPLT	when she should not	SWHERBD/TPHOT
when I remembered	WHEURPLD	when she should	SWHERBD
when I said	WHEUBS	when she shouldn't	SWHERBD/-PBT
when I say	WHEUBZ	when she thinks	SWHEPBGS
when I says	WHEUBSZ	when she understands	SWHEPBDZ/-S
when I shall	WHEURB	when she understood	SWH*EPBDZ
when I should	WHEURBD	when she wanted	SWHEPTD
when I should not	WHEURBD/TPHOT	when she wants	SWHEPTS
when I shouldn't	WHEURBD/-PBT	when she was	SWHEFS
when I think	WHEUPBG	when she was not	SWHEFS/TPHOT
when I think the	WHEUPBGT	when she wasn't	SWHEFS/-PBT
when I understand	WHEUPBD	when she wasn't	SWHE/WUPBT
when I understood	WH*EUPBDZ	when she will	SWHEL
when I want	WHEUPT	when she will go	SWHELG
when I wanted	WHEUPTD	when she would	SWHELD
when I was not	WHEUFS/TPHOT	when she would not	SWHELD/TPHOT
when I was	WHEUFS	when she wouldn't	SWHELD/-PBT
when I wasn't	WHEUFS/-PBT	when should	WH-RBD
when I wasn't	WH*EU/WUPBT	when the	WH-T
when I will	WHEUL	when was	WH-FS
when I will go	WHEULG	when were	WH-RP
when I would	WHEULD	when were the	WH-RPT
when I would not	WHEULD/TPHOT	when will	WH-L
when I wouldn't	WHEULD/-PBT	when will the	WH-LT
when is	WH-S	when would	WH-LD
when shall	WH-RB	when you	WHU
when she	SWHE	when you are	WHUR
when she believed	SWHEBLD	when you are not	WHUR/TPHOT
when she believes	SWHEBLS	when you aren't	WHURPBT
when she can	SWHEBG	when you aren't	WHUR/-PBT
when she cannot	SWHEBG/TPHOT	when you are the	WHURT
when she can't	SWHEBG/-PBT	when you believe	WHUBL
when she can't	SWHE/K-PBT	when you believe the	WHUBLT
when she could	SWHEBGD	when you believed	WHUBLD
when she could not	SWHEBGD/TPHOT	when you can	WHUBG
when she couldn't	SWHEBGD/-PBT	when you cannot	WHUBG/TPHOT
when she feels	SWHEFLS	when you can't	WHUBG/-PBT
when she felt	SWHEFLT	when you can't	WHU/K-PBT
when she had	SWHED	when you could	WHUBGD

when you could not	WHUBGD/TPHOT	where's	WR*S
when you couldn't	WHUBGD/-PBT	where've	WR*F
when you ever	WHUFR	whereabout	WR-BT, WRABT
when you ever go	WHUFRG	whereabouts	WR-BTS
when you ever had	WHUFRD	whereabouts	WRABTS, WRABT/-S
when you feel	WHUFL	where about	WR-/ABT
when you felt	WHUFLT	where are	WR-R
when you find	WHUFPBD	where are the	WR-RT
when you go	WHUG	whereas	WRAZ
when you had	WHUD	where as	WR-/AZ
when you had not	WHUD/TPHOT	whereat	WRAT
when you hadn't	WHUD/-PBT	where at	WR-/AT
when you hadn't	WHU/H-PBT	whereby	WR-B
when you happen	WHUP	where by	WR-/PWEU
when you happened	WHUPD	where can	WR-BG
when you have	WHUF	where can the	WR-BGT
when you have been	WHUFB	where could	WR-BGD
when you have been the	WHUFBT	where do you live	WROUL
when you have believed	WHUFBLD	where do you reside	WROURD
when you have gone	WHUFG	where do you work	WROURBG
when you have had	WHUFD	where else	WRELS, WR-/ELS
when you have not	WHUF/TPHOT	wherefore(s)	WR-FR(S)
when you haven't	WHUFPBT	where had	WR-D
when you haven't	WHUF/-PBT	where has	WR-Z
when you haven't	WHU/SR-PBT	where have	WR-F
when you have the	WHUFT	where have the	WR-FT
when you know	WHUPB	where he	WRE
when you know the	WHUPBT	where he believed	WREBLD
when you recall	WHURL	where he believes	WREBLS
when you recall the	WHURLT	where he can	WR*EBG
when you recalled	WHURLD	where he can	WRE/K-
when you recollect	WHURBG	where he cannot	WR*EBG/TPHOT
when you recollect the	WHURBGT	where he can't	WR*EBG/-PBT
when you recollected	WHURBGD	where he can't	WRE/K-PBT
when you remember	WHURPL	where he could	WREBGD
when you remember the	WHURPLT	where he could not	WREBGD/TPHOT
when you remembered	WHURPLD	where he couldn't	WREBGD/-PBT
when you said	WHUBS	where he feels	WREFLS
when you say	WHUBZ	where he felt	WREFLT
when you says	WHUBSZ	where he had	WRED
when you shall	WHURB	where he had not	WRED/TPHOT
when you should	WHURBD	where he hadn't	WRED/-PBT
when you should not	WHURBD/TPHOT	where he hadn't	WRE/H-PBT
when you shouldn't	WHURBD/-PBT	where he happened	WREPD
when you think	WHUPG	where he happens	WREPS
when you think the	WHUPBGT	where he has	WREZ
when you understand	WHUPBDZ	where he has not	WREZ/TPHOT
when you understood	WH*UPBDZ	where he hasn't	WREZ/-PBT
when you want	WHUPT	where he hasn't	WRE/HAPBT
when you wanted	WHUPTD	where he is	WRES
when you were	WHURP	where he is not	WRES/TPHOT
when you were not	WHURP/TPHOT	where he isn't	WRES/-PBT
when you weren't	WHURP/-PBT	where he isn't	WRE/S-PBT
when you weren't	WHU/W-RPBT	where he knows	WREPBS
when you were the	WHURPT	where he recalled	WRERLD
when you will	WHUL	where he recalls	WRERLS
when you will go	WHULG	where he recollected	WRERBGD
when you would	WHULD	where he recollects	WRERBGS
when you would not	WHULD/TPHOT	where he remembered	WRERPLD
when you wouldn't	WHULD/-PBT	where he remembers	WRERPLS
where *(as wd)*	WR-	where he said	WREBS
where'd	WR*D	where he say	WREBZ
where'll	WR*L	where he says	WREBSZ

where he shall	WRERB	where I remember	WREURPL
where he should	WRERBD	where I remembered	WREURPLD
where he should not	WRERBD/TPHOT	where I said	WREUBS
where he shouldn't	WRERBD/-PBT	where I say	WREUBZ
where he thinks	WREPBGS	where I says	WREUBSZ
where he understands	WREPBDZ/-S	where I shall	WREURB
where he understood	WR*EPBDZ	where I should	WREURBD
where he wanted	WREPTD	where I should not	WREURBD/TPHOT
where he wants	WREPTS	where I shouldn't	WREURBD/-PBT
where he was	WREFS	where I think	WR*EUPBG
where he was not	WREFS/TPHOT	where I think	WR-/EUPBG
where he wasn't	WREFS/-PBT	where I think the	WR*EUPBGT
where he wasn't	WRE/WUPBT	where I think the	WR-/EUPBGT
where he will	WREL	where I understand	WREUPBDZ
where he will go	WRELG	where I understood	WR*EUPBDZ
where he would	WRELD	where I want	WREUPT
where he would not	WRELD/TPHOT	where I wanted	WREUPTD
where he wouldn't	WRELD/-PBT	where I was	WREUFS
where I	WR*EU	where I was not	WREUFS/TPHOT
where I am	WREUPL	where I wasn't	WREUFS/-PBT
where I am the	WREUPLT	where I wasn't	WR*EU/WUPBT
where I believe	WREUBL	where I will	WREUL
where I believe the	WREUBLT	where I will go	WREULG
where I believed	WREUBLD	where I would	WREULD
where I can	WREUBG	where I would not	WREULD/TPHOT
where I cannot	WREUBG/TPHOT	where I wouldn't	WREULD/-PBT
where I can't	WREUBG/-PBT	wherein	WR-PB
where I can't	WR*EU/K-PBT	where in	WR-/TPH-
where I could	WREUBGD	where is	WR-S
where I could not	WREUBGD/TPHOT	whereof	WROF
where I couldn't	WREUBGD/-PBT	whereon	WROPB
where I feel	WREUFL	where on	WR-/OPB
where I felt	WREUFLT	where shall	WR-RB
where I find	WREUFPBD	where she	SWRE
where I go	WR*EUG	where she believed	SWREBLD
where I go	WR*EU/TKPWO	where she believes	SWREBLS
where I had	WREUD	where she can	SWREBG
where I had not	WREUD/TPHOT	where she cannot	SWREBG/TPHOT
where I hadn't	WREUD/-PBT	where she can't	SWREBG/-PBT
where I hadn't	WR*EU/H-PBT	where she can't	SWRE/K-PBT
where I happen	WREUP	where she could	SWREBGD
where I happened	WREUPD	where she could not	SWREBGD/TPHOT
where I have	WREUF	where she couldn't	SWREBGD/-PBT
where I have been	WREUFB	where she feels	SWREFLS
where I have been the	WREUFBT	where she felt	SWREFLT
where I have believed	WREUFBLD	where she had	SWRED
where I have gone	WREUFG	where she had not	SWRED/TPHOT
where I have had	WREUFD	where she hadn't	SWRED/-PBT
where I have not	WREUF/TPHOT	where she hadn't	SWRE/H-PBT
where I haven't	WREUFPBT	where she happened	SWREPD
where I haven't	WREUF/-PBT	where she happens	SWREPS
where I haven't	WR*EU/SR-PBT	where she has	SWREZ
where I have the	WREUFT	where she has not	SWREZ/TPHOT
where I know	WR*EUPB	where she hasn't	SWREZ/-PBT
where I know the	WREUPBT	where she hasn't	SWRE/HAPBT
where I know the	WR*EUPBT	where she is	SWRES
where I recall the	WREURLT	where she is not	SWRES/TPHOT
where I recall	WREURL	where she isn't	SWRES/-PBT
where I recalled	WREURLD	where she isn't	SWRE/S-PBT
where I recollect the	WREURBGT	where she knows	SWREPBS
where I recollect	WREURBG	where she recalled	SWRERLD
where I recollected	WREURBGD	where she recalls	SWRERLS
where I remember the	WREURPLT	where she recollected	SWRERBGD

© 2004 StenEd® Briefs & Phrases (Excerpted from StenEd's Realtime Professional Dictionary)

where she recollects	SWRERBGS	where you have been	WRUFB
where she remembered	SWRERPLD	where you have been the	WRUFBT
where she remembers	SWRERPLS	where you have believed	WRUFBLD
where she said	SWREBS	where you have gone	WRUFG
where she say	SWREBZ	where you have had	WRUFD
where she says	SWREBSZ	where you have not	WRUF/TPHOT
where she shall	SWRERB	where you haven't	WRUFPBT
where she should	SWRERBD	where you haven't	WRUF/-PBT
where she should not	SWRERBD/TPHOT	where you haven't	WRU/SR-PBT
where she shouldn't	SWRERBD/-PBT	where you have the	WRUFT
where she thinks	SWREPBGS	where you know	WRUPB
where she understand	SWREPBDZ	where you know the	WRUPBT
where she understands	SWREPBDZ/-S	where you recall	WRURL
where she understood	SWR*EPBDZ	where you recall the	WRURLT
where she wanted	SWREPTD	where you recalled	WRURLD
where she wants	SWREPTS	where you recollect	WRURBG
where she was	SWREFS	where you recollect the	WRURBGT
where she was not	SWREFS/TPHOT	where you recollected	WRURBGD
where she wasn't	SWREFS/-PBT	where you remember	WRURPL
where she wasn't	SWRE/WUPBT	where you remember the	WRURPLT
where she will	SWREL	where you remembered	WRURPLD
where she will go	SWRELG	where you reside	WRURD
where she would	SWRELD	where you said	WRUBS
where she would not	SWRELD/TPHOT	where you say	WRUBZ
where she wouldn't	SWRELD/-PBT	where you says	WRUBSZ
where should	WR-RBD	where you shall	WRURB
where the	WR-T	where you should	WRURBD
whereupon	WRUP, WR-/POPB	where you should not	WRURBD/TPHOT
wherever	WR*FR	where you shouldn't	WRURBD/-PBT
where was	WR-FS	where you think	WR*UPBG
where were	WR-RP	where you think	WR-/UPBG
where were the	WR-RPT	where you think the	WR*UPBGT
where will	WR-L	where you think the	WR/-UPBGT
where will the	WR-LT	where you understand	WRUPBDZ
where would	WR-LD	where you understood	WR*UPBDZ
where you	WRU	where you want	WRUPT
where you are	WRUR	where you wanted	WRUPTD
where you are not	WRUR/TPHOT	where you were	WRURP
where you are the	WRURT	where you were not	WRURP/TPHOT
where you aren't	WRURPBT	where you weren't	WRURP/-PBT
where you aren't	WRUR/-PBT	where you weren't	WRU/W-RPBT
where you believe	WRUBL	where you were the	WRURPT
where you believe the	WRUBLT	where you will	WRUL
where you believed	WRUBLD	where you will go	WRULG
where you can	WRUBG	where you would	WRULD
where you cannot	WRUBG/TPHOT	where you would not	WRULD/TPHOT
where you can't	WRUBG/-PBT	where you wouldn't	WRULD/-PBT
where you can't	WRU/K-PBT	whether *(as wd)*	WHR-
where you could	WRUBGD	whether every	WHR-FR
where you could not	WRUBGD/TPHOT	whether he	WHRE
where you couldn't	WRUBGD/-PBT	whether he believed	WHREBLD
where you feel	WRUFL	whether he believes	WHREBLS
where you felt	WRUFLT	whether he can	WHREBG
where you find	WRUFPBD	whether he cannot	WHREBG/TPHOT
where you go	WRUG	whether he could	WHREBGD
where you had	WRUD	whether he ever	WHREFR
where you had not	WRUD/TPHOT	whether he feels	WHREFLS
where you hadn't	WRUD/-PBT	whether he felt	WHREFLT
where you hadn't	WRU/H-PBT	whether he had	WHRED
where you happen	WR*UP	whether he happened	WHREPD
where you happened	WRUPD	whether he happens	WHREPS
where you happened	WR*UPD	whether he has	WHREZ
where you have	WRUF	whether he is	WHRES

whether or not I recall the	WHROEURLT
whether he knows	WHREPBS
whether he recalled	WHRERLD
whether he recalls	WHRERLS
whether he recollected	WHRERBGD
whether he recollects	WHRERBGS
whether he remembered	WHRERPLD
whether he remembers	WHRERPLS
whether he said	WHREBS
whether he say	WHREBZ
whether he says	WHREBSZ
whether he shall	WHRERB
whether he should	WHRERBD
whether he thinks	WHREPBGS
whether he understand	WHREPBDZ
whether he understands	WHREPBDZ/-S
whether he understood	WHR*EPBDZ
whether he wanted	WHREPTD
whether he wants	WHREPTS
whether he was	WHREFS
whether he will	WHREL
whether he will go	WHRELG
whether he would	WHRELD
whether I	WHREU
whether I am	WHREUPL
whether I am the	WHREUPLT
whether I believe	WHREUBL
whether I believe the	WHREUBLT
whether I believed	WHREUBLD
whether I can	WHREUBG
whether I cannot	WHREUBG/TPHOT
whether I could	WHREUBGD
whether I ever	WHREUFR
whether I feel	WHREUFL
whether I felt	WHREUFLT
whether I had	WHREUD
whether I happen	WHREUP
whether I happened	WHREUPD
whether I have	WHREUF
whether I have been	WHREUFB
whether I have been the	WHREUFBT
whether I have had	WHREUFD
whether I have the	WHREUFT
whether I know	WHREUPB
whether I know the	WHREUPBT
whether I recall	WHREURL
whether I recall the	WHREURLT
whether I recalled	WHREURLD
whether I recollect the	WHREURBGT
whether I recollect	WHREURBG
whether I recollected	WHREURBGD
whether I remember	WHREURPL
whether I remember the	WHREURPLT
whether I remembered	WHREURPLD
whether I said	WHREUBS
whether I say	WHREUBZ
whether I says	WHREUBSZ
whether I shall	WHREURB
whether I should	WHREURBD
whether I think	WHREUPBG
whether I think so	WHREUPBGS
whether I think the	WHREUPBGT
whether I understand	WHREUPBDZ
whether I understood	WHR*EUPBDZ
whether I want	WHREUPT
whether I wanted	WHREUPTD
whether I was	WHREUFS
whether I will	WHREUL
whether I will go	WHREULG
whether I would	WHREULD
whether or not	WHRORPBT
whether or not he	WHROE
whether or not he believed	WHROEBLD
whether or not he believes	WHROEBLS
whether or not he can	WHROEBG
whether or not he could	WHROEBGD
whether or not he feels	WHROEFLS
whether or not he felt	WHROEFLT
whether or not he had	WHROED
whether or not he happened	WHROEPD
whether or not he happens	WHROEPS
whether or not he has	WHROEZ
whether or not he is	WHROES
whether or not he knows	WHROEPBS
whether or not he recalled	WHROERLD
whether or not he recalls	WHROERLS
whether or not he recollected	WHROERBGD
whether or not he recollects	WHROERBGS
whether or not he remembered	WHROERPLD
whether or not he remembers	WHROERPLS
whether or not he said	WHROEBS
whether or not he say	WHROEBZ
whether or not he says	WHROEBSZ
whether or not he shall	WHROERB
whether or not he should	WHROERBD
whether or not he thinks	WHROEPBGS
whether or not he understand	WHROEPBDZ
whether or not he understands	WHROEPBDZ/-S
whether or not he understood	WHRO*EPBDZ
whether or not he wanted	WHROEPTD
whether or not he wants	WHROEPTS
whether or not he was	WHROEFS
whether or not he will	WHROEL
whether or not he will go	WHROELG
whether or not he would	WHROELD
whether or not I	WHROEU
whether or not I am	WHROEUPL
whether or not I am the	WHROEUPLT
whether or not I believe	WHROEUBL
whether or not I believe the	WHROEUBLT
whether or not I believed	WHROEUBLD
whether or not I can	WHROEUBG
whether or not I could	WHROEUBGD
whether or not I feel	WHROEUFL
whether or not I felt	WHROEUFLT
whether or not I had	WHROEUD
whether or not I happen	WHROEUP
whether or not I happened	WHROEUPD
whether or not I have	WHROEUF
whether or not I have been	WHROEUFB
whether or not I have been the	WHROEUFBT
whether or not I have had	WHROEUFD
whether or not I have the	WHROEUFT
whether or not I know	WHROEUPB
whether or not I know the	WHROEUPBT
whether or not I recall	WHROEURL

whether or not I recall the	WHROEURLT	whether or not you are the	WHROURT
whether or not I recalled	WHROEURLD	whether or not you believe	WHROUBL
whether or not I recollect	WHROEURBG	whether or not you believe the	WHROUBLT
whether or not I recollect the	WHROEURBGT	whether or not you believed	WHROUBLD
whether or not I recollected	WHROEURBGD	whether or not you can	WHROUBG
whether or not I remember	WHROEURPL	whether or not you could	WHROUBGD
whether or not I remember the	WHROEURPLT	whether or not you feel	WHROUFL
whether or not I remembered	WHROEURPLD	whether or not you felt	WHROUFLT
whether or not I said	WHROEUBS	whether or not you had	WHROUD
whether or not I say	WHROEUBZ	whether or not you happen	WHROUP
whether or not I says	WHROEUBSZ	whether or not you happened	WHROUPD
whether or not I shall	WHROEURB	whether or not you have	WHROUF
whether or not I should	WHROEURBD	whether or not you have been	WHROUFB
whether or not I think	WHROEUPBG	whether or not you have been the	WHROUFBT
whether or not I think so	WHROEUPBGS	whether or not you have had	WHROUFD
whether or not I think the	WHROEUPBGT	whether or not you have the	WHROUFT
whether or not I understand	WHROEUPBDZ	whether or not you know	WHROUPB
whether or not I understood	WHRO*EUPBDZ	whether or not you know the	WHROUPBT
whether or not I want	WHROEUPT	whether or not you recall	WHROURL
whether or not I wanted	WHROEUPTD	whether or not you recall the	WHROURLT
whether or not I was	WHROEUFS	whether or not you recalled	WHROURLD
whether or not I will	WHROEUL	whether or not you recollect	WHROURBG
whether or not I will go	WHROEULG	whether or not you recollect the	WHROURBGT
whether or not I would	WHROEULD	whether or not you recollected	WHROURBGD
whether or not she	SWHROE	whether or not you remember	WHROURPL
whether or not she believed	SWHROEBLD	whether or not you remember the	WHROURPLT
whether or not she believes	SWHROEBLS	whether or not you remembered	WHROURPLD
whether or not she can	SWHROEBG	whether or not you said	WHROUBS
whether or not she could	SWHROEBGD	whether or not you say	WHROUBZ
whether or not she feels	SWHROEFLS	whether or not you says	WHROUBSZ
whether or not she felt	SWHROEFLT	whether or not you shall	WHROURB
whether or not she had	SWHROED	whether or not you should	WHROURBD
whether or not she happened	SWHROEPD	whether or not you think	WHROUPBG
whether or not she happens	SWHROEPS	whether or not you think so	WHROUPBGS
whether or not she has	SWHROEZ	whether or not you think the	WHROUPBGT
whether or not she is	SWHROES	whether or not you understand	WHROUPBDZ
whether or not she knows	SWHROEPBS	whether or not you understood	WHRO*UPBDZ
whether or not she recalled	SWHROERLD	whether or not you want	WHROUPT
whether or not she recalls	SWHROERLS	whether or not you wanted	WHROUPTD
whether or not she recollected	SWHROERBGD	whether or not you were the	WHROURPT
whether or not she recollects	SWHROERBGS	whether or not you were	WHROURP
whether or not she remembered	SWHROERPLD	whether or not you will	WHROUL
whether or not she remembers	SWHROERPLS	whether or not you will go	WHROULG
whether or not she said	SWHROEBS	whether or not you would	WHROULD
whether or not she say	SWHROEBZ	whether she	SWHRE
whether or not she says	SWHROEBSZ	whether she believed	SWHREBLD
whether or not she shall	SWHROERB	whether she believes	SWHREBLS
whether or not she should	SWHROERBD	whether she can	SWHREBG
whether or not she thinks	SWHROEPBGS	whether she cannot	SWHREBG/TPHOT
whether or not she understand	SWHROEPBDZ	whether she could	SWHREBGD
whether or not she understands	SWHROEPBDZ/-S	whether she feels	SWHREFLS
whether or not she understood	SWHRO*EPBDZ	whether she felt	SWHREFLT
whether or not she wanted	SWHROEPTD	whether she had	SWHRED
whether or not she wants	SWHROEPTS	whether she happened	SWHREPD
whether or not she was	SWHROEFS	whether she happens	SWHREPS
whether or not she will	SWHROEL	whether she has	SWHREZ
whether or not she will go	SWHROELG	whether she is	SWHRES
whether or not she would	SWHROELD	whether she knows	SWHREPBS
whether or not you	WHROU	whether she recalled	SWHRERLD
whether or not you are	WHROUR	whether she recalls	SWHRERLS
whether or not you are able	WHROURBL	whether she recollected	SWHRERBGD
whether or not you are able to	WHROURBLT	whether she recollects	SWHRERBGS
whether or not you are able to say	WHROURBLTS	whether she remembered	SWHRERPLD

whether she remembers	SWHRERPLS	whether you will go	WHRULG	
whether she said	SWHREBS	whether you would	WHRULD	
whether she say	SWHREBZ	which *(as wd)*	KH-	
whether she says	SWHREBSZ	which are	KH-R	
whether she shall	SWHRERB	which are the	KH-RT	
whether she should	SWHRERBD	which can	KH-BG	
whether she thinks	SWHREPBGS	which cannot	KH-BG/TPHOT	
whether she understand	SWHREPBDZ	which could	KH-BGD	
whether she understands	SWHREPBDZ/-S	which feel	KH-FL	
whether she understood	SWHR*EPBDZ	which feels	KH-FLS	
whether she wanted	SWHREPTD	which felt	KH-FLT	
whether she wants	SWHREPTS	which had	KH-D	
whether she was	SWHREFS	which happened	KH-PD	
whether she will	SWHREL	which happens	KH-PS	
whether she will go	SWHRELG	which has	KH-Z	
whether she would	SWHRELD	which have	KH-F	
whether the	WHR-T	which have been	KH-FB	
whether you	WHRU	which have been the	KH-FBT	
whether you are	WHRUR	which have had	KH-FD	
whether you are able	WHRURBL	which have the	KH-FT	
whether you are able to	WHRURBLT	which he	KHE	
whether you are able to say	WHRURBLTS	which he believed	KHEBLD	
whether you are the	WHRURT	which he believes	KHEBLS	
whether you believe	WHRUBL	which he can	KHE/K-	
whether you believe the	WHRUBLT	which he could	KHEBGD	
whether you believed	WHRUBLD	which he feels	KHEFLS	
whether you can	WHRUBG	which he felt	KHEFLT	
whether you cannot	WHRUBG/TPHOT	which he had	KHED	
whether you could	WHRUBGD	which he happened	KHEPD	
whether you feel	WHRUFL	which he happens	KHEPS	
whether you felt	WHRUFLT	which he has	KHEZ	
whether you had	WHRUD	which he is	KHES	
whether you have	WHRUF	which he knows	KHEPBS	
whether you have been	WHRUFB	which he recalled	KHERLD	
whether you have been the	WHRUFBT	which he recalls	KHERLS	
whether you have had	WHRUFD	which he recollected	KHERBGD	
whether you have the	WHRUFT	which he recollects	KHERBGS	
whether you know	WHRUPB	which he remembered	KHERPLD	
whether you know the	WHRUPBT	which he remembers	KHERPLS	
whether you recall	WHRURL	which he said	KHEBS	
whether you recall the	WHRURLT	which he say	KHEBZ	
whether you recalled	WHRURLD	which he says	KHEBSZ	
whether you recollect	WHRURBG	which he shall	KHERB	
whether you recollect the	WHRURBGT	which he should	KHERBD	
whether you recollected	WHRURBGD	which he thinks	KHEPBGS	
whether you remember	WHRURPL	which he understand	KHEPBDZ	
whether you remember the	WHRURPLT	which he understands	KHEPBDZ/-S	
whether you remembered	WHRURPLD	which he understood	KH*EPBDZ	
whether you said	WHRUBS	which he wanted	KHEPTD	
whether you say	WHRUBZ	which he wants	KHEPTS	
whether you says	WHRUBSZ	which he was	KHEFS	
whether you shall	WHRURB	which he will	KHEL	
whether you should	WHRURBD	which he will go	KHELG	
whether you think	WHRUPBG	which he would	KHELD	
whether you think so	WHRUPBGS	which I	KH*EU	
whether you think the	WHRUPBGT	which I am	KHEUPL	
whether you understand	WHRUPBDZ	which I am the	KHEUPLT	
whether you understood	WHR*UPBDZ	which I believe	KHEUBL	
whether you want	WHRUPT	which I believe the	KHEUBLT	
whether you wanted	WHRUPTD	which I believed	KHEUBLD	
whether you were the	WHRURPT	which I can	KH*EUBG	
whether you were	WHRURP	which I cannot	KH*EUBG/TPHOT	
whether you will	WHRUL	which I could	KHEUBGD	

which I feel	KHEUFL	which she should	SKHERBD
which I felt	KHEUFLT	which she thinks	SKHEPBGS
which I had	KHEUD	which she understand	SKHEPBDZ
which I happen	KH*EUP	which she understands	SKHEPBDZ/-S
which I happened	KHEUPD	which she understood	SKH*EPBDZ
which I have	KHEUF	which she wanted	SKHEPTD
which I have been	KHEUFB	which she wants	SKHEPTS
which I have been the	KHEUFBT	which she was	SKHEFS
which I have had	KHEUFD	which she will	SKHEL
which I have the	KHEUFT	which she will go	SKHELG
which I know	KH*EUPB	which she would	SKHELD
which I know the	KH*EUPBT, KHEUPBT	which should	KH-RBD
which I recall	KHEURL	which side	KH-DZ
which I recall the	KHEURLT	which the	KH-T
which I recalled	KHEURLD	which was	KH-FS
which I recollect	KHEURBG	which were	KH-RP
which I recollect the	KHEURBGT	which were the	KH-RPT
which I recollected	KHEURBGD	which will	KH-L
which I remember	KHEURPL	which will go	KH-LG
which I remember the	KHEURPLT	which will the	KH-LT
which I remembered	KHEURPLD	which would	KH-LD
which I said	KHEUBS	which you	KHU
which I say	KHEUBZ	which you are	KH*UR
which I says	KHEUBSZ	which you are the	KH*URT
which I shall	KHEURB	which you believe	KHUBL
which I should	KHEURBD	which you believe the	KHUBLT
which I think the	KHEUPBGT	which you believed	KHUBLD
which I think	KHEUPBG	which you can	KH-/UBG
which I understand	KHEUPBDZ	which you could	KHUBGD
which I understood	KH*EUPBDZ	which you feel	KHUFL
which I want	KHEUPT	which you felt	KHUFLT
which I wanted	KHEUPTD	which you find	KHUFPBD
which I was	KHEUFS	which you had	KHUD
which I will	KH*EUL	which you have	KHUF
which I will go	KH*EULG, KHEULG	which you have been	KHUFB
which I would	KHEULD	which you have been the	KHUFBT
which is	KH-S	which you have had	KHUFD
which part	KH-PT	which you have the	KHUFT
which shall	KH-RB	which you know	KHUPB
which she	SKHE	which you know the	KHUPBT
which she believed	SKHEBLD	which you recall	KH*URL
which she believes	SKHEBLS	which you recall the	KH*URLT
which she can	SKHEBG	which you recalled	KH*URLD
which she cannot	SKHEBG/TPHOT	which you recollect	KHURBG
which she could	SKHEBGD	which you recollect the	KHURBGT
which she feels	SKHEFLS	which you recollected	KHURBGD
which she felt	SKHEFLT	which you remember	KHURPL
which she had	SKHED	which you remember the	KHURPLT
which she happened	SKHEPD	which you remembered	KHURPLD
which she happens	SKHEPS	which you said	KHUBS
which she has	SKHEZ	which you say	KHUBZ
which she is	SKHES	which you says	KHUBSZ
which she knows	SKHEPBS	which you shall	KHURB
which she recalled	SKHERLD	which you should	KHURBD
which she recalls	SKHERLS	which you think	KHUPBG
which she recollected	SKHERBGD	which you think the	KHUPBGT
which she recollects	SKHERBGS	which you understand	KHUPBDZ
which she remembered	SKHERPLD	which you understood	KH*UPBDZ
which she remembers	SKHERPLS	which you want	KHUPT
which she said	SKHEBS	which you wanted	KHUPTD
which she say	SKHEBZ	which you were the	KHURPT
which she says	SKHEBSZ	which you were	KHURP
which she shall	SKHERB	which you will	KH*UL

which you will go	KH*ULG	who he knows	WHOEPBS
which you would	KHULD	who he recalled	WHOERLD
whichever	KH*FR, KH-FR	who he recalls	WHOERLS
whininess	WHAOEU/	who he recollected	WHOERBGD
	TPH*EUPBS	who he recollects	WHOERBGS
whininess	WHAOEUPB/	who he remembered	WHOERPLD
	TPH*EUPBS	who he remembers	WHOERPLS
white *(as wd)*	WHAOEUT	who he said	WHOEBS
White *(as wd)*	WHAO*EUT	who he say	WHOEBZ
white-collar *(j)*	WHAOEUBG	who he says	WHOEBSZ
white collar	WHAOEUT/KHRAR	who he shall	WHOERB
white house	WHOUS	who he should	WHOERBD
White House	WHO*US	who he thinks	WHOEPBGS
WHO *(World Health Organization)*		who he understand	WHOEPBDZ
	W-RBGS/HO*	who he understands	WHOEPBDZ/-S
WHO	WHO*	who he understood	WHO*EPBDZ
who *(as wd)*	WHO	who he wanted	WHOEPTD
who'd	WHO*D	who he wants	WHOEPTS
who'll	WHO*L	who he was	WHOEFS
who's	WHO*S	who he will	WHO*EL
who've	WHO*F	who he will go	WHO*ELG, WHOELG
who are	WHOR	who he would	WHOELD
who are the	WHORT	who he wouldn't	WHOELD/-PBT
who believe	WHOBL	who I	WHO*EU
who believe the	WHOBLT	who I am	WHO*EUPL
who believed	WHOBLD	who I am	WHOEUPL
who believes	WHOBLS	who I am the	WHOEUPLT
who can	WHOBG	who I believe the	WHOEUBLT
who can the	WHOBGT	who I believe	WHOEUBL
who cannot	WHOBG/TPHOT	who I believed	WHOEUBLD
who can't	WHOBG/-PBT	who I can	WHOEUBG
who could	WHOBGD	who I cannot	WHOEUBG/TPHOT
who couldn't	WHOBGD/-PBT	who I can't	WHOEUBG/-PBT
who else	WHOELS	who I could	WHOEUBGD
whoever	WHOFR. WHO*FR	who I couldn't	WHOEUBGD/-PBT
who feel	WHOFL	who I feel	WHOEUFL
who feels	WHOFLS	who I felt	WHOEUFLT
who felt	WHOFLT	who I had	WHOEUD
who had	WHOD	who I happen	WHOEUP
who happened	WHOPD	who I happened	WHOEUPD
who happens	WHOPS	who I have	WHOEUF
who has	WHO*Z	who I have been	WHOEUFB
who have	WHOF	who I have been the	WHOEUFBT
who have been	WHOFB	who I have had	WHOEUFD
who have been the	WHOFBT	who I have the	WHOEUFT
who have had	WHOFD	who I know	WHOEUPB
who haven't	WHOFPBT	who I know the	WHOEUPBT
who have the	WHOFT	who I recall	WHOEURL
who he	WHO*E	who I recall the	WHOEURLT
who he believed	WHOEBLD	who I recalled	WHOEURLD
who he believes	WHOEBLS	who I recollect	WHOEURBG
who he can	WHOEBG	who I recollect the	WHOEURBGT
who he cannot	WHOEBG/TPHOT	who I recollected	WHOEURBGD
who he can't	WHOEBG/-PBT	who I remember	WHOEURPL
who he could	WHOEBGD	who I remember the	WHOEURPLT
who he couldn't	WHOEBGD/-PBT	who I remembered	WHOEURPLD
who he feels	WHOEFLS	who I said	WHOEUBS
who he felt	WHOEFLT	who I say	WHOEUBZ
who he had	WHOED	who I says	WHOEUBSZ
who he happened	WHOEPD	who I shall	WHOEURB
who he happens	WHOEPS	who I should	WHOEURBD
who he has	WHOEZ	who I think	WHOEUPBG
who he is	WHOES	who I think the	WHOEUPBGT

who I understand	WHOEUPBDZ	who think the	WHOPBGT
who I understood	WHO*EUPBDZ	who thinks	WHOPBGS
who I want	WHOEUPT	who understand	WHOPBDZ
who I wanted	WHOEUPTD	who understands	WHOPBDZ/-S
who I was	WHOEUFS	who understood	WHO*PBDZ
who I will	WHOEUL	who want	WHOPT
who I will go	WHOEULG	who wanted	WHOPTD
who I would	WHOEULD	who wants	WHOPTS
who I wouldn't	WHOEULD/-PBT	who was	WHOFS
who is	WHOS	who were	WHORP
who recollect	WHORBG	who were the	WHORPT
who recollect the	WHORBGT	who will	WHOL
who recollected	WHORBGD	who will go	WHOLG
who recollects	WHORBGS	who will the	WHOLT
who remember	WHORPL	who would	WHOLD
who remember the	WHORPLT	who would not	WHOLD/TPHOT
who remembered	WHORPLD	who wouldn't	WHOLD/-PBT
who remembers	WHORPLS	who you	WHOU
who said	WHOBS	who you are	WHOUR
who say	WHOBZ	who you are the	WHOURT
who says	WHOBSZ	who you believe	WHOUBL
who shall	WHORB	who you believe the	WHOUBLT
who she	SWHOE	who you believed	WHOUBLD
who she believed	SWHOEBLD	who you can	WHOUBG
who she believes	SWHOEBLS	who you cannot	WHOUBG/TPHOT
who she can	SWHOEBG	who you can't	WHOUBG/-PBT
who she cannot	SWHOEBG/TPHOT	who you could	WHOUBGD
who she can't	SWHOEBG/-PBT	who you couldn't	WHOUBGD/-PBT
who she could	SWHOEBGD	who you feel	WHOUFL
who she couldn't	SWHOEBGD/-PBT	who you felt	WHOUFLT
who she feels	SWHOEFLS	who you had	WHOUD
who she felt	SWHOEFLT	who you have	WHOUF
who she had	SWHOED	who you have been	WHOUFB
who she happened	SWHOEPD	who you have been the	WHOUFBT
who she happens	SWHOEPS	who you have had	WHOUFD
who she has	SWHOEZ	who you have the	WHOUFT
who she is	SWHOES	who you know	WHOUPB
who she knows	SWHOEPBS	who you know the	WHOUPBT
who she recalled	SWHOERLD	who you recall	WHOURL
who she recalls	SWHOERLS	who you recall the	WHOURLT
who she recollected	SWHOERBGD	who you recalled	WHOURLD
who she recollects	SWHOERBGS	who you recollect	WHOURBG
who she remembered	SWHOERPLD	who you recollect the	WHOURBGT
who she remembers	SWHOERPLS	who you recollected	WHOURBGD
who she said	SWHOEBS	who you remember	WHOURPL
who she say	SWHOEBZ	who you remember the	WHOURPLT
who she says	SWHOEBSZ	who you remembered	WHOURPLD
who she shall	SWHOERB	who you said	WHOUBS
who she should	SWHOERBD	who you say	WHOUBZ
who she thinks	SWHOEPBGS	who you says	WHOUBSZ
who she understand	SWHOEPBDZ	who you shall	WHOURB
who she understands	SWHOEPBDZ/-S	who you should	WHOURBD
who she understood	SWHO*EPBDZ	who you think	WHOUPBG
who she wanted	SWHOEPTD	who you think the	WHOUPBGT
who she wants	SWHOEPTS	who you understand	WHOUPBDZ
who she was	SWHOEFS	who you understood	WHO*UPBDZ
who she will	SWHOEL	who you want	WHOUPT
who she will go	SWHOELG	who you wanted	WHOUPTD
who she would	SWHOELD	who you were	WHOURP
who she wouldn't	SWHOELD/-PBT	who you were the	WHOURPT
who should	WHORBD	who you will	WHOUL
who the	WHOT	who you will go	WHOULG
who think	WHOPBG	who you would	WHOULD

108 © 2004 *StenEd*® Briefs & Phrases (Excerpted from StenEd's Realtime Professional Dictionary)

who you wouldn't	WHOULD/-PBT	Wisconsin	W*EU/W*EU
wholehearted	WHOEL/HARTD	with *(as wd)*	W-
wholeheartedly	WHOEL/HARTD/HREU	with reference	WREFRPBS
whomever	WHOPL/*FR	with reference to	WREFRPBS/TO
whomever	WHOPL/-FR	with regard(s)	WRARD(Z)
whomsoever	WHOPL/SO*FR	with regard to	WRARD/TO
whomsoever	WHOPL/SOFR	with respect	W-RPT
whose	WHOZ	with respect	WR-PT
whosoever	WHO/SO*FR	with respect to	W-RPT/TO
whosoever	WHO/SOFR	with respect to	WR-PT/TO
wicket	WEUBGT	with the	W-T
widower	WEUD/WER	with your	WUR
wiliness	WAOEU/HR*EUPBS	withdraw	WRAU
wiliness	WAOEUL/HR*EUPBS	withdrawal	WRAUL
will *(as wd)*	HR-	withdrawing	WRAUG
will be	HR-B	withdrawn	WRAUPB
will believe	HR-BL	withdraws	WRAUZ
will believe the	HR-BLT	withdrew	WRAOU
will ever	HR-FR	within *(as wd)*	W-PB
will find	HR-FPBD	within normal limits	W*PBL
will go	HR*G, HR-/TKPWO	within the	W-PBT
will have	HR-F	without	WOUT
will have been	HR-FB	witness *(as wd)*	W-PBS, W*PBS
will have had	HR-FD	witness excused	WEUBGS
will he say	HREBZ	(Witness excused.)	W*EUBGS
will I say	HREUBZ	(Witness nods.)	WO*DZ
will not	HR-PBT	witness stand(s)	W-PBD(Z)
will recall	HR-RL	WKT *(Written Knowledge Test)*	
will recollect	HR-RBG		W-RBGS/K*T
will remember	HR-RPL	WMD(s) *(weapon[s] of mass destruction)*	
will say	HR-BZ		W-RBGS/PH*D(Z)
will she say	SHREBZ	WMD(s)	W-PLD(Z)
will the	HR-T	wobbliness	WOB/HR*EUPBS
will want	HR-PT	wobbliness	WOBL/HR*EUPBS
will you describe	HRUDZ	woman	WOPL
will you please	HRUPLS	womanhood	WOPL/HAOD
will you repeat	HRURPT	womanize	WOPL/AOEUZ
will you say	HRUBZ	womanizer(s)	WOPL/AOEUZ/ER(S)
will your Honor	HRURPB	womanlike	WOPL/HRAO*EUBG
will your Honor please	HRURPBLS	womanly	WOPL/HREU
willed	HR-D	women	WEUPL
willful	HR-FL	won't	WOEPBT
willfully	HR-/TPHREU	wonderful	WOPBD/-FL
willfully	HR-FL/HREU	wonderfully	WOPBD/TPHREU
willfulness	HR-FL/*PBS, HR-/TPHR*PBS	wonderment	WOPBD/-PLT
		wooziness	WAO/S*EUPBS
willing	HR-G	wooziness	WAOZ/*PBS
willingly	HR-G/HREU, HR-/TKPWHREU	wooziness	WAOZ/S*EUPBS
		wordiness	WOR/TK*EUPBS
willingness	HR-G/*PBS	WordPerfect	WO*RD/PEFRT
will-less	HR-/HRES	workers' *(as wd)*	WORBG/ERS/AOE
wills	HR-S	workers' comp	WOFRP
wind *(as wd)*	WEUPBD	workers' compensation	WOFRPGS
windchill	W-FP	world *(as wd)*	WORLD
windchill factor	W-FP/TPABG/TOR	World *(as wd)*	WO*RLD
windiness	WEUPB/TK*EUPBS	World Court	WO*URT
Windows 95	W*EUPB/9/5	World War I	WORLD/WAR/1
Windows 98	W*EUPB/9/8	World War II	WORLD/WAR/2
Windows XP	W*EUPB/KP-RBGS/P*RBGS	worldliness	WORLD/HR*EUPBS
		worthiness	WOR/TH*EUPBS
wink	W*EUPBG	would *(as wd)*	WOULD
wiriness	WAOEU/R*EUPBS	wouldn't	WO*PBT
wiriness	WAOEUR/R*EUPBS	would've	WO*UF

© 2004 StenEd® Briefs & Phrases (Excerpted from StenEd's Realtime Professional Dictionary)

would-be	WO*UB
would be	WOUB
would be the	WOUBT
would believe	WOUBL
would believe the	WOUBLT
would feel	WOUFL
would find	WOUFPBD
would have	WOUF
would have been	WOUFB
would have believed	WOUFBLD
would have had	WOUFD
would have recalled	WOUFRLD
would have recollected	WOUFRBGD
would have remembered	WOUFRPLD
would have the	WOUFT
would he say	WOEBZ
would I say	WOEUBZ
would recall	WOURL
would recollect	WOURBG
would remember	WOURPL
would she say	SWOEBZ
would want	WOUPT
would you describe	WOUDZ
would you please	WOUPLS
would you repeat	WOURPT
would you repeat the question	WOURPGS
would you rephrase	WOUFRS
would you rephrase the question	WOUFRGS
would you say	WOUBZ
would you tell me	WOUPLT
would you tell us	WOUTS
would your Honor	WOURPB
would your Honor please	WOURPBLS
wpm *(words per minute)*	W*/P*PL
wpm	W*PL
wrinkle(s)	WR*EUPBG/-L(S)
wrinkled	WR*EUPBG/-LD
wrinkling	WR*EUPBG/-LG
write	WREU
writer	WREUR
writer	WREU/ER
writing	WREUG
writing	WREU/-G
written	WREUPB
written	WREU/-PB
wrongdoer	WROPBG/TKOER
wrongdoing	WROPBG/TKO*EUPBG
wrote	WRO
wrought	WRAUT
Wyoming	WAO*EU/WAO*EU
Wyoming	WEUFPLT
WYSIWYG *(what you see is what you get)*	WEUZ/SEU/WEUG
WYSIWYG	WEUZ/WEUG

X *(Roman numeral)*	10R
xerographic	SAO*ER/TKPWRAFBG
xerographically	SAO*ER/TKPWRAFBG/HREU
xerox *(often cap)*	SAO*ERBGS
XI *(Roman numeral)*	1/1R
XII *(Roman numeral)*	12-R
XIII *(Roman numeral)*	13-R
XIV *(Roman numeral)*	14R
XIX *(Roman numeral)*	19R
Xmas	KPHAS
x-rated	KPRAEUT/-D
x-ray	KPRAEU
XV *(Roman numeral)*	15R
XVI *(Roman numeral)*	16R
XVII *(Roman numeral)*	17R
XVIII *(Roman numeral)*	18R
XX *(Roman numeral)*	20R
XYZ	KP-RBGS/KWR*Z

y'all	KWRA*UL
Y2K *(Year 2000)*	KWR*BG
yada-yada-yada	KWRAD/KWRAD/KWRAD
yank	KWRA*PBG
Yankee	KWRA*PBG/KAOE
YBP *(years before present)*	KWR-RBGS/PW*P
yea *(as wd)*	KWRAE
yea or nay	KWRAERPB
yea or no	KWRAOERPB
year(s) *(as wd)*	KWRAOER(/-S)
year ago	KWRAERG
year ago	KWRAOERG
years ago	KWRAERGS
years ago	KWRAOERGS
year old	KWRAERLD
years old	KWRAERLDZ
-year-old *(suf)*	KWRAOERLD
-year-olds *(suf)*	KWRAOERLDZ
yellow *(as wd)*	KWREL/HROE
yellow light(s)	KWR-LT(S)
yes *(as wd)*	KWRE
Yes,	KWR*ERBGS
Yes.	KWR*EFPLT
yes or no	KWRORPB
yes, ma'am	KWREPL
yes, sir	KWRES
yes, your Honor	KWRURPB
yesterday(s)	KWRED(Z)
YMCA *(Young Men's Christian Association)*	KWR-RBGS/PH*RBGS/KRA*
YOB *(year of birth)*	KWR-RBGS/O*B
you *(as wd)*	KWROU
you'd	KWRO*UD
you'll	KWRO*UL
you're	KWRO*UR
you've	KWRO*UF
you are	UR
you are not	UR/TPHOT
you are the	URT
you aren't	URPBT
you believe	UBL
you believe so	UBLS
you believe the	UBLT
you believed	UBLD
you can	UBG
you cannot	UBG/TPHOT
you can't	UBG/-PBT
you could	UBGD
you ever	UFR
you ever been	UFRB
you ever been the	UFRBT
you ever had	UFRD
you feel	UFL
you felt	UFLT
you find	UFPBD
you have	UF
you have been	UFB
you have been the	UFBT
you have believed	UFBLD
you have had	UFD
you haven't	UFPBT
you have the	UFT
you have the right to remain silent	UFT/R*RS
you just want	UFPT
you just wanted	UFPTD
you know	KWRO*UPB
you recall	URL
you recalled	URLD
you recollect	URBG
you recollected	URBGD
you remember	URPL
you remembered	URPLD
you're welcome	KWROURBG
you said	UBS
you say	UBZ
you says	UBSZ
you shall	URB
you should	URBD
you think	UPBG
you think the	UPBGT
you understand	KWROU/UPBS
you want	UPT
you wanted	UPTD
you were	URP
you were the	URPT
you will	KWROU/HR-ULD
you would	ULD
your *(as wd)*	KWROUR
your best estimate	KWROURBTS
your Honor	KWROURPB
your Honor please	KWROURPBLS
your verdict	KWR-RBGT
yours *(as wd)*	KWROURS
yourself	KWRO*URS
yourselves	KWRO*URS/-S
yourselves	KWRO*URSZ
Yours truly	KWR-T
Yours very truly	KWR-FT, KWR*FT
YTD *(year to date)*	KWR-RBGS/T*D
YWCA *(Young Women's Christian Association)*	KWR-RBGS/W*RBGS/KRA*

zaniness	SA*EU/TPH*EUPBS
zaniness	SA*EUPB/TPH*EUPBS
zillion(s)	S*L(S)
zillionaire	S*L/TPHAEUR
zillionth	S*LT
zonk	SO*PBG
zoologist	SAO*LGS
zoology	SAO*LG
ZPG *(zero population growth)*	STK-RBGS/P*G
Zurich	SAO*URBG
zzz *(sleeping/snoring)*	STK*/STK*Z
ZZZ	STK-RBGS/STK*Z

StenEd Dictionaries

HARD COPY DICTIONARIES

Realtime Professional Dictionary (Item #551)
- Comprehensive listing of words and their conflict-free StenEd outlines.
- A must for all StenEd writers. Also an excellent reference for non-StenEd writers who want to eliminate their conflicts.
- Includes options, briefs, and phrases.
- Appendix includes a summary of StenEd writing principles as well as useful word lists such as cities, states, countries, compounds, soundalikes, and much more.

Reverse Dictionary (Item #552)
- Includes the words and outlines in the *Professional Dictionary* alphabetized by outline rather than by English.
- Use of this dictionary helps keep the students and teacher from inadvertently incorporating a potentially conflicting outline.
- Recommended and extremely valuable for students who have completed theory.
- A necessity for scopists.

Dictionary of Briefs & Phrases (Item #553)
- Includes a concise listing of the briefs and phrases contained in the more comprehensive *Professional Dictionary*.
- Designed to be a convenient "quick" reference, *not* a summary of the StenEd theory.

Medical Dictionary (Item #555)
- Contains conflict-free stenotype outlines for words contained in *Stedman's* and *Dorland's* medical dictionaries and medications contained in the *PDR*.
- Appendix contains comprehensive listings of medical acronyms and abbreviations; prefixes, suffixes, and roots; medical soundalikes; and more.
- Recommended and extremely valuable for all students taking any medical course.

Legal Dictionary (Item #556)
- Comprehensive listing of terms and their conflict-free StenEd outlines.
- Appendix contains listings of legal phrase elements and legal steno briefs.

TRANSLATING DICTIONARIES

StenEd® Main CAT (StenEd##) (Item #CAT01/02)
- Conflict free.
- Compatible with all CAT systems. (Available in most CAT vendor formats.)
- Translates all words in StenEd's *Professional Dictionary* plus much more.
- Includes legal terms; includes foreign terms commonly used in this country.

StenEd® Medical Job (MedSted##) (Item #MD01/02)
- Conflict free.
- Compatible with all CAT systems. (Available in most CAT vendor formats.)
- Translates all words in StenEd's *Medical Dictionary* plus more.
- Used as a job dictionary in conjunction with the main CAT translating dictionary.
- Best used in conjunction with StenEd's Main CAT translating dictionary (CAT01).

Note: ## refers to year of latest update.